ADVANCED SOCIAL MEDIA MARKETING

HOW TO LEAD, LAUNCH, AND MANAGE A SUCCESSFUL SOCIAL MEDIA PROGRAM

Tom Funk

Apress®

Advanced Social Media Marketing: How to Lead, Launch, and Manage a Successful Social Media Program

ISBN-13 (pbk): 978-1-4302-4407-3
ISBN-13 (electronic): 978-1-4302-4408-0

Trademarked names, logos, and images may appear in this book. Rather than use a trademark symbol with every occurrence of a trademarked name, logo, or image we use the names, logos, and images only in an editorial fashion and to the benefit of the trademark owner, with no intention of infringement of the trademark.

The use in this publication of trade names, trademarks, service marks, and similar terms, even if they are not identified as such, is not to be taken as an expression of opinion as to whether or not they are subject to proprietary rights.

While the advice and information in this book are believed to be true and accurate at the date of publication, neither the authors nor the editors nor the publisher can accept any legal responsibility for any errors or omissions that may be made. The publisher makes no warranty, express or implied, with respect to the material contained herein.

Distributed to the book trade worldwide by Springer Science+Business Media New York, 233 Spring Street, 6th Floor, New York, NY 10013. Phone 1-800-SPRINGER, fax (201) 348-4505, e-mail orders-ny@springer-sbm.com, or visit www.springeronline.com. Apress Media, LLC is a California LLC and the sole member (owner) is Springer Science + Business Media Finance Inc (SSBM Finance Inc). SSBM Finance Inc is a Delaware corporation.

For information on translations, please e-mail rights@apress.com, or visit www.apress.com.

Apress and friends of ED books may be purchased in bulk for academic, corporate, or promotional use. eBook versions and licenses are also available for most titles. For more information, reference our Special Bulk Sales–eBook Licensing web page at www.apress.com/bulk-sales.

Any ... ie author in this text is available to readers ... ACC LIBRARY SERVICES AUSTIN, TX ... your book's source code, go to www. apre

Dedicated to my wonderful and unusual extended family, especially our newest member, Harrison James Lee. And to the two beloved patriarchs who are no longer with us, Steve Funk and Chris Del Sesto.

Contents

About the Author

Tom Funk has been involved in ecommerce and online marketing since the emergence of the commercial internet in the mid 1990s. A senior marketing manager at Green Mountain Coffee Roasters, he has a wealth of experience in social media, online advertising, website usability, and more. Tom is a frequent speaker at industry conferences and events. His previous books include *Web 2.0* and *Social Media Playbook for Business*.

Acknowledgments

I'd like to thank all the businesses whose stories and experiences helped shape this book.

Thanks to Michael McHale at Subaru of America, and Chris Boudreaux of Accenture, for sharing their insights with me in interviews. My writing also benefited from best practices learned from Select Design, Gary Vayverchuck and the team at VaynerMedia, Shama Khabani of Marketing Zen Group, Ted Wright of Fizz Marketing, Seth Godin, and the Zappos Insights crew.

Thanks to Leslie Kennedy and Tina Rubio at Facebook for keeping us dialed into new developments, and getting me that coveted invite to a Facebook Hack. Thanks too, to Fred Tietze, Amanda Swan, and Myra Sack at Extole for helping us navigate refer-a-friend campaigns, and OpenGraph sharing.

I'd like to thank everyone who makes social media tick at Green Mountain Coffee Roasters, especially Kristen Mercure who keeps them all in line. Thanks to the folks on my Café Express social media team, Marybeth Longo, Rob Ouellette, and Riley Houser, who launched our program and pushed it to greater heights. Thanks to Brian Galloway, with whom it's such a kick to test all those shiny, new Facebook advertising options.

My editor, Jeff Olson, is a joy to work with. He knows his craft. He's smart, fast, and knows the care and feeding of those unpredictible beasts called authors. Thanks also to Rita Fernando and Tamsin Willard, for moving the project swiftly and smoothly from manuscript to finished product.

Thanks to the Sugarbush ski patrol, Dr. Eric Benz of Champlain Valley Orthopedics, and to Bristol Physical Therapy. (Note to self: Next time you're on deadline for a book project, try not to ski into a tree.)

Finally, thanks yet again to my incredible wife Elizabeth and three fantastic daughters Hannah, Molly, and Louisa. I couldn't have done it without you!

The Business Case

Understanding the Two ROIs of Social Media

Social platforms like blogs, Twitter, and Facebook make it almost effortless for businesses like yours to compose and post content to a potential audience of millions. It's faster and cheaper than large-scale publishing, promotion, or customer relations have ever been.

But it isn't free.

To use social media effectively today takes strategists, writers, community managers, graphic designers, app developers, and customer service reps. It all costs money, even before you throw in funds for brand monitoring and analytics tools, publishing and promotions software, buzz-building prizes and giveaways—or for paid social media advertising.

That's what Mark Zuckerberg and other social media moguls are staking their future on: the notion that businesses and organizations will pay big money for ads on social networks.

In short, corporate social media programs require *investment*. General Motors, which in 2012 pulled back its advertising from Facebook, has been spending a whopping $40 million a year to manage its social media efforts, of which $10 million is devoted to advertising.

If investment is necessary, bean counters and decision makers at your firm will want to know the *return* on that social media investment.

But despite the jumble of social media measurement tools that have emerged in recent years (see Chapter 8), measuring the impact of social media programs is an inexact science at best—and, at its worst, a nonscience, right up there with phrenology and bloodletting.

Nevertheless, online social presence and expertise are now a required, core competency of successful businesses and organizations. This book aims to clarify the business case for social media, share best practices of brands large and small, and give practical help to marketers on everything from social media advertising to online damage control and operations management—and, not least, how to measure the impact of it all.

The Power of Social Media

Before they loosen the corporate purse strings, those holding them will say, "Show me the impact social media have on reputation and the bottom line." In answering, start here. Statistics eloquently tell some of the story. Social media can be a boon for brand equity, customer loyalty, and business performance. Various studies have found the following:

- 74% of consumers have a more positive brand impression after interacting with a company through social media

- Purchase likelihood increases 51% after a customer clicks the "like" button

- When they receive good customer service, social media users tell three times as many people about it as do nonusers of social media

- 83% of people who complained about a given company on Twitter "liked or loved" a response by the company

- 90% of consumers trust product reviews from people they know; 70% trust reviews from people they don't know

- 40% of social media users "like" businesses in order to receive special discounts and promotions

- Facebook fans of a brand spend twice as much as those who are not Facebook fans

The business benefits of social media aren't limited to the realms of marketing and brand equity. Major efficiencies and productivity gains are to be had from faster and more interactive communication—between companies and consumers, among consumers, and in social-media-driven collaborations within a company.

McKinsey Global Institute, the research arm of business consulting firm McKinsey & Company, reckons that better communication and collaboration via social media could add $1.3 trillion to the global economy.

"These technologies are successful when influential people are role models, using them and explaining them," says Michael Chui, coauthor of the McKinsey study "The Social Economy: Unlocking Value and Productivity Through Social Technologies."[1]

As I'll explain in Chapter 7, social media are a pivotally important channel in the new area of customer relationship management, or CRM. Today, when customers want to reach businesses to ask a question, express gratitude, or lodge a complaint, they don't just reach for the phone or ping the customer service e-mail address. Increasingly, they also post on brand social media pages, or the web at large. Integrating social media, enterprise-wide, as a communications and customer relations channel is one of the key challenges and opportunities faced by organizations today.

In all stages of the customer relationship life cycle, online social media platforms are now playing a crucial role. Here are a few of the ways social media are part of the conversation:

- **Awareness, Knowledge, Consideration, Selection:** Before purchases are made, conversations about what brands to buy take place online, and the proliferation of customer ratings and reviews influences buyers, along with the sharing of purchases and recommendations. Companies profit through increased online visibility in search, video, mobile, and the blogosphere. More and more companies are profiting from free sampling campaigns, coupons, and sweepstakes. Increasingly, social media are driving customer awareness, influencing customer research and willingness to try new products, and inspiring purchase decisions and recommendations.

- **Satisfaction, Advocacy, Loyalty:** After purchases are made, social networks are the new CRM channel, a place to publicly resolve complaints, receive testimonials, and deepen consumer engagement. Brands build equity with their social media fan bases and encourage loyalty through member-exclusive discounts, building of personal relationships, corporate social responsibility, cause-related marketing, and more.

---

[1] "The Social Economy: Unleashing Value and Productivity Through Social Technologies," Michael Chui, James Manyika, Jacques Bughin, Richard Dobbs, Charles Roxburgh, Hugo Sarrazin, Geoffrey Sands and Magdalena Westergren, McKinsey Global Institute, 2012, www.mckinsey.com/insights/mgi/research/technology_and_innovation/the_social_economy.

Depending on your industry, acquiring a brand-new customer can cost hundreds of dollars. That's why *retaining loyal customers* is crucial for your bottom line.

Beloved Brands Thrive in Social Media

As an employee or consultant, I've been fortunate to work for a number of beloved brands, including The Vermont Teddy Bear Company, Green Mountain Coffee, Wine of the Month Club, Terry Precision Bicycles, and others. Brands like these resonate with consumers because they have a unique story to tell, a story with an emotional dimension. Such brands are positioned to thrive on social media.

Currently I work for Green Mountain Coffee Roasters, Inc., in the direct-to-consumer division of the specialty coffee business, selling single-serve Keurig K-Cup packs online at www.GreenMountainCoffee.com and through a direct-mail catalog. Together, Keurig and Green Mountain Coffee, plus portfolio and licensed brands including Tully's Coffee, Barista Prima Coffeehouse, Café Escapes, Newman's Own Organics, and others, maintain active social media programs totaling well over two million fans (many of whom, no doubt, overlap among brands).

I'm responsible for the online community of our Café Express Savings Club—a 250,000-strong group of loyal consumers who opt to have their coffee automatically delivered to their homes or small offices every month or so.

In July 2012, NetBase measured social media chatter to generate a "passion index" of coffee brands, and our company's Keurig single-cup coffee brewer ranked as the most beloved coffee-related brand among users of social media. That is, 91% of social media buzz was distinctly "love it" positive. (Within the coffee category, Starbucks dominated the conversation by a mile. Fully 89% of all coffee-related social media mentions were of Starbucks. However, the sentiment of those conversations straddled the "like it" and "love it" quadrants.)

Meanwhile, Green Mountain Coffee was named "coffee brand of the year" in a 2012 Harris Poll EquiTrend study.

I mention this not to boast but to acknowledge that bigger, better-known brands enjoy some advantages in social media over smaller, lesser-known ones. Consumers often come to Facebook or Twitter seeking them out, perhaps driven by a customer service need, desire for exclusive discounts, or mere curiosity.

That said, it's not how *well known* you are that drives your social media reputation. It's how *well loved* you are. Big, established brands have a head start in social media because their brand attributes are personalized in the minds of consumers, and an emotional relationship already exists between merchant and consumer.

This isn't to say that smaller, niche brands don't enjoy some tangible advantages in social media:

- Niche and special-interest brands cater to smaller, more tightly defined audiences and subcultures. These groups are by nature passionate. Often, they're already a bona fide community, perfectly suited for social networking.

- Smaller niche businesses are usually faster-reacting, more agile, and more entrepreneurial than big enterprises. Culturally, they're a good fit for the pace and style of social media.

- Social media marketing is still a low-cost arena, where content is king, and guerrilla marketing and "earned media" (word-of-mouth buzz and free media coverage) can sometimes make a bigger, better impression than a humongous media buy.

Whether your customer community is big or small, the glue holding it together is authentic consumer devotion to your brand—and the products and services you sell. Your social media fans will buy more from you and are more likely to spread the good word about you than customers who haven't connected with you on social media.

■ **Note** While big companies have some advantages in the social media sphere, small companies have real strengths, like built-in communities and better-targeted audiences, that fit the social media space well and let you amplify your ad spend considerably.

Leveraging the Network Effect

Thanks to what's called the "network effect," initial awareness of your brand and its reach will be multiplied many times over by participation on social media websites. Here's an example of how it works: for the Café Express Savings Club, we have a Facebook community of about 80,000 fans. Each member of Facebook has, on average, about 300 friends. When our fans see our posts in their Facebook news feeds, if they choose to "like," comment on, or share them, our reach begins to extend to all their friends. As a result, our 80,000 fans give us a network reach of about *23 million people.*

Go into the Facebook Insights stats package yourself, and see what the reach of your Facebook fan page is—you'll probably find it is over 300 times your fan base. As we'll discuss later, it's a challenge to actually *reach* your "reach" (any given wall post will get to only about 16% of fans); nevertheless, it's inspiring to think that a free medium can give you publishing and relationship access to an audience that huge.

Friends-of-fans reach is valuable because friends typically share similar tastes and demographics—making them good potential customers.

Three Vital Ingredients and "Social Proof"

Awareness, *personality*, and *relationship* are the first three vital ingredients for social media success.

It's not much different, really, from what makes you willing to confirm a Facebook friend request from an individual person: (1) you know who they are, (2) you like them, and (3) there's some form of bond between you. These are the same assets a brand brings from the outside world and uses to establish its social media program.

Another aspect of the network effect is *social proof.* The likes, shares, and comments your brand inspires become powerful peer recommendations—and a demonstration of strength in numbers.

What happens next—strategic building of a network and interaction between a brand and its fans—determine whether a company leverages its brand capital to be as successful in the social media world as it is outside of it, or whether it squanders that precious capital.

There are many examples of brands squandering their capital, demonstrating that they just "don't get" social media, appearing out of touch, uncool, even soulless or greedy. In Chapter 7, I share a handful of examples of corporate social media screw-ups, some of which were speedily repaired by smart damage control, others of which were bungled and allowed to become full-blown fiascos.

Think about your advertising and public relations budget—hundreds of thousands of dollars at least, or perhaps many millions of dollars. If you're willing to spend that kind of money building a positive brand image, personality, and "cool factor" in paid media, why wouldn't you make concerted efforts to promote and protect that same precious brand identity across online social media—where over half of Americans of all ages are spending leisure time every single day?

Setting Goals and Tactics

As I detail in Chapter 8, a corporate social media program must establish tangible goals and measure progress toward those goals. I establish goals for business social media using the following categories:

- Brand engagement, advocacy, and loyalty
- Lead generation
- Sales
- Customer service

Different businesses will have different goals or priorities. Nonprofits may replace sales with donations. Entertainment companies, online games, or other applications may be more interested in views or downloads to drive ad dollars.

For each goal, you'll deploy a number of social media tactics. For instance, sales goals can be served by promotional wall posts, member-exclusive discounts, social couponing, refer-a-friend campaigns, ad campaigns, social shopping integrations, or full-fledged Facebook commerce.

Customer service may be accomplished by wall posting, one-to-one interaction with community members, "surprise and delight" campaigns to soothe disgruntled customers, and brand monitoring of the social sphere at large.

One-to-one customer relationship management fosters repeat buying and advocacy from your best customers. It detects and defuses potential customer service and public relations problems before they turn nasty. Since much of this customer care occurs in public, on your Facebook or Twitter wall, it bolsters the reputation of your brand, showing that you're trustworthy, ethical, and able to appeal to prospective customers.

Customer Service 2.0

Speaking of customer service, let's recognize how dramatically the landscape has shifted in our Web 2.0 world. Customer satisfaction plays out on public walls before the eyes of thousands or even millions. Consumers are more powerful than ever, with their gripes or praise reaching big networks with the click of a mouse. And sprinkled among ordinary consumers is a new breed of hyperconnected influencers, with thousands of friends and followers, publishing highly ranked blogs and maintaining contacts in the traditional media. These are the folks who have the power to make or spoil a campaign, product, or sometimes even a brand.

Here's a story demonstrating how things have changed. One Monday morning, I arrived at the office to a string of e-mails and a couple of voice messages concerning a website snafu. In the middle of the night, when new content had been pushed to our website, a glitch caused one of our products, a bulk 80-count box of Caribou Coffee K-Cup packs, to appear with a price of $0.00.

What a deal!

Of course, it was obviously an error. When added to the shopping cart, the correct price appeared at checkout and in confirmation e-mails. However, the possibility of receiving a $60 product for free set off a frenzy, with word spreading in minutes across social media and deal sites like FatWallet, Slickdeals, and other online communities. We received hundreds of orders. Our discussion boards were awash with frantic speculation about whether the zero price would be honored, the full price charged, or the orders cancelled.

We quickly fixed the pricing error on the website. But what to do about the orders in the system?

Our web team, customer care leads, and social media managers had been tuned into the online social media conversation. We monitored its tone and trajectory. We could see both opportunities and risks, depending on our response.

While nobody wants to ship free goods, after a brief huddle, we acknowledged that our brand image, customer relationships, and reputation for fair dealing were also important considerations. The deal sites are large and thriving communities, and they appeal to a segment of our customer base, including some very loyal but price-conscious customers.

We decided to credit the orders received, shipping one free 80-count box of Caribou Coffee per customer, along with a friendly e-mail explaining the website glitch while owning up to it and thanking them for their business. The result? We avoided backlash from any spurned consumers—and because most of them considered the free box an unexpectedly generous gesture, we bolstered our reputation for going above and beyond.

The consumer response, shared publicly on those same discussion boards, left no doubt that our decision was the right one for brand image, customer advocacy, and future sales. Here are just some examples:

- "I am very impressed with your customer service. I'll look only to you guys to reorder [K-cup packs] in the future."

- "Thank you very much. This is a good decision and shows your commitment to exceptional customer service, and I will use you again in the future."

- "Wow, nice touch, folks. Customer for life."

- "Wow, that is unbelievable customer service! You have just made a new regular out of me."

- "Wow! This is pleasantly unexpected—I don't think I've ever seen such great customer service!"

- "That is just awesome. Few and far between retailers will stand up when a mistake is made. You have a customer for life."

The lesson learned here was that, in the new public square of social media, doing the right thing can win you not just a single customer here or there, but public devotion (and future business) from an entire online community group.

■ **Tip**   Good deeds are amplified in the online world (as are bad deeds). Consider mistakes opportunities to gain new and repeat customers.

How to Calculate Social Media ROI

Now that we've established the business case for developing and maintaining a strong social media program, let's answer, head on, one of the myths you'll hear often, maybe even from your boss. The biggest complaint made about social media marketing is that its impact, the return on investment (ROI), is unquantifiable. In a study by Econsultancy and Adobe,[2] a mere 12% of companies reported that they could track the impact of social media on revenues or the bottom line.

Fully 57% of companies could report metrics no deeper than engagement, such as the number of followers, comments, and time spent on social pages.

Worryingly, one in five companies described the state of their social media analytics as "almost none."

---

[2] "Marketers Still Can't Tie Social to Bottom Line," *eMarketer*, September 12, 2012, www.emarketer.com/Article.aspx?R=1009340&ecid=a6506033675d47f881651943c21c5ed.

I believe there are four practical approaches to measuring the impact of social media marketing. Together they provide a good, although not perfect, picture of your ROI.

- **Audience response:** Track everything that's trackable. As a digital medium, social is more easily quantified than you may think. Your website analytics, and the metrics provided by social networks, can measure impressions, interactions, visits, app downloads, event RSVPs, e-mail signups and other leads, coupon downloads, refer-a-friends, fundraising or sales— whether produced organically or through social media advertising. In your customer database, identify leads and prospects as having originated from social media. When they convert, allocate some of the sale to the social channel, along with directly tracked campaign and referral sales, for a valid ROI calculation.

- **Impression valuation:** PR managers have long calculated the value of "earned media" impressions, or the impressions if a free media mention had been bought as a paid ad. While it's a fuzzier and usually much bigger number than audience response, this ad value of impressions is a decent, established precedent for social media managers to use as well. Your impressions in social media include your own posts, consumer "likes" and comments, reviews and ratings, YouTube video views, and more. Sum up all these social media impressions, divide by 1,000, then multiply by a typical banner advertising cost-per-thousand, or CPM (usually around $10). This provides an easy ballpark measure of the reach and positive impact of your social media program.

- **Attitude & usage:** If you can afford to commission them, "attitude & usage" (or A&U) consumer research surveys are a great way to track the evolving visibility and reputation of your brand and how it's being affected by all your efforts, including social media. You can also track social brand mentions, customer-generated product ratings and reviews, and other signals of brand equity. While this is not strictly an ROI calculation, showing a correlation between social media impressions and positive brand image is an entirely valid exercise. Improved brand equity always means improved business performance.

- **Cost savings:** Some organizations have shifted substantial costs for telephone call-centers onto cheaper social channels. Consumer insights teams can gain free and instant feedback from online communities rather than paying for a focus group. Marketers can forgo some traditional advertising and promotional expense, and business-to-business (B2B) teams may be able to skip some business travel or conference-going by hosting webinars or Google+ hangouts, or by doing wiki-style online collaboration.

- **Loyalty impact:** Probably the biggest ROI contribution of social media is the enhanced relationship between brand and consumer. It's a chicken-and-egg question whether social media engagement creates brand loyalty, or the other way around, as the most loyal consumers gravitate to a brand's fan page. Either way, though, if you're not there to return your customer's love, the opportunity is lost. Assume a conservative 50% improvement in customer retention, positive brand sentiment, spending, or lifetime value when you turn an ordinary customer into a brand advocate. Grow your Facebook and other online communities in raw numbers and as a percentage of your customer base, and you should see an improvement in customer loyalty and bottom-line revenue.

  Pull data from your Facebook wall to identify active members by name and location, and match them up with your consumer database. With a cell of flagged "Facebook loyalists" in your database, benchmark their buying patterns against the customer base as a whole. This exercise quantifies the added value of your Facebook fans. Invest in growing that fan base and cultivating a positive relationship with members, and the ROI is easily calculated. Say this year's Facebook community represents 10% of your customer base, and its members yield 50% more revenue than average. If next year's community makes up 15% of your (growing) customer base, the business will generate 2.5% more sales overall, thanks to its more loyal and engaged customers.

To do the ROI math, start with your paid advertising, determining your return on ad spending, or ROAS, for each campaign and your social media advertising program as a whole. Compare the cost of sales, leads, and clicks to your other marketing channels. I've found that while social media advertising underperforms search-engine advertising when measured on a strict sales basis, it outperforms when lead acquisition is taken into account: that is, when your campaign produces sweepstakes entrants, catalog requesters, or e-newsletter subscribers who are later converted to customers via e-mail marketing or another channel.

Sum up all your social media program costs, including staff, software, and design and development services. My prediction is that you will find the tangible business benefits outweigh the expense—and the many intangible benefits further tip the scales. Hard though it can be to quantify, I've seen ample evidence that social media marketing is a high-ROI undertaking that compares very favorably with other online marketing and with traditional media.

The Other ROI: Risk of Ignoring

Perhaps most important, if your organization isn't maintaining an active presence on social media, you're ceding valuable territory to your competitors. By being absent from the conversation, you create the impression you're irrelevant, unhip, even backward. From a practical perspective, if you're not learning by trial and error today, you can't be successful in social media tomorrow. An important aspect of corporate social media programs at this stage is learning from experience, building skills, and establishing core competencies in what is still very much an emerging field.

In essence, there are four key reasons your business must be involved in social media and why you must hold yourself to the same standards of excellence there that you do in other media and CRM platforms:

- Social media are big. Today, 91% of online adults use social media regularly. Virtually everyone is there.

- In a jaded and distracted era, social media stand out as a unique opportunity to build a *personal connection* with your brand loyalists.

- You can (and should) let fans do the selling for you. Some 92% of people trust the recommendations of friends and family. Only 47% still trust TV, radio, and newspapers.[3]

- Your competitors are there. An estimated 88% of businesses with 100 or more employees are now using social media for

---

[3] "Nielsen: Global Consumers' Trust in 'Earned' Advertising Grows in Importance," Nielsen, April 10, 2012, www.nielsen.com/us/en/insights/press-room/2012/nielsen-global-consumers-trust-in-earned-advertising-grows.html.

marketing purposes.[4] You need to be among them—and you should be executing with the best of them.

■ **Note** Ignore social media at your peril. Most of your competitors are at least dipping their toes in the social media pool—if they haven't already dived in head first.

Summary

Social media offer an affordable, fast, and high-impact way to promote your business, bolster your brand image, and strengthen ties to your most ardent customers. True, it remains challenging to make ironclad return on investment calculations for the social channel. For one thing, the social media environment is still geared more toward entertainment, interaction, and personal connection than toward immediate commercial transactions. Therefore, you'll have to place some faith in less tangible signs of business benefit: exponentially increased reach to prospective customers, improved access to existing customers, and the potential for greater agility in detecting and resolving customer service issues. These are the levers that drive tangible business results: e-mail signups and other leads, increased lifetime value of loyal customers, the influence of positive brand messages, and product ratings and reviews. The ROI is one degree removed, but it is real and growing.

Next, I will explore best practices for managing a corporate social media marketing program, so that you can make these business benefits start working for your bottom line.

---

[4] "Is Social Media Marketing at a Saturation Point?" eMarketer, August 17, 2012, www.emarketer.com/Article.aspx?R=1009273.

Best Practices

What Makes for a Winning Program

Think of your social media effort as a business within a business. As you would with a start-up business or a major internal initiative, write a project charter and business plan for your social media program. This is important for the following reasons:

- Social is still a new medium, whose goals and measurements won't be understood or embraced across the enterprise unless you document them in writing, and

- The fast pace of change and frequent emergence of new social platforms and tactics means you need to define your priorities—and stay disciplined in pursuit of those priorities.

I know most readers of this book have a corporate social media program already under way. I suspect, though, that few have a written plan in place. I'm not trying to insult your intelligence by suggesting you go back to square one, but the fact is, at whatever stage you are with your social media efforts, if you lack a plan document, it's time to write one.

In Appendix A, I've drafted a mock social media program plan for a fictional company, Ends of the Earth Tours. Use it as a jumping-off point to codify your program's mission, goals, strategy, tactics, budget, operations plan, and other vital elements. As you proceed, you'll also follow the valuable research steps of assessing and benchmarking the competition and the size of your market in social media.

Formal planning will get your program started with a well-thought-out path to success. If your organization is already active in social media, a written plan you draft now will ensure that your strategic vision is clear and that your campaigns and daily practices stay on target to meet the big-picture goals. Yes, the social media landscape, technologies, opportunities, rivals, and partners will change all along the way. Like any good plan, yours will be a living document that you can revise and keep relevant.

What's the Big Idea?

Like a business, a new product line, or anything you want to sell to the public, your social media program needs a mission statement: what you're going to accomplish in the online social space, and why anyone should care.

Your business has a mission statement. If you're a start-up entrepreneur, you have a well-honed elevator pitch. You're just waiting for that opportune moment with a potential angel investor, when you can quickly explain your product or service and why it's such a blockbuster opportunity.

Think of the "unique selling proposition," or USP, for your main business. No doubt it is largely applicable to your online social efforts, but it will need tweaking. It defines what special benefit you offer and why that matters to the customer. It's not a feature of what you sell, but the benefit provided to your customers. The best USPs make strong, defensible claims.

They are often word-smithed down to a catchy phrase that conveys the core benefit. For Zappos, the USP is "Powered by Service." BMW's is "The Ultimate Driving Machine." And for years, the USP for FedEx was "When it absolutely, positively has to be there overnight."

USPs start with a customer benefit statement, in the following form: "For [the target market] the [name of your brand] is the [unique or superlative positioning and benefit], because [why should the consumer believe you?]."

Here's an example:

> For one-legged pirates, the Single Shoe Emporium is your trusted source for single right or left shoes—because we're one-legged pirates just like you.

Now apply the same formula to your social media mission: "For [the target market] the [name of your brand] online community is the [unique or superlative positioning and benefit of the community], because [why should the consumer believe you?]."

What's telling about this exercise is that, for most brands, the social community is not about selling a product or service—it's about establishing a vibrant network around an important topic, cause, interest, or area of expertise.

PetSmart's social media program, for example, isn't about moving lots of dog and cat food. Rather, the company says, "Our goal is to provide you with the best possible Facebook community to share your love and passion about pets." That translates into a steady dialogue of pet owner Q&A and terabytes of uploaded photos of adorable puppies and kittens.

Coca-Cola puts the focus squarely on the consumer, not itself, calling its Facebook presence "a collection of your stories showing how people from around the world have helped make Coke into what it is today."

Patagonia's online community is not about clothes but about climbing, surfing, and other extreme sports—and the conservation we'll need to practice to ensure such outdoor recreations will still be around tomorrow.

As with these iconic brands, your brand community must stand for something bigger than merely selling stuff—and it's that greater identity that should govern your social media approach.

I should point out that a good business mission statement does not always lend itself to anchoring the "big idea" of a thriving social media community. FedEx, for instance, is a successful business and a terrific brand, but its Facebook community is an uneasy jumble of public customer service complaints, sponsored motor-sports news, and "green"-themed corporate social responsibility. It doesn't quite gel.

For your business (or personal brand) to catch on and be successful, especially in the noisy and crowded social media scene, you need a clear brand identity and personality.

Be a storyteller. Express yourself colorfully, perhaps with humor or attitude, and always with authenticity. Wear your passions, business ethics, and social consciousness on your sleeve.

"The number one reason people fail at social media marketing is they don't have a solid foundation," points out Shama Kabani, author of *The Zen of Social Media Marketing* (BenBella Books, Inc., 2012) "They don't have a brand, they don't understand the outcome they provide, and they have absolutely no way of differentiating themselves from the competition."

Before your company plunges any further into social media marketing, make absolutely sure you and your team can articulate what's special about your business and how you'll leverage that specialness in social media. Among the hundreds of millions of real people engaging on social networks, why will anyone feel passionate about *you?*

Social Media Strategy

Kabani, who founded and runs the social media agency The Marketing Zen Group, developed an "ACT" framework for a successful online and social media strategy. The acronym stands for "Attract, Convert, and Transform"— and I find it a useful framework for positioning an online business. To paraphrase Kabani:

- **Attract:** To attract likely prospects, you must stand out from a crowded field with a clear and unique brand, a strong value proposition, worthwhile content, social proof (testimonials and an active, emotionally engaged community), and an appealing incentive for individuals to sign up for emails or fill out an inquiry form.

- **Convert:** Optimize the design and user experience on your social platforms and your website, so you successfully convert browsers to buyers.

- **Transform:** Build a bona fide personal and emotional connection with your customers or clients. Doing business with you should be no mere transaction. It becomes a relationship with your brand, one that inspires and rewards a passionate following, loyalty, and brand advocacy.

That's a good way to view your overall business plan, your web presence, and your social media program. Social media marketing is a strategic effort to continually deepen the relationship between your business and its audience. You're constantly nurturing your audience, encouraging them to graduate from prospects to buyers to loyalists.

One Channel, Many Functions

Virtually anything your business or organization attempts to do today—be it a promotion, a market research project, a human resources initiative, customer service, investor relations—deserves the amplification and reach of social media.

For businesses, social media serves as a channel for several different functions:

- Customer service

- Customer engagement and brand-equity-building

- Promotion and customer retention

In my work at Green Mountain Coffee Roasters, my fellow marketers and I frequently discuss where social belongs in our integrated promotions calendar. The calendar outlines our entire year's major promotional events, seasonal holidays, and new product or category launches. Each promotional campaign merits a concerted push from multiple marketing channels: e-mail, catalog or other direct mail, paid search ads and online banners, affiliate marketing, press releases, and on-website promotional messaging.

Social also belongs in that marketing mix. Today we message any major promotion or product launch on Facebook, Twitter, and our blog. Depending on the promotion, you might also amplify the message on other networks or niche platforms: YouTube, Groupon, Foursquare, Pinterest, and others.

Any business that has or aspires to have a strong personal connection to its audience must establish a robust presence in social media. There it must commit to four things:

- **A customer-oriented culture** that combines responsiveness, personality, and authenticity. The aim is to respond to customer comments, questions, and complaints immediately, just as you would in your inbound customer service e-mail and call center. Your customer orientation will also help you find the "influentials"—your most active brand loyalists, who serve as self-appointed ambassadors and help you in a multitude of ways, doing the vast majority of posting in your community, blogging to their own large circle of influence, making referrals to friends, offering helpful consumer feedback and testimonials, and so on.

- **Content planning,** just as a periodical publisher would do. When you're active in social media, you need a posting schedule for Facebook, Twitter, and your blog that keeps your page fresh and your brand front and center in the activity feeds of your fans and followers. (Remember, 90% of your fans will never return to your page, so they'll only see your posts in their feed.) Content plans encompass what you'll say in your social spaces, as well as multichannel promotions and events to which you'll invite your community.

- **Promotion of your social space.** If you build it, they won't come—unless you invest thought, time, and some money in promotion. I'll detail in Chapter 4 exactly how you can drive traffic to your social media pages, both with paid advertising and for free with cross-network promotion and "earned media."

- **A retention plan** to keep community members coming back. The biggest boon of the social media revolution—its massive and exponentially growing scale—is also its Achilles heel. The sheer number of people, messages, and fan pages makes for massive overload. It guarantees that most of your fans will have only a fleeting engagement with you online, then move on to other things. For most organizations, Facebook and the other social media platforms are a customer engagement opportunity, not a place to troll for prospective customers or hit them with a sales pitch. For that reason, you'll want to use social media to get to know your existing customers better, thank them and reward them for their patronage, and give them a unique window into the inner workings and culture of your business. Make them feel special, appreciated, and part of something important—a business or brand that stands for something.

In Chapter 9, I'll talk more about advanced social media campaigns, retention techniques including "surprise and delight," loyalty badging, sweepstakes, free samples, polling and feedback campaigns, ambassador programs, "gamification," and more. With these tools in hand, you'll be able to ramp up your social media program so it serves existing members well and attracts newcomers.

Listening

But enough about you. Yes, before you dive into social media, you have to know what your business stands for and how it will translate its value and identity into the social media realm. But the process will also depend on an outward focus, and this means a listening ear directed at your consumers.

The best thing you can do for your corporate social media program is be a great listener. Employ social media monitoring tools like Hootsuite, Tweetdeck, or SocialMention—or simply perform regular Twitter searches—to stay abreast of social media conversations about your brand, industry, and competitors. You'll learn the hot-button topics on the minds of your audience, and start to identify the most active and influential people inside your community and in the social sphere at large.

Planning

High-impact social media campaigns involve many moving parts, both within the social media landscape and in traditional media. These campaigns will call upon players in your marketing, legal, customer service, and operations departments. They require technology development and a number of weeks or months of lead time.

As a result, a social media program requires disciplined planning in advance. You'll need to employ some of the following processes:

- Daily community management staffing plan

- Monthly publishing schedules

- Research, survey, and customer insights projects

- Promotions and campaign strategy briefs

- Creative design briefs and production

- Technology requirements: writing, vendor selection or in-house development, user-experience testing, user acceptance testing (UAT) testing/debugging

- Budgeting and reporting

Community Management

Facebook would be the first to tell you that merely having a brand page won't guarantee traffic to it. It takes daily posting of engaging content that inspires interactions. Here are Facebook's suggestions for winning posting practices:[1]

1. Post once a day to maximize reach. Posting too frequently reduces the amount of time needed to distribute each Page post to your audience.

2. Express your core message within the first 90 characters of your post to ensure your audience sees it when your Page post becomes an ad or sponsored story. Longer messages will be truncated.

3. Post at the optimal time. Only you know what's right for your business, and you can use your Page Insights to figure out what's working. Many restaurants find that posting between 7 am and 12 pm is ideal, while retailers find that posting between 8 am and 2 pm works best. People engage with Pages the most between 9 pm and 10 pm, and the 18-24 age demographic is the most engaged during this time.

It's important to digest this information, because as businesspeople, we have attention spans that are often biased toward what occurs during the workweek and during business hours. With social, you need to adopt an always-on, 24/7 x 365 mindset, and, to some degree, you need to staff to support it by

---

[1] Facebook, "Reach Generator," www.facebook.com/business/fmc/guides/reach.

monitoring your social media community off hours and on weekends, with either internal staff or an external agency that explicitly commits to some nontraditional work hours.

You can use a social publishing tool so you can write posts ahead of time and schedule them to be published to Facebook, Twitter, your blog, and so forth during off hours. But to be quickly responsive to comments and questions—and to any potential social media crises that might emerge—you'll need to staff to support a nontraditional schedule.

Everything about Facebook is huge: it is a deluge of postings scrolling constantly at a billion or so people, worldwide, 24 hours a day. Every new message in the activity feed is quickly scrolled offscreen by a parade of subsequent messages. For your company's updates to stand out from the crowd and appear on your fans' radar, you must strive for high *interactivity*—the more people are commenting on and "liking" your posts, the better. Each comment and "like" amplifies your reach.

Compare these two scenarios for two equally popular brands, each with 10,000 Facebook fans:

- Both brands post to their pages, and their stories are seen by 15% of fans = 1,500 people.

- Brand X gets a post response rate, or "virality," of 0.75%, while brand Y's more fun, useful, or provocative post stimulates a 2.5% response.

- Each brand's fans have 350 friends apiece, roughly the Facebook average.

- Brand X inspires 11 fans to create 3,800 new stories across Facebook.

- Brand Y inspires 38 fans to create 13,300 new stories across Facebook.

The same principles hold true for Twitter. Two Twitter accounts can have an equal number of followers and even generate the same number of tweets, but the one that inspires the most retweets, direct replies, and use of its hashtag will generate far more impressions.

When you do post to Facebook, Twitter, or LinkedIn—even when you upload a video to YouTube—you should invite interaction. Ask what your fans and followers think. Solicit feedback. When community members post to your Facebook wall, listen carefully to what they say, and respond to them with answers or gratitude.

■ **Note**   When you post to your social media hot-spots, invite interaction. It will multiply the reach of your story, engaging your existing fans and helping to attract new ones.

The most interactive posts for us at Green Mountain Coffee's Café Express Savings Club (our automatic coffee delivery service) tend to be questions about member's lives, families, fond memories, favorite daily habits, recipes. Coffee, tea, and cocoa aren't always the focus of the conversation. But these drinks have strong associations for getting energized, taking a break, and relaxing—so they're more a jumping-off point to a bigger conversation than an end in themselves.

Tactically, you can stimulate interaction with polls, open-ended questions, invitations to share photos or videos, simple games like "What's different in these pictures?" or "Guess the number of jelly beans." The simplest engagement technique, though, is responding to member comments in a way that draws more responses and becomes a real dialogue. Our social media agency, VaynerMedia, has good instincts for posts that will stimulate response. And VaynerMedia is always testing and comparing posts for their impact on "likes," comments, and "shares."

■ **Tip**   While you strive for fan interaction, be aware that Facebook's terms of service prohibit you from offering promotions or rewards to users in exchange for "liking" a wall post, commenting, or uploading a photo. For complete Facebook Pages Terms, see www.facebook. com/page_guidelines.php.

A true community inspires interactivity not just between members and the brand, but also among members. It's very satisfying to see members answering each other's questions, supporting each other's comments, and congratulating winners of contests and sweepstakes.

I love the way Gardener's Supply encourages engagement with the master gardeners who buy its products. Rather than try to sell something (although the company does periodically post sales and special offers to its Facebook community), Gardener's Supply mostly shares gardening tips and recipes and asks questions such as:

- "What's your idea of a perfect pickle?"
- "Anyone else getting a good garlic crop?"
- "Anyone have tips for beet germination success?"

These are topics its fans care about, questions whose answers enliven the conversation on the wall and benefit the audience by making them more informed and successful gardeners.

The National Hockey League is another best-practice example. Virtually every Facebook post the League makes is tailored to get the greatest response from the 2.5 million opinionated fans who have friended the league. Which free agent will turn the Canadiens around? Who will step up to fill the holes in the Flyers' defense? Who has the best playoff beard? The NHL asks fans to vote for the goal, save, and hit of the season, and encourages fans to "like" posts to pay tribute to stars like retiring Red Wings captain Nicklas Lidstrom. It's all calculated to drive the maximum interaction—which is good for the community and good for organic growth via stories appearing in the news feeds of friends.

Although some of my examples come from large businesses, remember that building an online community isn't about *quantity*—it's about *quality*. Many organizations, from college alumni offices to bicycle tour operators, deliberately focus on smaller niche communities and invitation-only groups on Facebook or LinkedIn. When your network consists of a tight group of people with common interests—such as alums from the same graduating class, or folks signed up to pedal through Tuscany—you can unlock the most powerful benefits of social media: personal connection with and among your consumers, information sharing, word-of-mouth brand advocacy, and customer loyalty.

Pursuing and Cultivating "Influentials"

Call them "influentials": they are ambassadors, tastemakers, connectors, brand advocates, loyalists. Not all members of a fan community are equal: some are substantially more active and boast wider reach, with bigger friend networks, stronger reputations, perhaps an active blog readership (or even print media readership or other bricks-and-mortar constituencies). Their opinion carries greater weight and influence.

These influentials can make a difference, especially to a smaller, newer, or niche-focused online community. When you are building and cultivating a social network of customers and fans, don't just blindly solicit everyone you can reach. Do a little homework.

I'll get into more platform-specific ideas in Chapter 3, but here are some ideas on how to find and cultivate influential community members on Twitter:

1. Search for people tweeting about your company, brands, market or industry, rivals, or the topic you specialize in. Whether it's

beer, bras, bike tires, or business school, your industry already has a thriving community of experts on Twitter. Follow them.

2. Over a period of weeks, keep searching and following people that specialize in your area of interest until you have at least 50.

3. Develop a list of the top 10 or 20 people who have the best potential to be your brand ambassadors. These will be the Twitterers who:

   a. Obviously love your brand and speak highly of it without being prompted to.

   b. Tweet frequently and do it well—with energy, authority, and personality. Perhaps they are behind trending topics or hashtags in your industry.

   c. Have lots of followers. Ideally these followers are themselves interested in your business; they're active and widely followed on Twitter. That's the network effect!

   d. Earn the most retweets and replies.

5. Actively engage with these core Twitter community members, using @ replies and retweets to commend them for good posts, or thank them for flattering posts about your company or brand.

6. Meanwhile, post your own tweets, establishing yourself as an interesting voice in your area of expertise. Some of these star Twitter community members will begin following you as soon as you follow them; others may not notice you until you retweet @ reply or otherwise engage them.

7. Once you have the beginnings of a relationship, cultivate it through meaningful back-and-forth. Ask how you can help them. In my experience, we have featured influentials on our blog, rewarded them with "surprise and delight" campaigns offering free products, and reached out directly with requests for input.

The reasons for all this microfocus on the core people who make up your Twitter followers are as follows:

1. It's the best way to build a *community* worthy of the name—not just a faceless and disengaged list of Twitter handles, but a core circle of like-minded people who truly feel connected with you and the larger mission of your brand or organization.

2. The resulting connection and passion of your follower network ensures that when you post, your messages are more likely to be noticed, retweeted, and replied to. This interaction extends your reach, which is the path forward to organic growth.

In short, if at the start you do the slow, hard work of recruiting the influentials, your community's second-phase growth will be easier and more naturally linked to the network effect of Twitter.

On Facebook, communication is a bit harder, since a brand or company fan page can't make friend requests. If you are connected as admin to the fan page, however, you can use your personal profile to suggest that your friends "like" the page. As of fall 2012, fans can direct-message to brand pages, and brands can direct-message a fan—but the communication must be initiated by the fan.

Communications preferences between Facebook fans and brands are a rapidly evolving landscape, however. Grocery store chain Fresh & Easy sometimes performs customer service by having its Facebook admins reach out to particular fans via their personal accounts, always identifying themselves as Fresh & Easy employees, in order to address a fan's question, complaint, or concern voiced on the Facebook wall. "Some situations call for a more personal approach than what you can do with a wall post reply," says Nicole DeRuiter, Fresh & Easy's social media manager. "It blows people away when they notice the [Facebook] message is from our brand."[2]

Here are some other ideas for finding and connecting with influential Facebook members:

- In choosing admins for your Facebook fan page, find a number of people who are known in the industry or publicly associated with your brand. They could use their personal profiles, but often it's more effective and presents less conflict if these people have separate "business" profiles that they can reserve for their business persona.

- These admins will research and seek out influential customers, critics, journalists, and business partners and connect with them individually on Facebook. Similar to the rules of engagement on LinkedIn, these can be professional relationships rather than personal ones, but they all should be people known to your admins.

---

[2] Christopher Heine, "Facebook's New Direct Messaging Has Brands Talking," *ClickZ*, March 2, 2012, www.clickz.com/clickz/news/2156896/facebooks-direct-messaging-brands-talking.

- Admins will then suggest that their friends "like" the page.

- Meanwhile, your role as a social media manager, is to tap your consumer database and internal industry contacts to send a direct e-mail to suggest they "like" your page. These should be your best customers, people already known to you, with whom you genuinely want to interact on Facebook. The point is to build a tight network of engaged fans and brand advocates as the heart of your online community.

Promoting Your Online Community

Facebook offers three basic ways to build your audience:

- Invite friends,

- Share your page, and

- Employ paid Facebook advertising.

These are in order of scalability. Inviting your few hundred friends is a nice start, but it's only a start. Sharing extends your impact, allowing you to post about your page on your own timeline, a friend's timeline, in a group you belong to, or in a private message. Again, these techniques can get a community started, but they don't scale—and you need to be judicious in what you share and with whom. Never spam your friends!

With the initial alpha community established, now you want to build up a big audience of loyal fans. Communities do reach critical mass, where the "friends of fans" reach extends toward the million-plus mark. At that point, all you need to do is post, and your community will grow, by hundreds of fans a day. Why? Every post you make, assuming it has the hallmarks of good, provocative, interactive content, will inspire a number of comments and "likes." These comments and "likes" are broadcast across Facebook to all the friends of fans. The same occurs with Twitter posts that are enthusiastically retweeted.

Best practices for promoting your online community:

- First, prominently display on your website the logos of Facebook, Twitter, Google+, and YouTube or other social icons. Subtle little footer icons are getting to be common practice, but I'd challenge you to think bigger. Take a cue from Redbox, which dedicates a full 20% of its footer real estate, about four square inches, to large, eye-catching icons for Facebook, Twitter, its SMS "Text Club," and mobile apps for iPhone and Android. Importantly, Redbox includes a call to action ("Stay in Touch") and a consumer value proposition ("Preview & Reserve Movies!").

- Consider integrating those icons by using widgets or via an application programming interface (API), so users never have to leave your website in order to "like," "pin," or "follow" you.

- Display those same logos in the header or footer of the e-mail newsletters and promotional campaigns you send to your house e-mail list. Don't forget to do this in automatic transactional messages like shipping confirmations as well as in your promotional e-mails.

- Display social media URLs—and value propositions—in your catalog, sales collateral, or other direct mail.

Early on, seek to do something out of the ordinary, something worthy of word-of-mouth buzz or media mention. There's a fine line between catchy and gimmicky, but I must say I am a fan of novel promotional campaigns that have cut through the noise to celebrate and reward the growth of online communities. Here are some grassroots, low-budget, guerrilla marketing efforts that have made a splash:

- For every 1,000 "likes" it receives, Dog Bless You (www.facebook.com/exploredogs) donates a service dog to a needy US veteran.

- British artist Greg Burney (@gregburney) pledged to draw tiny profile portraits of his first 3,000 Twitter followers.

- The guys at College Humor promised, via a YouTube video, to wear a "beard of bees" when their Facebook page (www.facebook.com/collegehumor) hit a million "likes."

The first time someone does a campaign like this, it's genius. The second time? Ho-hum. It's copycatting, and it has no impact. So I present these ideas not as blueprints, but as challenges to you to think creatively.

Already it's quite common for brands to celebrate milestones for numbers of followers or "likes" by giving away prizes or money (usually in the form of gift cards). I wouldn't discourage it—I do it myself for programs I'm involved with—but it is getting harder to make much of an impact with small giveaways.

■ **Note**   By all means, celebrate milestones such as half a million "likes" or 15,000 Twitter followers. But make sure the celebration or reward is unique and newsworthy. For instance, when Porsche reached one million Facebook fans, it unveiled a 911 race car in Facebook colors, emblazoned with tiny images of its fans.

Tapping the Network Effect

The dawn of the commercial Internet in the 1990s introduced some radical business ideas, including the idea of viral growth: through the power of person-to-person e-mail—"word of mouse"—businesses could reach exponentially more consumers than ever before, at zero incremental cost. That was a stunning notion indeed for businesses accustomed to printing and mailing catalogs, buying expensive airtime, and doing other traditional marketing.

Alas, the novelty faded when marketers realized it was *hard* to create the next viral smash YouTube video. E-mail inbox fatigue eventually set in, discouraging folks from forwarding to (or spamming) their friends.

The rise of social networks reignited viral growth without relying much on e-mail. Social media provide frictionless, viral transmission of all sorts of trends, fads, memes, offers, and gossip. Social networks thrive by making it ridiculously easy and tempting to pass something on to your entire network. Likewise, it's ridiculously easy for everyone downstream to "like," comment, retweet, and otherwise amplify your message to their own friend networks.

But just because the platforms are designed to create virality doesn't guarantee they will work for you—because there's so much competing noise. For instance, only a small fraction of your fans or followers will ever see a given post in their activity feed, for two reasons:

- The platforms deliberately throttle back the volume of shared activity to a level manageable for users, and

- Even when a given post is delivered to the news feed, some fans will never see it if they don't log onto the site frequently enough.

In fact, according to Facebook, *the average post from a brand fan page reaches only about 16% of fans.*

That's one reason Facebook has been so successful with its "Sponsored Stories" ad unit (see Chapter 5). Basically, Facebook charges advertisers to deliver their posts to more eyeballs.

But there is another way: create great, meaningful content that people feel impassioned about and good about sharing.

Tap into primal human emotions and passions: humor, sex, love, greed, compassion, patriotism, sports, and adventure.

Be Remarkable

In other words, what makes for a virally successful social media campaign is much the same as what makes for a successful brand. Frank Goedertier, professor of Brand Management and Marketing at the Vlerick Leuven Gent Management School in Belgium and a visiting scholar at the Kellogg School of Management, argues that a successful brand must have eight key attributes. These attributes are equally crucial for a winning social media campaign. Like a successful brand, a successful social media campaign must be:

- **Memorable**
- **Meaningful**
- **Likeable**
- **Transferable** (from one social platform to another)
- **Protectable** (by copyright and trademark)
- **Authentic**
- **Simple**
- **Adaptable** (to rapid change)[3]

Particularly in social media, with its distracting plethora of stimuli, with its nearly a billion users and its bias toward fluffy diversions, focus on the first three attributes for your campaign: memorable, meaningful, and likeable.

Think about the words of Seth Godin, marketing guru and best-selling business book author, and his persistent call to *be remarkable*. Following that call is not easy to do—but it's the only thing to do.

"Artists never hold back," says Godin. "They know they'll never be on that stage again. They say, 'This is my shot.'"

---

[3] Matt Symonds, "The 8 Keys to Successful Branding," *Forbes*, May 30, 2012, www.forbes.com/sites/mattsymonds/2012/05/30/the-8-keys-to-successful-branding-why-mad-men-and-bourbon-are-not-going-to-cut-it/.

"The only thing that's going to work, that's going to scale, is the thing that's remarkable—*the thing worth making a remark about.*"[4]

What's heartening to me is that something remarkable and authentic *really is happening* between some brands and their customers. Sure, a lot of hype and hyperbole is swirling around social media at the moment. But at its best, social media marketing allows brands to reveal their human side and connect unforgettably with the values, interests, and concerns of their customers.

Target, for instance, kicked off one back-to-school season with a charitable campaign aimed straight for the hearts of America's moms: "Help us give up to $2.5 million in support of schools," exhorted Target's Facebook page, to its 16 million fans.

I'll explore Target's campaign strategy and execution in detail in Chapter 9. But for now, simply understand that to cash in on the network effect in social media, you've got to follow these key rules:

- Your brand must stand for something special.

- Your social media campaigns must capture the imagination and passions of your fans.

- You must make sharing frictionless and fun. Issue a strong call to action, offer rewards or incentives, and provide an encouraging feedback loop (or "gamification" of some sort) to make participation satisfying—even a little addictive.

Summary

The best practices we've discussed here will help you build your social media program on a rock-solid foundation. Your program will be centered on a meaningful "story" about your brand, a story that should matter personally to your audience and inspire them to join and participate in your online community.

You will encourage member engagement through careful listening, a customer-service orientation, smart posting practices, and careful cultivation of your most influential fans. With those basic disciplines in place, you're ready to drill into the specifics of the leading platforms and find out how to turn them to your advantage.

---

[4] Seth Godin, remarks at First Round Capital Ad Summit 2012, New York, May 3, 2012.

CHAPTER

3

The Platforms
Choosing and Prioritizing Your Networks

As a business or organization wanting to make an impact through social media, on what platforms will you be active? How will you allocate your time between them?

Today there are countless social media sites, for the mass market or the smallest of niches. There's Badoo, Bebo, Delicious, Reddit, and StumbleUpon. There's Classmates.com, Gays.com, and HR.com. There's Ryze, Xanga, Yammer, and Yelp. Or how about Flickr, Flixster, Friendster, and Fubar?

How can you make sense of the different purposes, demographics, and cultures of the major social networks? One clever answer, "Social Media Explained," from the perspective of donuts, was scrawled on a whiteboard and shared on Instagram in 2012 by Douglas Wray[1]:

Facebook:	*I like donuts*
Foursquare:	*This is where I eat donuts*
Instagram:	*Here is a vintage photo of my donut*
YouTube:	*Here I am eating a donut*
LinkedIn:	*My skills include donut eating*
Last FM:	*Now listening to "Donuts"*
Google+:	*I'm a Google employee who likes donuts*

Wray's posting charted a mini-viral success story among social media and web geeks. But while it neatly pigeonholes the major platforms, it doesn't fully answer our question.

---

[1] Douglas Wray, "Social Media Explained," http://instagram.com/p/nm695/.

Interactive social features have been a part of the Internet since before the World Wide Web, back in the days of bulletin boards and chat rooms. Among the earliest innovations of Amazon.com in the 1990s were user-generated book reviews and ratings.

Although the web has been social all along, it's only been in the past decade that dedicated social networks have zoomed into multimillion-user prominence. Many of the early darlings fizzled: Friendster, MySpace, and Second Life are just some of the communities that failed to maintain their early momentum or live up to their hype.

But Facebook changed everything. Virtually from its birth in 2004, it was a force to be reckoned with, and by 2008 it had unseated MySpace as the biggest social network. By 2010, in fact, it became the most visited site on the entire web, ousting Google.

I won't try to catalog all the networks out there or give you step-by-step advice on how to prosper in each. My goal is to zero in on the major platforms, the ones that deliver the greatest return for your efforts and investment. I'll focus on how they compare with each other in market share, specialty, and audience—and, I hope, get you thinking about how they can work together to allow you to derive maximum impact from your finite time and resources.

Social Media Market Share

As an organization, if you were to engage on just one social network, it would have to be Facebook, which dwarfs its rivals in both membership size and the passion of its audience (as measured by visits and time on site). But being on Facebook alone would be a mistake. You owe it to your business to participate on multiple networks. You should be using the strengths of the different platforms—and the different missions and mindsets of the people on them—so that you can achieve the following goals:

1. Your brand's social presence is essentially wherever consumers seek it

2. You satisfy a breadth of consumer needs, including research, customer service, amusement, and immersion in the brand experience

3. You amplify, echo, and support your key campaigns and brand messages consistently across multiple media

4. You leverage the fixed costs of social media (program strategy, policy establishment, planning and staffing, analytics and technology investments) across a broader reach

Some social platforms excel as conduits for news, trends, and gossip. Others specialize in professional networking or rich media sharing. While every platform overlaps the user base of the others, users may be in a different mindset or have a different mission when they visit each one.

▤ **Note** Facebook now captures 63% of all social media visits and an even higher share of online time. If you're active on only one social network, Facebook is the one to choose.

When you crank up your social media program in the comprehensive, purposeful ways I'll describe in this book, you generate millions of mostly free impressions seen by your customers and prospects. If you have a great brand, and if you're ethical, authentic, humble, energetic, and creative, the vast majority of those brand impressions will be positive. You'll create a personal face for your business—a persona that consistently reflects your brand's values, participates in relevant online conversations wherever they are found, and is attuned to the distinct culture and atmosphere of each major social network.

While I do advocate that you be "essentially everywhere," I don't mean you should be active on every single network or social media site. For one thing, it would be impossible. There are countless me-too social media plays out there today, all vying for the very limited leisure time of members—and dollars of advertisers.

An analogy to search engines may be helpful. Search marketers long ago discovered that if you stopped with Google AdWords, you left some money on the table. Despite their smaller size, Yahoo and Bing remained platforms you couldn't ignore for ROI and incremental reach.

But there was little additional benefit to building and managing search programs for second- and third-tier engines like Ask, AOL, FindWhat, and so on. You were already reaching 90% of searchers, so why expend time, effort, and money chasing the remaining 10%? Soon, lower-tier search engines began syndicating Google ads on their results pages, and the battle was over.

The same holds true for social networks. A brand can reach the lion's share of all social media users, and can be exposed to almost two-thirds of all social media visits, solely by establishing a Facebook presence. Twitter, YouTube, and a few well-chosen others can nicely round out the picture.

It takes time for brands to learn each unique social media neighborhood and begin to feel at home. The smallest networks aren't worth your attention as a marketer—unless they are special-interest sites directly aligned with your market niche, which I'll discuss later in the chapter.

Facebook is by far the dominant network, vacuuming up **63%** of social media visits. YouTube captures **20%**, and the rest manage only single-digit market shares (see Figure 3-1).

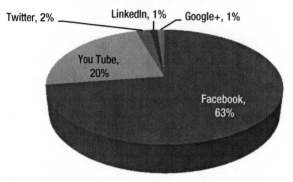

Social Media Market Share
by share of visits

Twitter, 2%　　LinkedIn, 1%　　Google+, 1%

You Tube, 20%

Facebook, 63%

Figure 3-1. Facebook is the 800-pound gorilla when it comes to total visits to social media sites. Facebook's dominance is even greater when measured by the amount of time users spend on each site.[2]

- I know, from the brands I work on professionally, that your business's Facebook fans, Twitter followers, YouTube subscribers, and Google+ followers will generally reflect these proportions. Facebook fans dwarf Twitter followers, while Google+, YouTube, Pinterest, and the others hardly register. However, there are important distinctions: some brands, especially celebrities, publishers, bloggers, and thought leaders, over-index on Twitter. That's because Twitter is such a popular and effective clearinghouse for information, trends, gossip, and news.

- On YouTube, subscribers are a poor measure of a brand's impact. Views are a better metric—although views align better with "reach" than "followers" when comparing YouTube with other networks.

To examine the idea of effort versus reward, I compared several leading brands in a variety of industries, including Coca-Cola, Toyota, Levi's, Lady

---

[2] Priit Kallas, "Top 10 Social Networking Sites by Market Share of Visits," August 2012, www.dreamgrow.com/top-10-social-networking-sites-by-market-share-of-visits-august-2012/.

Gaga, and others (see Table 3-1). I found that, on average, these brands' social media fan bases broke down as follows:

- 78% Facebook followers

- 18% Twitter fans

- 2% Google+ circles

- 1% YouTube subscribers

Table 3-1. Impact Comparison of Leading Social Media Platforms

Community	Facebook	Twitter	Google+	YouTube	TOTAL
Coca-Cola	46,622,757	590,343	2,490	75,654	47,291,244
Relative share	99%	1%	0%	0%	
Lady Gaga	53,075,813	28,117,376	3,290,737	529,182	85,013,108
Relative share	62%	33%	4%	1%	
Levi's	13,272,427	75,545	935	2,403	13,351,310
Relative share	99%	1%	0%	0%	
Los Angeles Lakers	14,430,340	2,650,426	802,545	4,510	17,887,821
Relative share	81%	15%	4%	0%	
Patagonia	185,175	63,260	217	7,776	256,428
Relative share	72%	25%	0%	3%	
Prada	1,849,283	6,771	2,179	7,424	1,865,657
Relative share	99%	0%	0%	0%	
Platform share of visits	63%	2%	1%	20%	

Obviously, Facebook is the 800-pound gorilla of the space. But with its nearly one billion global members, and the constant flood of newsfeed "stories," it can be difficult for a business to truly make an impact and cut through the noise on Facebook.

Twitter and LinkedIn, on the other hand, offer great tools for identifying potential connections and interacting with them one-to-one and in groups. Especially for niche markets, or for business-to-business (B2B), the advantages of Twitter and LinkedIn in building tighter, more personal communities compensate for their more limited reach.

The lesson here: invest your time, strategic energy, and money proportionally to the "market share" of these social media networks. But take into account the special affinities of your brand and marketplace. Visual brands should favor YouTube and Flickr. Authors, bloggers, and publishers should overweight Twitter. Business-to-business companies should overweight LinkedIn.

So, you'll complement Facebook with Twitter and other platforms. Depending on what market your business is in—say, whether it's B2B or B2C (business to consumer), whether it's highly visual, or whether it operates local retail stores—will determine on which other platforms you'll find your most receptive audiences. As with an effective marketing mix or a diversified media buy, a good social media program recognizes these truths:

- Each social platform has its unique strengths, weaknesses, culture, and audience.

- Being active on multiple platforms increases the likelihood you will reach—and make a memorable impression on—your target customer.

- Being active on multiple platforms lets you serve up the whole array of what fans are looking for: entertainment, engagement, customer service, exclusive deals, social proof in the form of customer testimonials, images and video, customer-generated reviews, recipes, and so forth.

Engagement vs. Marketing

This book is devoted to social media *marketing*, but many of the topics I'll cover have more to do with consumer engagement, customer service, and building brand equity than with direct-response advertising. People participate in social media for fun. They're eager to connect with friends and family, and they're increasingly willing to bring trusted brands into that circle of relationship. But there are limits to the connection people really want with companies on social media. Consumers have intangible but real boundaries when it comes to receiving promotional pitches through social channels.

One good way to reach your online community with new products, deals, and offers is to leverage the power of word of mouth. Consumers feel better about, and place more trust in, the purchase advice they get from friends. Social networks are a great place to pursue word-of-mouth marketing, build brand reputation, deepen your relationship with existing customers, and practice a soft sell.

E-mail and direct mail remain the dominant ways to sell to your customers. Yet, a surprising 20% of consumers say they have made a purchase in response to a marketing message on Facebook (see Figure 3-2).

Research has demonstrated a strong correlation between people "liking" a brand on social media and doing more business with that brand. However, a 2012 study found that many consumers are lukewarm about receiving promotional messages from brands they "friend."[3] While 40% of social media users "like" businesses in order to receive special discounts and promotions, another 40% say they don't believe that "liking" a brand on Facebook entitles the brand to market to them via the newsfeed. Clearly, the commercialization of social media is a touchy subject and a rapidly evolving one!

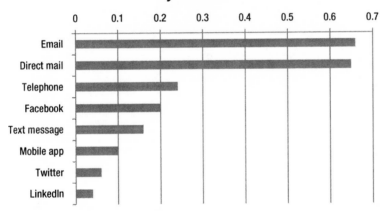

Consumers Who Have Purchased in Response to a Marketing Message, by Channel

Figure 3-2. While more traditional direct marketing tactics still dominate, a surprising 20% of consumers report making a purchase in response to a marketing message on Facebook.[4]

---

[3] ExactTarget, "The 2012 Channel Preference Survey, Report #14," August 2012.

[4] Ibid.

TEEN (15–17) CHANNEL PREFERENCE

While crafting the social media strategy of your organization, be sure to look down the road. Today's teens are tomorrow's adult consumers. Their preferences for online activity and communications? Think immediate gratification: more mobile, more social, more text messaging, and more instant messaging (IM).[5]

- 84% use e-mail at least once a day

- 82% text at least once a day

- 78% use Facebook at least once a day

- 51% check in using location-based services like Foursquare at least once a day

- 46% chat via instant messaging at least once a day

- 39% use smartphone messaging apps like WhatsApp at least once a day

- 32% use Twitter at least once a day

Facebook

Facebook keeps getting richer, as a user experience and as a place for businesses to build communities and advertise for customers. The site continues to grow because new users, merely curious at first, often become addicted to the site. Contrast that with many other social networks, where curious newcomers tend to kick the tires, get bored, and quit coming back.

The list of top business Facebook pages, measured by "likes," is dominated by celebrities, games, entertainment, and utilities. With buzz, critical mass, and momentum on their side, these multimillion-fan communities are growing by thousands of "likes" a day. Table 3-2 shows the top 15 as of September 2012.

[5] Ibid.

Table 3-2. Top 15 Business Facebook Pages.[6]

Rank	Page	Total Likes
1	Facebook for Every Phone	131.0 M
2	Facebook	71.8 M
3	Texas HoldEm Poker	64.9 M
4	YouTube	62.4 M
5	Eminem	60.9 M
6	Rihanna	60.1 M
7	The Simpsons	54.5 M
8	Shakira	54.3 M
9	Lady Gaga	53.2 M
10	Michael Jackson	51.7 M
11	Coca-Cola	49.9 M
12	Harry Potter	46.9 M
13	Cristiano Ronaldo	48.1 M
14	Family Guy	48.0 M
15	Justin Bieber	46.4 M

Among consumer product brands, the top Facebook and Twitter presences include Coca-Cola, Disney, Converse, Starbucks, Red Bull, Oreos, Skittles, McDonalds, Pringles, Walmart, Victoria's Secret, Target, iTunes, Xbox, Monster Energy, Subway, Nutella, Adidas, and Levi's, each with 10 to 30 million fans apiece.

Facebook offers a hard-to-beat mix of features. Brand pages and tabs are far more customizable than on other networks. The platform does a good job supporting text posts, photo sharing, video sharing, events, groups, bricks-and-mortar places, applications and more.

Social calls to action (liking, commenting, joining, sharing, downloading) are prominent in the site experience, and they generate strong ripple effects that

[6] Brittany Darwell, "Top 25 Facebook Pages September 2012," Inside Facebook, September 3, 2012, www.insidefacebook.com/2012/09/03/top-25-facebook-pages-september-2012/.

can be beneficial for brands. Social plug-ins make it easy to bring Facebook social features (such as the *Like* button) to your website and amplify your impact through the Facebook network. This system of adding social features to third-party websites was introduced as Facebook Connect, and is now known under the broader and more powerful toolset Facebook for Websites. I'll explore this opportunity in greater depth in Chapter 10.

Especially powerful is Facebook tab development through its open API and app development framework. Whether you're seeking to support a simple e-mail newsletter signup, or something more ambitious like an online sweepstakes, you can do it. App development like this is a great way to enhance your business page—and, as long as it's accompanied by clear opt-in messaging, to bring member data back into your house file to build future relationships.

One of the things I like best about Facebook is the ambitious application development that goes on within it and through its huge and vibrant app developer community.

Mail a Postcard, for instance, is a new Facebook partnership with Postagram, in limited beta, which lets users send their Instagram photos to friends as printed postcards through regular postal mail for 99¢ per card.

For now, Mail a Postcard only allows individuals to mail their own photos to friends; it doesn't work for public photos or photos from Facebook pages. So it's not immediately useful for companies and brands, but it is a development I'm watching eagerly. Any company sending out millions of catalogs or direct-mail pieces would likely be interested in directing some of its print media budget to a more social, personalized postcard mailing to its Facebook community (perhaps with fan-exclusive offers), or encouraging mailings between fans and their friends.

As I'll discuss in Chapter 5, Facebook has rolled out very powerful advertising options. Given all the free functionality of the site, the fast pace of continued enhancements, the third-party developer community, and the emerging advertising options, I believe Facebook is an ideal proving ground for any company's social media efforts.

Twitter

Not everybody "gets" Twitter. Of the 300 million individuals who have signed up, only about half are active. While Twitter users account for about 20% of all Internet *users*, the site garners just a single-digit share of all *visits* to social media sites. In other words, Twitter is visited less frequently by its members than are the "stickier" networks, namely Facebook and YouTube.

Twitter users' minimal time on site could further the impression that the network is an also-ran. But that impression would be mistaken.

Part of Twitter's appeal is efficiency: its stripped-down 140-character posts and messages, simple keyword and hashtag-driven searches, and clean, scrolling activity feed can deliver a wealth of information in minutes or even seconds. Twitter is part microblogging service, part social network. It excels as a special-interest news aggregation tool, a trend-spotting engine, and a vehicle for finding, following, and connecting with like-minded people.

Twitter is one of the least *reciprocal* of social networks: unlike Facebook or LinkedIn, where friends and connections communicate one-to-one, Twitter's "followers" model encourages thousands and even millions of users to subscribe to the posts of the most influential voices in the Twitter community.

■ **Tip**   Twitter is more of a publishing platform than a social network. To flourish on Twitter, target a clear topical niche and bring out your inner *People* magazine editor—zero in on trending topics in your market and craft headlines that will grab your readers' attention.

That characteristic makes some high-profile Twitter accounts more like a brand page on Facebook—and also something of a "Publishing 2.0" model, the vanguard of digital journalism. Some of the best fits for Twitter are providers of news, expertise, tips, insight, inspiration, and gossip.

Major brands, celebrities, and other high-profile personalities are often impersonated or copycatted by unauthorized, unofficial Twitter profiles. Twitter combats the practice by bestowing a blue checkmark "verified badge" on authentic profiles. But don't expect a verified badge if you're just a regular Joe—these badges are mostly added for VIPs on a "don't call us, we'll call you" basis. Says Twitter of its verification program: "We concentrate on highly sought users in music, acting, fashion, government, politics, religion, journalism, media, advertising, business, and other key interest areas. We verify business partners from time to time and individuals at high risk of impersonation."[7]

That said, if you detect fake or misleading profiles of your company or brand, or of high-profile people in your organization, do reach out to Twitter to see if the company will verify your username.

While the biggest accounts on Twitter belong to celebrities like Justin Bieber, Shakira, and Kim Kardashian, the network is ideal for smaller, niche players to find, follow, and start interacting with their own special-interest audience. I've

---

[7] Twitter, "FAQs About Verified Accounts," www.twitter.com/help/verified.

found that Twitter can be a challenging platform for B2C businesses to reach critical mass, but it's a great place for B2B businesses and individuals.

Facebook makes it easy to attract hundreds and thousands of fans, but the platform makes it difficult to communicate directly with them. Twitter, on the other hand, allows you to publicly message anyone—and to directly message any of your followers.

The beauty of Twitter is how easy it is to find experts, bloggers, tastemakers, real-world journalists, specialists, and consultants. By tracking Twitter conversations, hashtags, and trends for your own keywords, you can speedily identify influential people in your industry or marketplace. Follow them, retweet them when you like their stuff, and reach out to them with comments on their tweets.

If you're a B2B professional using Twitter, you can boost your profile by publishing thoughtful posts about your industry. You can follow and connect with business journalists, conference organizers, professional organizations, potential vendors, partners, and future customers.

Twitter has developed an API so outside developers can integrate their applications with it, but the platform is a lot simpler than Facebook—it's still basically a messaging platform and news aggregator. Twitter's mission statement is clear. It urges users to "Find out what's happening, right now, with the people and organizations you care about."

Twitter's value proposition to businesses is that the platform can provide "brand lift," CRM, and direct sales.

These are the best ways to leverage Twitter's power:

- Develop a publishing presence with an elevator pitch that makes it appealing to follow. If you can't squeeze all your messaging into one clear theme, consider establishing multiple Twitter feeds. Dell Computer, for instance, maintains dozens of mission-specific handles, for Dell Outlet, Dell Home, small business, customer care, investor relations, corporate social responsibility, all its different multinationals, and of course the personal handle of founder Michael Dell.

- Monitor the "Twitterverse" for brand mentions, and follow active Twitter users in your market. Following others is the best way to gain followers.

- Retweet positive brand messages posted by your followers and brand loyalists.

- Run occasional trend campaigns, where you encourage (or even incentivize) followers to retweet your message if they like or support it.

- Customize your profile-page background.

- Add Twitter logos and widgets to your site.

- Amplify your message with Twitter advertising programs like Promoted Accounts, Promoted Tweets, and Promoted Trends (see Chapter 6).

Retweeting is coin of the realm on Twitter, and it's the best evidence that your message is resonating with its audience. Here are strategies to get more retweets and generate viral word of mouth:

- Channel your inner *People* magazine editor. Compose Tweets that are catchy and compelling, including "top 10" lists, tips, bests and worsts, and so forth.

- Tweet at the right time: day of the week and hour of the day are critical if you want attention. Your Tweets should appear onscreen when your followers are awake and most likely to be looking at their Twitter feed

- Don't batch your tweets. Even if you write most of your posts in concentrated bursts, that's not the way to publish them—a steady cadence is best.

- Use popular, trending hashtags if they're relevant to your market. And invent and promote your own hashtags.

- Periodically update, revise, and repost your own Tweets. You may feel you're repeating yourself, but 99% of your followers will miss your posts the first time around. That's just the way Twitter rolls ... er, scrolls.

Although it's tempting to automate for the sake of efficiency, I don't recommend that you put your following or replying on autopilot. There are too many spammers out there to make it sensible for businesses to auto-follow whoever follows them. The same goes for "thanks for the follow" automatic messages. Hold yourself to a higher standard. Big or small, your program should have as its goal the establishment of real interactions with real stakeholders in (and potential ambassadors for) your brand. Taking a few seconds to see who each new follower is, and sending each one a (slightly) customized welcome message, will pay off in enhancing the strength of your network.

Remember, Twitter is part social network, part "microblog" publishing platform. When you follow a group of people, companies, and organizations, you're subscribing to a newsfeed. Twitter is where users go to take the pulse of current events, politics, pop-culture trends and memes, sports chatter, celebrities, industry news, or special interests.

When your business or organization establishes itself on Twitter, therefore, you become a publisher, streaming information—and ideally some inspiration— to your followers.

On a smaller scale, Twitter is also an effective person-to-person messaging platform, one that has partly replaced e-mail and IM for its most firmly entrenched denizens.

Google+

Frankly, there's still no clear map for what success looks like for a business on Google+. Sure, the Google+ member base grew faster than any product or service Google has launched in its entire history. The network reached ten million users in a stunning *16 days*. It grew a lot faster than Facebook did at the same point in its history. (Twitter took 780 days and Facebook 852 days to get to ten million.)

But despite the millions who suddenly signed up for Google+, few are deeply engaged with the community yet. Research from comScore recently found Google+ members spend a mere 3 minutes a month on the network. The figure for Facebook is a hefty 405 minutes a month. And here's another hint that all is not well with Google+: it's not exactly an inspiring message when your VP of engineering asserts that the network is "not a ghost town."[8]

Yet you can't dismiss Google+. The platform remains an important place to test, learn, and optimize. Some Google+ innovations, like Hangouts (interactive online video chats), could prove to be important behavior-changing and trendsetting developments. Others, like Circles, were quickly copied by other platforms and may not remain much of a differentiator. Thus far, these are the most attractive elements of the Google+ play:

1. It can offer benefits in search engine optimization (SEO). Google calls its new approach to social search "Search, plus Your World." A robust Google+ network can benefit your organic search presence in four ways:

---

[8] Nick Bilton, "Countering the Google Plus Image Problem," *The New York Times*, March 6, 2012, http://bits.blogs.nytimes.com/2012/03/06/google-defending-google-plus-shares-usage-numbers/.

    a. *Personal Results.* Google+ photos and posts from the searcher and his or her personal network rise to the top of that user's organic search results. That feature enables Google+ users to "search across information that is private and only shared to you, not just the public web," says Jack Menzel, director of product management at Google Search.

    b. *Profiles in Search.* Google+ profiles are crawled and ranked. They appear in both autocomplete and organic results, favoring people within the user's network or those whom the user might be interested in following.

    c. *Pages in Search.* Google+ pages are crawled and appear in search results. In fact, Google+ content seems favored by Googlebot (hmmm, whodathunk?).

    d. *Social Signals in Search.* Google's organic search-ranking algorithm now incorporates not just links and on-page content, but also "social signals" of a page's popularity. One recent study found that high organic ranking is more strongly correlated with the number of Google +1's that a page has received than with the number of Facebook "likes" it has received.[9]

2. As I'll explore in Chapter 6, Google+ offers compelling integration with your AdWords paid search ads, which should boost click-through rate and even conversion rate. When you link your AdWords account with your Google+ page, your ads display "social annotations"—showing the destination site's total Google +1's (which are equivalent to "likes" on Facebook) and spotlighting those from friends of the searcher.

3. Google+ offers exposure across other Google account features and YouTube video hangouts. As ExactTarget put it in a research report, "We're curious to see whether Google's continued integration of Google+ into its other messaging channels—

---

[9] Paul Huggett, "Google +1s Have a Stronger Correlation to High Ranking URLs than Facebook Likes," Stickyeyes, www.stickyeyes.com/insights/seo/google-1s-have-a-stronger-correlation-to-high-ranking-urls-than-facebook-likes/.

Gmail, Google Chat, and Android mobile devices—will deliver on the promise of the 'social inbox.'"[10]

4. Google+ Circles and its interactive, real-time video Hangouts are real innovations that have taken today's social networks up a notch.

■ **Tip** To delve into the nitty-gritty of how-to and strategy for community building and sharing on Google+, check out Guy Kawasaki's e-book: *What the Plus! Google+ for the Rest of Us* (Guy Kawasaki, 2012), http://www.guykawasaki.com/what-the-plus/.

LinkedIn

LinkedIn is the world's biggest professional networking site, with over 175 million members worldwide. If you're a business-to-business company, LinkedIn should sit front and center of your corporate social media efforts. Even if you're in B2C, LinkedIn has a valuable role to play in building your own personal brand and in helping you connect with vendors, resources, and partners to help you successfully run your social media program.

When I worked in the digital agency world, as VP of marketing for Timberline Interactive, LinkedIn was an important part of my outreach to the e-commerce industry at large and to particular e-comm professionals. Building a strong, coherent, industry-focused network is the heart of success on LinkedIn.

Whether you're an expert in network security, political fundraising, or Pilates, LinkedIn is an ideal way to broadcast your expertise to potential new clients, industry media, conference organizers, and even the mainstream media. Posting good information—whether it's something original that you wrote on your blog, or whether you're sharing the insights of others—boosts your profile as an expert in your field. You can also link these posts to your Twitter account.

Participating in LinkedIn Groups and LinkedIn Answers furthers your professional reputation. You can drill into special-interest topics, connect with other members, and be recognized with "Best Answer" badges.

Impending industry conferences and commentary about trending hot topics in business generate a buzz on LinkedIn that is unlike that of the other social networks. Being part of that conversation makes you better informed and ultimately more valuable in your job.

---

[10] ExactTarget, "The 2012 Channel Preference Survey, Report #14," August 2012.

On LinkedIn, you can signify your openness to career opportunities, new ventures, consulting offers, business deals, and the like. LinkedIn is *de rigueur* for job seekers and recruiters, although unlike Monster.com, LinkedIn is much more than just a career site.

If you work in B2B sales and marketing, it's natural to view LinkedIn as an opportunity to reach business prospects. I firmly agree. But I caution you to observe one cardinal rule: never send a sales inquiry in the form of a connection request on LinkedIn. LinkedIn best practices are clear. You should only seek to connect with people you actually know. I frequently receive connection requests from salespeople I have never met, and I ignore them every time.

Tip On LinkedIn, request a connection only with people you know. People are attuned to disguised selling and will resent it.

Once I am actually doing business with someone, if that person is a valued member of my professional network, by all means I'll connect with him or her on LinkedIn. If you want to make a sales inquiry, do your research on LinkedIn, but reach out via phone or email or by an InMail.

LinkedIn maintains company pages, but they're pretty blah—functioning more like business directory entries than interactive brand pages. The site recently pepped up its home-page functionality, displaying industry-specific news and images attuned to each user's industry focus. But at the heart of it, LinkedIn's real attraction remains its ability to help its members build their professional networks and enhance their professional reputation.

For more on how to employ LinkedIn as part of a B2B marketing program, I recommend *LinkedIn for Business: How Advertisers, Marketers and Salespeople Get Leads, Sales and Profits from LinkedIn*, by Brian Carter (Que Publishing, 2012).

Another good read, although less about LinkedIn than about career development in the new economy, comes from LinkedIn founder Reid Hoffman and coauthor Ben Casnocha: *The Start-Up of You: Adapt to the Future, Invest in Yourself, and Transform Your Career* (Crown Business, 2012).

Building a healthy network of contacts on LinkedIn is a worthy mission for any B2B professional. On LinkedIn, your network means people connected, within three degrees of separation, to your friends. With 800 or so connections, I have over 15 million people in my network. That's a stunning number. Today when I search the site, most people with whom I want to connect are inside that circle.

YouTube

With online video, brands and their products come to life. YouTube, which is second only to Facebook for social media visits, is a boon to visual brands, including big fashion, entertainment, music, sports, and lifestyle brands.

Popular (and expensive) television campaigns like "Old Spice Guy," "Unpimp Your Auto," and anything from Victoria's Secret enjoy additional free airtime in the form of millions of views on YouTube. Brands in niche businesses can make effective use of YouTube videos, from viral success stories like BlendTec's "Will It Blend" series or the Dollar Shave Club.

■ **Tip**   While all marketers cherish the hope that their YouTube video will "go viral," that's as unlikely as hitting a grand slam. Instead, focus on hitting singles: create fun, relevant videos that connect with your target audience. Even without viral popularity, YouTube videos can benefit your brand image, boost search-engine visibility, and amass a "cookie pool" for Google AdWords advertising.

Humbler but still effective examples include how-to videos from Home Depot, tutorials from crafting shops, tips from investment newsletters, music videos from independent bands, or stunts like Wine of the Month Club's founder demolishing bottles of substandard wine by using them as bowling pins. While niche videos don't attract millions of views, they do find qualified audiences, reaching the people who are most likely to buy or spread the word.

One remarkable YouTube cultural trend is the *haul video*. Especially popular among shopping-obsessed teen girls, these user-generated YouTube videos feature shoppers displaying and talking about all the cool new outfits, shoes, and accessories they just purchased at the mall or online. The most popular practitioners of haul videos enjoy fan bases of thousands of subscribers and can rack up millions of video views—inspiring comments, video responses, and other positive word of mouth both for the YouTube personality and the brands he or she favors.

Haul video star Bethany, who goes by the YouTube handle Macbarbie07, is a perfect example—a teenage girl whose YouTube channel has attracted nearly a million subscribers and over 100 million video views. She posts several times a week on fashion and beauty—showing off her latest buys, displaying her new haircut or makeup, and giving a video tour of her bedroom decor. A typical Bethany haul video showcases clothing from PacSun, H&M, and Urban Outfitters, generating feedback like "I love your sense of style, want ALL your clothes for the new school year :)" and "I went to H&M a couple weeks ago and got the same pants."

According to a study by Google and Compete, 2012 marks the first time that more than half of clothing purchases—57%, to be exact—are transacted online or influenced by online research and price comparison. Video is playing a powerful role in this equation.

"We're seeing massive changes in the use of digital, mobile devices, and video in driving apparel sales," said Todd Pollak, Google's industry director for retail. "Four out of ten shoppers who watched a product video online later visited the store online or in person. And 34 percent of clothing shoppers are likely to buy after watching an online video ad, versus only 16 percent after watching an ad on TV."[11]

Consumers using video to research products and services spend more and buy more frequently. About 25% of video users bought apparel more than six times in six months. Some 28% of video researchers spent more than $500 on apparel in six months—compared to a mere 2% among those who don't use video to research their purchases.

Younger shoppers, ages 18 to 34, are more than twice as likely as older shoppers to rely on video to decide what products to buy.

Another advantage for brands with a robust presence on YouTube is the integration of advertising options from YouTube parent company Google. In Chapter 6, I'll go into more detail, but for now the valuable thing to know is that you can serve remarketing ads to people who have watched your videos. You drop cookies on your YouTube video viewers, and then later show Google Display Network ads to them as they navigate the web at large.

YouTube is not the only video network in town—the mobile video app Socialcam is soaring in usage, for instance—but it is still the biggest. Advertising synergies with Google and social integration with Google+ can be expected to increase, making YouTube an important element of most social media plans.

---

[11] Laurie Sullivan, "Clothing Haul Videos Hit YouTube, Lead To Rising Retail Sales," *Online Media Daily*, MediaPost, August 13, 2012, www.mediapost.com/publications/article/180628/clothing-haul-videos-hit-youtube-lead-to-rising-r.html#ixzz29C77Hdf1.

Pinterest

Pinterest, the online pinboard especially popular among women, was the social media darling of 2011. The fastest site ever to get to 10 million users, Pinterest is still growing at double digits, but its rocket-ship ride slowed dramatically in 2012. Still, the site has 20 million users, most of them in the coveted female demographic, devoted to interests like fashion, interior design, cooking, and recipes. Pinterest is now the third most popular social network by visits, after Facebook and Twitter.

It's no wonder marketers sat up and took notice.

Just look at who's on the site and what they're passionate about:

- 68% are women
- 50% have children
- 50% are ages 25 to 44
- 28% have high household income of $100,000+

And the hot topics for pinboards:

- Beauty
- Fashion and jewelry
- Interior decor
- Food and cooking
- Weddings
- Travel
- Photography

What's special about Pinterest is that it has elevated cool but otherwise ordinary people into highly influential tastemakers. Graphic designers, "fashionistas," architects, interior decorators, crafters, cooks, homemakers—these are the types of people who rise to stardom on Pinterest. The heavy hitters generally create a few dozen boards with a few thousand pins. They can have hundreds of thousands of followers apiece. Some are approaching a million.

At this point, Pinterest accepts no advertising. So, if you want to participate and expose your products to the Pinterest audience, you'll have to join the site and start pinning items. Organizations and brands like Threadless, Scholastic books, Birchbox, Volvo, Homes.com, UNICEF, and AMC Theaters are doing interesting things on Pinterest, including movie promotions, fundraising campaigns, "pin to win" sweepstakes, and more.

If your business appeals to women consumers, and it's visual, you're in the sweet spot for Pinterest.

As with Twitter, the growth of your Pinterest community depends on the clarity and popularity of your interests, how frequently you pin, whom you choose to follow, how much promotion you do, and how well you integrate Pinterest with your main website.

Pinterest's member growth is real, and the female-centric nature of the site makes it especially attractive to businesses, because women make 85% of brand purchase decisions. Women are more social than men, especially when it comes to shopping—and their already considerable financial might will grow dramatically in coming years.

"Over the next decade, women will control two-thirds of consumer wealth in the United States and be the beneficiaries of the largest transference of wealth in our country's history. Estimates range from $12 to $40 trillion," says Claire Behar, senior partner at the marketing and public relations firm Fleishman-Hillard New York. "Many boomer women will experience a double inheritance windfall, from both parents and husband. The boomer woman is a consumer that luxury brands want to resonate with."[12]

Let's not overstate the female-centric nature of Pinterest, though. The 8.5 million men using the site are nothing to scoff at. Indeed, Pinterest may represent an ideal audience for markets where husbands and wives work together to make major purchase decisions. "Pinterest is good for us," says Michael McHale, director of corporate communications at Subaru of America.[13] With boards dedicated to motor sport, vintage Subarus, camping, dogs, and other lifestyle interests, plus "Fan Friday" owner-submitted car portraits, the Subaru of America Pinterest account really captures the full sweep of the brand and how it factors in the emotional life of its fans—male and female alike. Subaru's "Longevity" pinboard features scores of owner-submitted photos of venerable Subaru odometers, like Frankie Prato's 1999 Impreza showing 488,314 miles and still going strong. Whether you're a performance car enthusiast or a soccer mom, what's not to love about that?

Yet, Pinterest is still new and unproven. Impossible though it seems to its adherents, Pinterest could be a mere fad. The site currently offers very few business-specific offerings, either for hosting a brand presence or for advertising. Your legal department may have intellectual property concerns

---

12 Sheconomy, "Marketing to Women: Quick Facts," www.she-conomy.com/facts-on-women.
13 Michael McHale, in discussion with the author, October 5, 2012.

about the Pinterest model and warn you to pin only your own content and not the content of others.

For these reasons, I recommend a test-and-learn approach to Pinterest. It is a vibrant, different, and exciting social media phenomenon. Brands that set up a presence on Pinterest will benefit by forging a connection with one of the most coveted consumer demographics anywhere.

Foursquare

Foursquare is a mobile app used by some 20 million consumers to find, check in on, and interact with local establishments. Nearly a million businesses are represented on Foursquare, which has notched over two billion check-ins in the company's brief history.

■ **Note**   Social media marketing isn't just for e-commerce companies. Bricks-and-mortar businesses can flourish by claiming their location page on Foursquare, interacting with customers, and offering Foursquare specials for newcomers and regulars. As online activity continues to migrate from the desktop to the smartphone, Foursquare's reach and value will only increase.

Adoption of mobile applications to interact with local businesses (and other patrons) is still young and still poised for explosive growth. A 2012 survey by Intuit found that only about 18% of smartphone owners use check-in apps, but that number represents a 50% upswing from the prior year. Some 25% of businesses agree that check-in apps are an important phenomenon, up from a mere 2% in 2011.

Owners of local establishments have a lot to gain by engaging with their regulars and prospective customers on Foursquare.

First, claim your business location. One benefit of doing so is the cling window decal Foursquare will send you to display in your front widow to encourage patrons to check in.

Then, it's time to start offering specials, posting updates, encouraging check-ins, and befriending and interacting with patrons.

The key to a successful Foursquare presence is to encourage lots of check-ins. To do that, tap into the four main motivations of users: fun, fame, friendship, and, well, greed.

Fun and fame are served by the *gamification* elements of the Foursquare app. With Foursquare's points system, leaderboard, and badging system, users feel encouraged to check in. Rewarded both for first-time check-ins and for becoming a regular, a Foursquare user has it both ways.

Foursquare supports seven types of specials for a business owner to promote to its clientele. It charts these deals on a continuum of customer acquisition versus customer retention:

- **Newbie Special.** Unlocked for a first-time check-in. ("Welcome new customer! Save 10% off anything in the store, today only.")

- **Friends Special.** Unlocked when a set number of Foursquare friends check in together. California Pizza Kitchen, for instance, offered a 20% meal discount when three friends checked in as a group.

- **Flash Special.** Like an early bird or happy hour special, this is unlocked for the first people to check in after a specific hour. The first ten Foursquare users to check into Penn Museum's 2011 Summer Nights series received a free drink. The Sports Authority awarded a $20 gift card for its first check-in after 11 a.m.

- **Swarm Special.** A group discount, it's unlocked when a given number of people are checked into the same location at once. They don't need to be friends on Foursquare.

- **Check-In Special.** A frequent-buyer reward, this offer is unlocked every time the customer checks in.

- **Loyalty Special.** Foursquare says this can be "like a coffee shop punchcard where you might get something free on your tenth check-in." Another angle is unlocking a special for those who check in frequently in a given period, say three times in a week.

- "Mayor" Special. "Mayors are royalty," says Foursquare, so there's an offer type exclusively for them. As there is only one "mayor" per establishment (your most frequent customer of the past 60 days), you can afford to go big. The Avalon Hollywood nightclub lets its "mayor" under the velvet rope, *sans* cover charge, naturally. The Redwood, California, Whole Foods Market gives the "mayor" a free cup of coffee every visit and a free slice of pizza every tenth visit.

For more ideas on how businesses are employing Foursquare specials, check out the company blog: http://blog.foursquare.com/2011/03/09/a-whole-new-world-of-specials/.

At the time of this writing, Foursquare had just launched Local Updates, messages that appear in the *Explore* tab to communicate to your fans with news, specials, and exclusive offers.

Foursquare is also piloting its first-ever advertising offering: Promoted Updates, which will also be displayed in the *Explore* tab. These will be quite similar to Local Updates, except for the heading "Promoted." Foursquare selected 20 merchants for the pilot, including Best Buy, Old Navy, Walgreens, Miami's Standard Spa, and Starwood Hotels.

"We've been developing these two in parallel for a while," says Foursquare product manager Noah Weiss. "Local Updates are really about engaging with your existing customers when they're in the feed, when they're nearby." Promoted Updates, on the other hand, "are about showing your business more prominently, hopefully with a compelling piece of content, in the Explore tab, which is where our users go when they're actually looking for ideas for what to do next in the real world."14

By the way, Foursquare isn't just for local businesses anymore. Bravo, Red Bull, History Channel, Louis Vuitton, and The New York Times Company are among the first to develop Foursquare Pages presences tied not to a physical location but to a brand. Pages enable brands to share a stream of "Tips," status updates and photos, and be liked and followed by Foursquare users. Brands can even offer custom badges like the "Historian" badge from History Channel, which requires users to follow the brand, then check into two historical locations from the "Tips" feed in order to unlock the badge.

It's early yet to know the impact on brands of Foursquare Pages, which the company describes as "a free way to make your mark on Foursquare," explaining that "our 20,000,000 strong community can see your tips when they're out exploring." I'm inclined to agree it's a worthwhile new frontier for brands. Create a presence, if only to grab the real estate and see what comes of it.

By no means does Foursquare have the bricks-and-mortar social landscape all to itself. Mainstream networks Facebook and Google+ now have check-in functionality. Special-interest networks like Yelp and IMDb let you share with friends that you've checked into a restaurant or movie theater. But at this

---

14 VentureBeat, "With Promoted Updates, Foursquare helps advertisers push people into stores," http://venturebeat.com/2012/07/24/foursquare-promoted-updates/#VtL4HcT0TDWIHe1J.99.

juncture, I'd say increasing use of local business apps will be a net good for all the players—the rising tide that lifts all boats, as consumers become more acclimated to the fact that their phones are the ticket for researching, finding, getting deals from, and engaging with local businesses.

Niche Networks

Whatever your market, there probably exist specialized social networks dedicated exclusively to you and your audience. For example, the Ravelry online knitting and crocheting community works wonders for the folks at Yarn.com. Photographers, artists, designers, fashionistas, and other visual types will want to be active on places like Flickr, Etsy, CafePress, and Zazzle. The travel and tourism industry has TripAdvisor, WAYN, and other travel communities. Authors and readers meet on Goodreads, LibraryThing, and Amazon. Foodies and restaurant-goers gravitate to Yelp, Epicurious, and Serious Eats. Specialist communities like these can make for fruitful, tightly targeted social media outreach.

What these networks lack in size, they make up for in focused sense of community—and the halo that your brand may cultivate simply by being an active part of a tighter, more tribal group. Depending on your market, you may find that your time spent building community on a niche site is far more valuable than building it on the big, mainstream platforms.

Proprietary Networks

Thoughtful businesspeople ask themselves whether it makes sense to invest time and money to build their online community on a platform they don't own. Why create a thriving community on Facebook, Twitter, or YouTube, where all the interactions, all the search engine juice, all the customer contact information and permission, and much of the goodwill, are a feature of someone else's domain? If those platforms disappeared, so would your community. If those platforms, currently free, suddenly decided to charge you for activity on your fan page, what choice would you have?

What if they sold access to your fans to the highest bidder among your rivals? That's already happening, courtesy of Facebook advertising—and it's only going to increase, both in volume and in targeting precision.

"Build versus buy" is a crucial question to ask yourself about any technology platform: do the benefits of creating custom software suited directly to your needs merit the much higher cost, time investment, technical demands, and ongoing commitment to upgrades?

For most organizations, the answer will be a resounding "no." Building a custom social media platform is a significant design and technology challenge. If it's successful and grows rapidly, it becomes an infrastructure and bandwidth challenge (and if it *fails* to grow, that's a different problem). Once it's launched, the need for enhancements and upgrades never ceases.

Yet despite the obstacles, some companies have built impressive proprietary networks, including Bodybuilding.com's weightlifting and bodybuilding forum, the Nike+ fitness community, and Fiskars's "Fiskateers" scrapbooking and crafting community. Some e-commerce sites, like Fab.com and The Clymb, incorporate social elements to such a degree that they've inspired a new coinage, "social shopping."

These proprietary networks succeed because their members are truly passionate, their needs are specialized, and it pays to build functionality expressly for them.

If you serve a specialized market and possess core competency in technology development, a proprietary social network may be the right path for you.

If not, you still have options. Inexpensive software tools like Ning enable anyone to easily host a niche community with basic functionalities like blogs, photo and video sharing, groups, events calendars, and discussion forums. A few examples I like are the networking and careers website New Media Social, the nonprofit Social Actions, the Brooklyn Art Project, and Expedition Republic, the online community for outdoor apparel company Mountain Hardwear.

You can also take advantage of social widgets and increasingly powerful API development tools offered by Facebook, Twitter, LinkedIn, and other platforms to build rich social hooks right into your website. That way, you gain the benefits of social sharing and the network effect of the membership bases of the big networks without driving customers and browsers away from your site—and without having to become a software company yourself.

In Chapter 10, I have more on adding social features to your website.

Blogging

Blogs were the first meaningful wave of social media: cheap, instant publishing platforms enabled with commenting functionality, to turn one's readership into a bona fide online community. Despite its somewhat old-school aura, blogging remains today a highly relevant and effective way to build your personal brand and connect to an audience of like-minded prospects, media, or potential business partners.

Admittedly, in recent years blogs have become overshadowed by the huge rise in social networks.[15] Business participation on Facebook and Twitter is soaring, while support for corporate blogs has leveled off. Among *Fortune* 500 companies, 73% now maintain corporate Twitter accounts and 66% have Facebook pages, while the share of those companies with corporate blogs has been essentially flat for four years, at 28%.

However, Google and other search engines love blogs. The mostly text content of blogs is easily parsed by search engine crawlers. Assuming you update your blog frequently, with posts every day or two, the search bots will learn to crawl it frequently and reward the latest posts with high rank. As with news stories, blog posts can rise quickly to the top of relevant search results, although they often decline after the initial pop.

Search engine algorithms score the links between sites as if they were "votes" for the quality and importance of each page. Because blogs are by nature richly interlinked to and from other content on the web, Google rewards popular blogs with high page rank.

Given all this, a well-regarded blog can quickly deliver online visibility. Whether your business specializes in woodworking tools, artisanal cheeses, or day trading, a blog dedicated to your topic can bring you valuable web traffic, visitors searching for precisely what you offer.

Interestingly, some of these searchers aren't just ordinary consumers. They may also include journalists, conference organizers, and potential business partners—people with the ability to give you national media publicity, professional recognition, or valuable new co-ventures.

As a blogger, stay focused on your area of specialty, in which you are (or can become) a recognized expert. Post regularly—daily if possible. When I worked at an e-commerce marketing agency, I once performed a test where I increased my blogging frequency to daily (from once in a blue moon). The results were immediate:

- Crawl frequency increased dramatically
- Organic search traffic grew 56%

---

[15] Nora Ganim Barnes, Ph.D., Ava M. Lescault, MBA, and Justina Andonian, "Social Media Surge by the 2012 Fortune 500: Increased Use of Blogs, Facebook, Twitter and More," Charlton College of Business Center for Marketing Research, University of Massachusetts Dartmouth, www.umassd.edu/cmr/socialmedia/2012fortune500/.

- Without any prompting, my posts began being syndicated on places like Online Marketing Connect and Who's Blogging What

- My LinkedIn profile garnered 50% more views

- Business inquiries and speaking offers increased

For businesspeople wanting a firmer toehold in the blogosphere, I recommend *Naked Conversations: How Blogs Are Changing the Way Businesses Talk with Customers*, by Robert Scoble and Shel Israel (John Wiley & Sons, Inc., 2006).

If you like to write and can commit yourself to a regular publishing schedule, I recommend you add a blog to your social media arsenal. The rise of Facebook, Twitter, and other social media does not make blogging obsolete—it simply gives a blogger more platforms on which to publish and a wider audience to cultivate.

Mobile

Which social networks people use is just half the question. How they access them—whether via laptops and desktops, or by tablets or mobile devices—is also a key strategic consideration. ComScore Media Metrix reported in 2012 that almost 40% of mobile users visit social media using their mobile devices. And the proportion is rapidly growing. In sheer numbers, the mobile audience for social networking is approaching 100 million people.

The convergence of mobile and social is a big deal, and it has already spawned its own slightly laughable bit of marketing jargon: *mocial*.

Four of every five mobile minutes are spent using apps as opposed to browsing the web. Table 3-3 shows the top 15 apps (for iOS, Android, and Research In Motion combined).[16]

---

[16] comScore, "comScore Introduces Mobile Metrix 2.0, Revealing that Social Media Brands Experience Heavy Engagement on Smartphones." May 7, 2012, www.comscore.com/Press_Events/Press_Releases/2012/5/Introducing_Mobile_Metrix_2_Insight_into_Mobile_Behavior

Table 3-3. The Top 15 Mobile Apps

Rank	Application	Users
1	Google Maps	70M
2	Facebook	63M
3	YouTube	51M
4	Android Market	50M
5	Google Search	45M
6	Gmail	38M
7	Apple iTunes	33M
8	Cooliris	29M
9	Yahoo! Weather	23M
10	Words With Friends	23M
11	Yahoo! Stocks	22M
12	Angry Birds	16M
13	Pandora Radio	10M
14	The Weather Channel	9M
15	Temple Run	7M

Social media apps, where networking and sharing are central to the experience, are indicated in bold. These games aren't inherently social—they aren't real-time multiplayer games—but with Twitter integration baked in, sharing of high scores has become a pop culture trend that nicely demonstrates the synergy of mobile and social. Even celebrities, like NBA star LeBron James and singer Mary J. Blige, have tweeted scores to their 10 million or so followers:

> *"I got 1,032,164 points while escaping from demon monkeys in Temple Run. Beat that! t.co/bRr0HnMx"—LeBron James*

Looking only at purely social sites, Table 3-4 shows the top six, with Facebook capturing the lion's share of visits and total minutes of usage.[17]

Table 3-4. The Top Six Social Sites

	Total Unique Visitors (000)	% Reach of Online Users	Average Minutes per Visitor
Facebook	78,002	80.4%	441.3
Twitter	25,593	26.4%	114.4
LinkedIn	7,624	7.9%	12.9
Pinterest	7,493	7.7%	52.9
Foursquare	5,495	5.7%	145.6
Tumblr	4,454	4.6%	68.4

Note the appearance of Foursquare in the table. Platforms like Foursquare and Yelp, which emphasize local businesses, are naturals for mobile, where on-the-go customers are searching for nearby services.

The more essential that social media become to their daily lives—and the more addictive the platforms are—the more people will rely on the "anywhere, anytime" nature of mobile devices to post on and interact with social media. As you contemplate the platforms and your approach to them, be sure to combine "mission critical" tasks (product ratings and reviews, retail store locators, price comparisons, coupons, photo sharing, and more) that your audience will want to access via mobile.

Starbucks is an example of a smart and ambitious mobile/social strategy. The coffeehouse chain offers mobile apps for iPhone and Droid with transactional, local search, and sharing features. Get directions to the closest Starbucks, reload value onto your Starbucks Card, track your rewards balance, or send a friend an e-gift card. By April 2012, Starbucks had already processed 42 million payments via its mobile apps.

Starbucks also recently partnered with Foursquare for a mobile fundraising promotion with the AIDS-fighting charity (RED) called Rush to Zero. When

---

[17] comScore, "comScore Introduces Mobile Metrix 2.0, Revealing that Social Media Brands Experience Heavy Engagement on Smartphones," press release, May 7, 2012, www.comscore. com/Press_Events/Press_Releases/2012/5/Introducing_Mobile_Metrix_2_Insight_into_ Mobile_Behavior/.

consumers checked into any Starbucks location using Foursquare, Starbucks contributed $1 to the global fight against HIV-AIDS. Starbucks planned to donate up to $250,000.

Whether you plan to satisfy your customers' on-the-go needs directly through an app or mobile website, or through your presence on mobile-optimized social media—or both—mobile behaviors should feature prominently in your social media strategy.

Summary

There are literally several hundred social networks and social media websites out there. In this chapter, I've explored the top seven: Facebook, Twitter, Google+, YouTube, LinkedIn, Pinterest, and Foursquare. Between them, these "magnificent seven" cover almost 100% of the social media audience. More important, they run the gamut of different strengths you'll need to draw on depending on your brand and its market—whether you're B2C or B2B, e-commerce or bricks-and-mortar, targeting males or females, and so on.

Choosing your platforms and deciding how you'll allocate time, effort, and budget between them is like being a pro baseball manager, rostering a team of stars and utility players.

Beyond the big seven, will you find value in smaller platforms like Yelp or Reddit, or in even tinier niche platforms targeted directly at your special interest? Will publishing your own corporate blog add important reputational benefits, plus valuable SEO "link bait"? Quite possibly, yes.

My aim has been to point out where the biggest opportunities lie. These are the places to build your core online community and perform daily "organic" community-management activities: posting text and images on your wall and interacting with your fans and followers.

From here, I'll cover paid social media advertising, more ambitious social campaigns, and other tactics to really grow and optimize your online community—and show you how to measure your progress.

4

Advertising and Promotion

Buy Social Placements that Work—and Avoid the Money Pits

People log into their favorite social network for fun, relaxation, connection, and perhaps to consume news or information. They aren't there for ads.

Turn on the hard sell, and you'll be disappointed. However, if you adopt a new marketing mindset, social media advertising can be fruitful indeed. Focus on driving word-of-mouth endorsement, brand engagement, and qualified leads, and you can drive big numbers at great return on ad spending (ROAS).

Social networks encourage low-key, conversational marketing, and serve as a conduit for person-to-person buzz.

And that personal focus comes at a perfect time, because traditional advertising and selling are in trouble.

Money spent on online advertising has now eclipsed that bastion of old-school media, newspaper ads. But even online advertising is under pressure. Consumers are deluged with more commercial impressions than ever before, with overflowing e-mail inboxes, banner ads on every web page, and ads before every video.

We live in a jaded, impatient, overworked, and suspicious age. Ordinary people don't trust ads or the marketers behind them. When shopping for goods or services, what they do trust, overwhelmingly, are recommendations from friends.

It's no surprise that we trust the judgment of people closest to us. But amazingly, in the social media age, the opinions of *strangers* are nearly as powerful.

And that's where social media shines for marketers: allowing word of mouth to do the selling in a relaxed, personal, noncommercial way. The ads you run in social media are embedded in the fabric of the online community. Your campaign truly succeeds, gains extra traction and reach, through the "shares," "likes," comments, and other social interactions it earns.

We're now witnessing a turning point in commerce—where ordinary consumers engaging in social media trust each other more, and could be more influential for you, than traditional advertising.

I have five guidelines to help you identify the highest-return social advertising options and optimize your performance as you go along:

1. Start with a top-line budget

2. Establish measurable goals

3. Allocate money and time between core platform and test-and-learn campaigns

4. Test constantly

5. Rebalance efforts and budget based on return

Let's look at each in more depth, as well as touch upon the idea of social media burnout, promotions and "earned" media, and a dark side of social media spending—fan or "like" buying.

Your Social Ad Budget

How much should you spend on social media advertising? I allocate about 3% of my annual online advertising budget to social platforms, chiefly Facebook. Coincidentally, Facebook currently has about a 3% market share of all online ad spending.

Note that I'm talking exclusively about advertising expenses—media buying—not the costs of maintaining and staffing to support an online presence, creative design, and so forth.

Estimates of social media ad spending vary widely, but overall they suggest that in the United States today, marketers spend somewhere between 5% and 10% of their online ad budgets on social ads. In other words, in 2012, social advertising represented an estimated $2.0–3.5 billion of the overall $35–40 billion in online ad spending.

Because consumers spend about 15% of their online *time* on social media, some experts argue that current media budgets are underallocated to social. A survey by Buddy Media found that ad media buyers plan to increase spending on social advertising: while two-thirds of respondents currently dedicate less than 5% of their ad budgets to social, most expect in the next two years to be allocating 5–15% to social media.[1]

I concur that the slice of our ad budget pie dedicated to social advertising will grow over the next few years. Some companies are already there: the social shopping site Fab.com disclosed that fully 75% of its ad dollars are allocated to social media sites.[2]

In making budgeting decisions, marketers will inevitably have to balance the proven, high, immediate ROI of direct-response search and remarketing ads (think Google AdWords and Yahoo/Bing adCenter) with the less direct, brand-building and lead-generating benefits of social ads.

To manage a successful social media ad spend, you need the discipline of a fixed monthly budget that forces you to plan in advance, tailor promotions to seasonal peaks, pursue the best opportunities—and say "no" to the many marginal ones. Note that I'm talking specifically about *advertising* budgets. You must also budget your overall social media operating expense (see Chapter 5).

Goals and Tests: Where Are Social Ad Dollars Going?

Advertisers are spending their money where the overwhelming majority of users are spending their time: Facebook.

In a survey of media buyers, a resounding 86% of those who intended to advertise in social media planned to do so on Facebook (Figure 4-1).[3] Some

---

[1] Shawn Hess, "BuddyMedia Gears Up for Asia-Pacific Social Media," WebProNews/Business, June 12, 2012, www.webpronews.com/buddymedia-gears-up-for-asia-pacific-social-media-2012-06.

[2] Jason Goldberg, founder and CEO of Fab.com, "I'm Long on Facebook," Aug. 24, 2012, www.betashop.com/post/30096841223/im-long-on-facebook.

[3] GO-Gulf.com, "Global Online Advertising Spending Statistics," www.go-gulf.com/blog/online-ad-spending.

39% and 36%, respectively, planned to advertise on Twitter and YouTube. LinkedIn was in the ad budgets of 21% of media buyers, while Google+ attracted spending from just 18%.

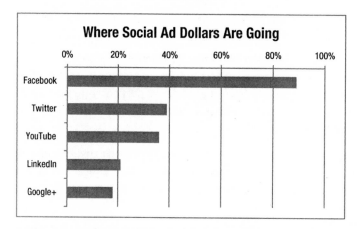

Figure 4-1. Of media buyers who intended to advertise on social media sites, fully 86% planned to advertise on Facebook. Source: GO-Gulf.com.

In Chapter 3, we noted that Facebook dominates the landscape with a 63% share of all social media visits. Facebook also does well when measured by time on site, averaging over 12 minutes per visitor (Table 4-1). By that metric, Facebook is competitive with YouTube and Pinterest, whose content is famously "sticky." Twitter, by contrast, serves its visitors with efficient summaries of scrolling news—resulting in short three-minute visits.

Table 4-1. Average Time Spent on Top Social Media Sites[4]

Site	Average Time on Site
YouTube	16.4 minutes
Pinterest	15.8 minutes
Facebook	12.1 minutes
Twitter	03.3 minutes

Given the disproportion in size and audience makeup of the top social media platforms, and the stark performance differences you'll inevitably see, you'll need to be disciplined about budgeting and goal setting.

---

[4] comScore, "State of the U.S. Internet in Q1 2012," June 14, 2012, www.comscore.com/Press_Events/Events_Webinars/Webinar/2012/State_of_US_Internet_in_Q1_2012.

- **Allocate 90% of your budget to core strategic platforms and 10% to "test and learn."** Tests are at the heart of successful marketing innovation, but too much test-and-learn on second-tier networks is the kiss of death. Unless you establish clear budget guidelines, you'll waste time and squander your attention on a crowd of small, "me too" social platforms with no ability to really move the needle. They simply don't reach enough people, and whatever reach they offer is seldom unique; it's easily duplicated on major platforms. Be disciplined, set limits for how much money and time you'll spend on small platforms, and you'll never fall victim to social media "shiny object syndrome."

- **Establish quantifiable goals.** Before rolling out an ad-supported social media campaign, state your objectives up front: we expect 12,000 new Facebook fans, say, and 10,000 contest sign-ups, of which 9,000 will opt into our e-mail program. We expect 100 new buying customers, or leads tracked directly from social media links, and X number of brand impressions from news-feed activity and retweets. Every campaign has its vital signs; they could be votes, poll responses, game-plays, dollars donated to a cause, customer-uploaded content, tell-a-friend referrals, free sample requests. With experience, you'll learn what to expect for ad cost, click-through, and conversion rate. You'll be able to establish benchmarks for efficient *cost per fan*, *cost per lead*, and *cost per order* metrics. You can also set less tangible but still trackable goals: survey-driven customer satisfaction levels or brand awareness and usage, positive sentiment, brand mentions—before, during, and after the campaign.

Remember, every dollar you spend on social media advertising will come out of some other marketing "bucket." By setting up a fixed budget, establishing clear goals, tracking results, and redirecting funds based on performance, you'll never be caught off balance by these three innocent questions from your boss:

- What are we spending on social media ads?

- What are we getting for our money?

- Is that good?

Measure Results—and Rebalance

Buyer, beware. Sure, your friendly account rep at Facebook or any other ad-supported social network wants to see you succeed so you'll become a long-term client. But don't expect him or her to worry about your ROAS. You, and only you, are accountable for the return on your ad dollars.

Whether your principal goal is to drive fan acquisition, e-mail newsletter or sweepstakes sign-ups, sales, free sample requests, or brand awareness and positive perception, you can measure it. Establish your goals, in raw numbers and in performance ratios, and broadcast them to your team in advance.

■ **Tip** It's important to establish a unit cost for the most trackable goals of a social media ad campaign, like cost per fan, cost per app download, or cost per e-mail sign-up. The key is to track the conversion rate of those social media leads to paying customers—via e-mail marketing, say. Then you can calculate your social media customer acquisition cost.

Always structure your social media ad campaigns as A/B tests. Review daily results, and optimize toward the winning media-pricing, offer, or creative model. You'll be surprised by how much variance can exist between two different ad images, headlines, calls to action, or other elements. Some of what you'll learn will be counterintuitive. For instance, I once ran a Facebook ad campaign for a sweepstakes contest; we found that ads promoting our online community (and not even mentioning the sweepstakes) generated more "likes" *and* more sweepstakes entries than the ads that pitched the sweepstakes explicitly.

Social media advertising is still in its infancy, with different ad units, targeting options, and pricing models still very much in "public beta." You can't prosper in this new landscape without making a few mistakes. Facebook itself puts it nicely in its motto: "Move fast and break things." If you're going to fail (and sometimes you will), do it quickly, react, and move on—testing new tactics, kicking the tires on new platforms, pulling ad dollars from poorly performing platforms and campaigns, and doubling down on the winners.

Combatting Social Media Fatigue

You shouldn't neglect an ironic new opportunity for social media ad campaigns: poking fun at social media.

There's no question that for many people, the hype surrounding social media is a touch overdone. Toyota recently seized on this trend—and the generational tensions stoked by Facebook's rise—with a series of clever television ads by Saatchi & Saatchi for the Toyota Venza crossover.

In one, a worried twenty-something woman sits alone at her kitchen table, browsing Facebook and addressing the camera. Having read "the majority of an article online" that reported "older people are becoming antisocial," she was aggressive about getting her parents onto Facebook. Alas, they have only 19 friends (losers!). The ad cuts to footage of her baby-boomer parents, off-roading in their Venza and mountain biking with friends. Their daughter, still at home looking at pictures of puppies on Facebook, concludes happily, "I have 687 friends! This is living."

I love it—it's funny, ironic, light, but makes a worthwhile point about lifestyle. And I doubt many younger people would be offended on behalf of their generation. We all believe we use Facebook in a healthy, balanced way. Regardless of age, most viewers wouldn't identify with the daughter in this spot. She is a caricature of lameness, and most viewers know she represents a certain type of social media addict, not all people of her generation.

The double irony is that many of the ad's impressions have been on social media. I heard it on Pandora, saw it on YouTube, then searched and found a post about it on a marketing blog. Much of the buzz and discussion about it will take place on social media. But afterward, we'll all go mountain biking, right? This is living!

Another fun twist was Victoria's Secret's 2010 offer of free-with-purchase, limited-edition bikini panties emblazoned across the seat with the Facebook thumbs-up icon and the slogan "You Like This." This exclusive offer was available with a printable coupon only after consumers "liked" the brand on Facebook.

(Facebook member-exclusive offers, by the way, are a great tactic to generate enthusiasm and underscore a sense of exclusivity and the privilege of membership—a strong answer to the natural question, "Why would I join your fan page? What's in it for me?")

These examples point out that sometimes the best way to play the social media trend is with a bit of self-awareness, irony, and self-deprecating humor. It can be an excellent way to stand out from the herd.

Promotion and "Earned Media"

While this chapter has focused almost entirely on paid advertising, advertising and *promotion* are inextricably linked. Your major advertising campaigns should be echoed simultaneously in other channels, including traditional and online press releases.

■ **Tip** Even prominent journalists do some research online, looking for specialists, experts, and "talking heads" among the blogs and on professional networks like LinkedIn. If you cultivate good social media visibility in your field or market, you could find yourself tapped for an interview out of the blue.

Blog networks are an interesting fusion between social media and paid promotion. Today, most of the biggest, most influential blogs are no longer labors of love but are supported by advertising and sponsorship. In my experience, specialty networks like BlogHer and SheBlogs, both of which aggregate "mommy bloggers" and other female-targeted blogs, can reach a valuable audience. The most attractive opportunities here are for sponsored sweepstakes and promotions, as well as packages that combine sponsorship with editorial coverage.

"Earned media" is a term that has arisen to describe free media coverage, the unpaid exposure in online and traditional media when your "story" catches on.

Giveaways and sweepstakes are not paid advertising, but they require many of the same budget-setting rigor and results tracking. Perhaps you're trying to get 10,000 free samples into the hands of bona fide prospects likely to buy your product in the future. Or maybe you want to promote a big sweepstakes, to collect qualified leads to opt into your e-mail newsletter. Promotions like these will typically be supported by both free and paid media.

Don't Go There

Major and minor social networks and platforms are scrambling to fill their coffers (and in the case of newly public companies, to justify their high but tumbling stock prices). The resulting landscape offers far more ad-buying opportunities than the potential advertiser—that's you—can or should pursue.

As Donald Trump famously observed, "Sometimes, your best investments are the ones you don't make."

■ **Note** Scams and frauds are alive and well on social media. Whether to dupe individuals or businesses, fake profiles abound—Facebook recently purged a whopping 83 million of them.

Stay away from operations that offer to add thousands of fans to your accounts in a matter of 24 or 48 hours, for flat-fee packages starting as low as $97. Sure, these firms claim to be on the up-and-up, and that no one will ever know that you "bought" your fans. But the tactics used by many fan-sellers are cheesy, manipulative, and bad for brands. That's counterproductive if your goal is to create positive brand associations and build authentic connections with brand loyalists and genuine prospects.

Most social fan-driving schemes are pretty simple:

1. Establish armies of fake profiles. Since sex sells, many, like the Twitter-deleted @jennieBHottie, are on the sexy side.

2. Use those fake profiles to follow the paying customer accounts.

3. Build huge but empty audiences through auto-following and friend requests.

4. Tweet and direct-message followers to promote "likes" and follows of the paying accounts.

The Mitt Romney 2012 campaign got a black eye when news outlets reported something fishy about @mittromney's sudden one-day jump of 117,000 Twitter followers. Online security firm Barracuda Labs identified a number of causes for suspicion:

- Followers jumped 17% in a single day

- 80% of the profiles were under three weeks old

- 23% had never tweeted

- 10% of the accounts had already been suspended by the time the story hit

"We believe most of these recent followers of Romney are not from a general Twitter population," wrote Barracuda Labs research scientist Jason Ding, "but most likely from a paid Twitter follower service."[5]

It's unknown whether follower-buying occurred, or who might be responsible—the campaign itself, a supporter, or even a rival's dirty tricks campaign. But the message is clear: shortcuts to social media success will blow up in your face. Such tactics make you look lazy and clueless at best, sleazy and dishonest at worst. The results—thousands of zombie followers that disappear the

---

[5] Barracuda Labs, "Fake Facebook Accounts, Fake Romney Followers: The Underground Economy of Social Networks," Aug. 3, 2013, www.barracudanetworks.com/ns/news_and_events/?nid=575.

moment Twitter gets wise to the abuse—do nothing to build real community or further your business goals.

The same scams occur on Facebook. National Public Radio reported on a service selling 1,000 "likes" for $75.[6] Although that business claimed its "likes" came from bona fide accounts, fake accounts are a centerpiece of some schemes. "Right now on the black market, you can actually buy and sell bundles of Facebook account credentials," Ben Zhao, computer science professor at UC Santa Barbara, told the reporters. "Tens of dollars or hundreds of dollars, for hundreds or thousands of Facebook accounts."

I'm not dismissing all services or agencies that claim they can help you get more exposure on social media. But if a firm is promising to add thousands of fans or followers to your accounts for a few bucks in the space of mere days or weeks, be afraid. Be very afraid. That's no way to build a truly brand-focused online community of real people interested in you and in each other.

If it sounds too good to be true, it probably is.

Summary

One of the main attractions of social media—especially for smaller companies, start-ups, and others with few dollars to spend—has been the access to millions of consumers, free. But can you still make an impact without spending ad dollars on Facebook and the rest?

While it's still true that social offers a great, free platform on which to publish and interact with fans, I believe most midsize and larger businesses have recognized that "organic" fan growth only gets you so far. In my experience, organic "likes" (from wall posts and "stories") tend to account for only 10–20% of new fans—while the other 80–90% come from ad-supported campaigns like sweepstakes and giveaways.

To truly expand your impact and make the most of promotions and other campaigns, you'll need to harness paid media in addition to free.

The major social networks now provide a bewildering array of new advertising options. In Chapter 5, I'll move on from the general role of social media advertising to specifics on running ads on Facebook, Twitter, LinkedIn, and other platforms—and how you can make the most of the new social advertising opportunities without losing your shirt.

---

[6] Steve Henn and Zoe Chace, "For $75, This Guy Will Sell You 1,000 Facebook 'Likes,'" NPR, May 16, 2012, www.npr.org/blogs/money/2012/05/16/152736671/this-guy-will-sell-you-sell-you-1000-facebook-likes.

Facebook Advertising

The Biggest Audience, the Most Ad Options— and Some Risks to Navigate

For years, Facebook was disdainful of calls to monetize its hundreds of millions of users, focusing instead on adding features and building critical mass. But today, as a public company, Facebook has been adding advertising options at a furious pace.

Not to be cynical, but the emerging Facebook value proposition to businesses looks something like this:

- Build your page on Facebook (free)

- Pay to build your fan base

- Pay to engage with your fan base

- Pay to engage your existing customers when they are on Facebook

Given the pace of change, this chapter is meant to explore the major advertising opportunities on Facebook today, help you understand aspects of targeting and best practices that won't change, and give you a frame of reference to assess the new units that will inevitably be introduced in coming months. We'll cover:

1. Marketplace ads

2. External URL ads

3. Facebook Object ads

4. Page Post ads

5. Sponsored Stories

6. Promoted Posts

7. Facebook Offers

8. Facebook Sponsored Search Results

9. Facebook Exchange remarketing ads

10. Custom Audiences

11. Action spec targeting

12. Facebook Premium ads

■ **Note** Facebook advertising options change fast. To stay abreast of the latest developments, visit the official Facebook advertising page www.facebook.com/marketing and leading blogs like www.insidefacebook.com, www.techcrunch.com, and www.mashable.com.

Managing Your Facebook Ads

Before we dig into the ad offerings, let me point out that Facebook supports a number of different levels of engagement for its advertisers, depending on the size of their ad budget, sophistication of the tools required, and willingness to do self-service. Facebook is ramping up ad opportunities very quickly, and its sales and support staff is challenged to keep up. That's likely one reason why, when it launched Facebook Exchange remarketing, the company selected several partner agencies to help sell the program, get clients onboard, and execute campaigns.

Your options as an advertiser are to self-serve using the online Ads Manager or to be a "managed account." Managed account status is reserved for bigger brands spending hundreds of thousands of dollars or more on Facebook ads annually—or for brands perceived to have the potential to do so. These bigger companies are assigned ad reps, they receive strategic consulting, and they get access to Facebook Premium ad units I'll discuss later. These companies may merit some Facebook schmoozing—or even a coveted invite to watch a "Hack," a mass all-nighter of frenzied code-writing at headquarters in Menlo Park.

Most advertisers, though, will be self-service accounts. Facebook Ads Manager is a fairly efficient, browser-based tool to create, track, and manage your ads. The ad units available via self-serve are called Marketplace Ads and Sponsored

Stories. If you want to create 20 or more ads at once, use the Power Editor (see sidebar).

POWERING UP

Using Facebook Ad Management Tools

Anyone can get started advertising on Facebook right away with a cost-per-click campaign. But given Facebook's rapidly growing advertising options, scaling up can require more powerful tools. Here are your Facebook ad management options, in increasing order of sophistication:

Ads Manager: This is a basic, intuitive way to manage Facebook ads manually using your web browser. Build campaigns and ads, upload images one at a time, and control budgets and bids.

Power Editor: To manage several ads efficiently, download the free Power Editor software. If you already use Google AdWords Editor, you'll find Power Editor a cinch for creating and uploading Facebook ads in bulk and for converting to and from Excel spreadsheets if desired. Documentation: http://ads.ak.facebook.com/ads/FacebookAds/Power_Editor_2012.pdf

Third-party platforms: Kenshoo, Marin, Clickable (Syncapse),and BuddyMedia are just a few of the cloud software platforms you can invest in to build, publish, manage, and track ad campaigns—not just on Facebook but across multiple social media networks—from one central dashboard. They employ the Facebook Ad API as well as APIs of the other major networks. Traditional web analytics platforms like Adobe Digital Marketing Suite (Omniture) have also expanded into social ad management and search engine marketing (SEM).

Facebook Ad API: Prefer building to buying? If you have access to developers, you can create, manage, and measure your Facebook ads via an API (application programming interface). It's also the framework for B2B companies to build Facebook ad-serving applications. Facebook says you should go the Ad API route if:

1. You manage your own ad spend, and have many accounts or many ads;

2. You need a scalable alternative to Facebook Ads Manager;

3. You are an advertising tool vendor serving small and medium-sized businesses, and you manage ads from multiple sources (like Facebook and other online advertisers); or

4. You are an ad agency managing budgets and campaigns for multiple clients.

Marketplace Ads

On Facebook, "Marketplace" is a collective term that describes a variety of ad options that appear in the right-hand column of most Facebook pages under the heading "Sponsored." Some variations of these ads can appear within the newsfeed as well.

You start by choosing something to advertise:

1. External URLs, e.g., YourDomain.com

2. Facebook pages you admin, e.g., Acme Widget

3. Facebook applications

4. Places, e.g., Blue Plate Diner, Mytown, KS

5. Events, polls, wall posts, videos, photos, or other "Facebook Objects"

On Facebook, anything that you can post to your wall can now also be sponsored as a paid ad. During the ad-create flow, you can select either an external URL, your brand as a whole, or specific posts or entities. You can choose to promote either those entities themselves or the *interactions* your fans are having with them—the stories generated when they like, share, download, comment upon, or otherwise interact with your content. This latter option, the other main type of ad unit, is called Sponsored Stories.

Tip Curious about which Facebook advertisers are targeting your own likes, interests, demographic, gender, and other identifying characteristics, right now? Go to www.facebook.com/ads/adboard. You'll get insights into targeting and see good examples of headlines, ad images, and copywriting.

External URLs

With Marketplace ads, Facebook allows advertisers to send clicks to an external URL, which launches in a new window.

Unfortunately, the bias of both Facebook and its users seems decidedly to favor remaining within the Facebook experience and seldom venturing off to other websites. Or, as Ben Pickering, CEO of the Vancouver-based Facebook development firm Strutta puts it, "In general, advertising on Facebook is more effective at driving behavior on Facebook."[1]

(However, as I'll explore later in the chapter, the new Facebook Exchange, or FBX, *remarketing ads* do seem to be successful at driving Facebook users off-site at a reasonable ROAS.)

In my experience, the cost per click (CPC) for external URL campaigns is significantly higher than for on-Facebook ads that drive users to a fan page, app downloads, events, and so forth. A 2012 Social Fresh survey of Facebook advertisers yielded similar findings: the average CPC for ads leading off-Facebook was $1.08, compared with $0.70 for on-Facebook entities—or a whopping 54% more.[2]

The average Facebook CPC for all advertisers surveyed was $0.80.

Facebook entities also have the advantage of having *Like* buttons directly on their ads—so when a user sees your ad, she needn't leave the page in order to become a fan of your brand.

■ **Tip**   You can add social activity to your external URL ads. When you enter an external website as a destination, Ads Manager searches for a Facebook page related to that website. If you find a match, you'll see a "Related Pages" check box. Check the box, and your ad will include social activity related to your Facebook page.

Facebook Object Ads

It can be a bit frustrating to pay Mark Zuckerberg and company simply to move members from one place to another within Facebook.com. But if you promote events, or have high-engagement apps like sweepstakes, giveaways, newsletter signups, or games, Facebook Marketplace ads and Sponsored Stories can be an affordable way to drive qualified leads—leads who later will visit your website and convert to customers.

Object ads have the same specs and appear in the same location as other Marketplace ads, but they promote engagement with Facebook "objects," namely:

---

[1] Ben Pickering, "How to Use Facebook Ads: An Introduction," Social Media Examiner, May 3, 2012, www.socialmediaexaminer.com/how-to-use-facebook-ads-an-introduction/.

[2] Brittany Darwell, "Survey Suggests Facebook Advertising Benchmarks: $0.80 CPC, 0.041 percent CTR," Inside Facebook, April 4, 2012, www.insidefacebook.com/2012/04/04/survey-suggests-facebook-advertising-benchmarks-0-80-cpc-0-014-percent-ctr/.

- Applications
- Events
- Pages

Page Post Ads

You can also gain likes and promote engagement with specific content elements posted to your brand's Facebook wall. Anything that you can post, you can promote in a Facebook page post ad:

- Text
- Video
- Photo
- Link
- Question
- Event

■ **Tip**   Facebook's nine-page PDF doc outlines best practices for page post ads: http://fbrep. com//SMB/Page_Post_Best_Practices.pdf.

Page post ads have a nice feature to help your ads stay fresh: during the ad-create flow, you'll see a check box labeled, "Keep my ad up-to-date by automatically promoting my most recent post." This option automatically turns your latest wall post into a page post ad or Sponsored Story, replacing the prior ad.

Sponsored Stories

On Facebook, when people connect with a page, app, or event, it creates a "story" that their friends may see in their newsfeeds. When these stories are about your Facebook objects, you can pay to promote the stories so they gain greater reach—and more people will see them when their friends have engaged with you. Sponsored stories can be about:

- "Likes" of a page
- Engagement on a page such as likes, shares, or comments on a post, votes on a question, and check-ins at a place

- Joins of an event

- Installs, uses, or plays of an app or game

- Likes or shares of an external website or link

Sponsored Stories can appear in either of two locations: in the right-hand column or within the newsfeed of your fans. In the right-hand column, they appear under a "Sponsored Stories" header. When in the newsfeed, Sponsored Stories bear a "Featured" link, which, when clicked, displays the explanation, "You are seeing this because you like Acme Widget. A sponsor paid to feature it here."

Sponsored Story ads promote interactions between people and entities that exist on Facebook: a page, event, application, place, video, photo, or album— even a single wall post. Sponsored Stories enjoy some advantages over other ad types:

- Sponsored Stories attract more attention, thanks to the profile picture of a user's friend.

- They carry the weight of *social proof*, an implicit recommendation from a friend. "Brenda Johnson likes American Express" or "Juan Castro plays Words With Friends" or "Althea Wood is going to San Antonio Zombie Walk" are powerful endorsements.

- At Facebook's discretion, they can appear not just in the right-hand column, but within the newsfeed too—which is a more natural, trusted, and higher-engagement placement.

"The basic idea is that ads should be content," says Mark Zuckerberg. "They need to be essentially just organic information that people are producing on the site."[3]

A Sponsored Story includes the profile picture of the person who made the action and the action performed, plus the names of other people in your network who have previously liked or interacted with the Facebook entity that sponsored the story.

Be aware that to run Sponsored Stories successfully, you must have an established fan base of some size—because these ads appear only in the newsfeeds of friends of your fans. If you have very few fans, you won't reach many friends of fans.

---

[3] David Kirkpatrick, *The Facebook Effect: The Inside Story of the Company That Is Connecting the World* (Simon & Schuster, 2010).

Wait, you ask, if these stories already appear free in the newsfeeds of my fans, why would I want to pay?

You pay because the initial, free distribution doesn't reach enough eyeballs. Sponsored Stories ensure that "likes" and other interactions generate more word of mouth than could happen organically. You're paying for faster growth of your fan base, among the universe of like-minded friends of fans. It's not dissimilar to the concept behind Promoted Posts, which I'll talk about next.

Promoted Posts

It's a win when fans "like" your brand page. But don't expect them to come back for a visit. Research has found about 90% of users who "like" a brand on Facebook *never return* to view or engage with your wall.

That means the newsfeed is your only lifeline to your fans. But if you have 10,000 fans, and you post religiously several times a day, how many of them actually see what you're posting?

A mere 16%, according to comScore, and Facebook itself. Many posts are filtered out of the newsfeed in a deliberate move by Facebook architects to deliver a more manageable user experience. Posts that do get through are often missed by users.

Promoted Posts are a means to reach more of your fans, for a fee.

Whether you're a page admin or an individual Facebook user, you can promote any of your recent posts (within the past three days) by clicking the *Promote* button below the post.

Because they are essentially the same format served in the same places as organic newsfeed posts, Promoted Posts enjoy a much higher engagement rate than Marketplace ads.

"Organically, you get anywhere from 15 percent to 20 percent of your fans," says Gokul Rajaram, "In order to reach the remaining 80 to 85 percent, sponsoring posts is important."[4]

Promoted Posts replaces an earlier product called Reach Generator, which was an ad-serving utility exclusively for Premium advertisers, which allowed them to pay a flat fee to reach a set percentage of their fan base.

---

[4] Zach Rodgers, "Inside the World of Gokul Rajaram, Facebook's Ad Architect," AdExchanger, September 5, 2012, www.adexchanger.com/social-media/inside-the-world-of-gokul-rajaram-facebooks-ad-architect/.

Like many of Facebook's ad offerings, Promoted Posts is a rather ingenious system to get you to pay for attention on-site—and to move Facebook users from one section of the site to another, from the other guy's stuff to yours.

Adding Social Activity to Ads

When your ad points to pages, events, "stories" and other Facebook real estate, those objects automatically display a Facebook *Like* button, which is a great element for encouraging a response without having to pull users away from whatever Facebook activity they're enmeshed in. (They can still also click on your ad to view your page.)

You can also add the *Like* button by going to any page you manage and clicking on "Build Audience" in the admin panel, then selecting "Create an Ad."

Actions on Facebook are powerful and relatively frictionless. In addition to "Join" for an event, "Use Now" for downloading an app, and "Like" for virtually any Facebook content, app developers can define their own custom actions, like "Play," "Get Recipe," "Clip Coupon," "Enjoy," "Get", "Crave," "Want," and more. You can also target these custom actions for ad-serving using the action spec (more on that later in this chapter).

Sponsored Stories have been well received by most advertisers and Facebook users alike—although not by everyone. A class-action lawsuit was recently brought against Facebook, contending that Sponsored Stories violated the rights of users by making them, in effect, unpaid endorsers whenever their "likes" or other actions are used in a paid ad. A court ruled in 2012 that Facebook must make clear to users which of their actions are used to generate advertisements seen by their Facebook friends. Users must also be given controls to opt out. For Facebook users under 18, parents must have the opportunity to opt-out their children.

That said, this ad unit has not ignited the criticism that Facebook has sometimes faced in years past from consumer advocates and privacy watchdogs. The times, they are a changin'.

Targeting

Your targeting options will differ somewhat depending on what ad unit you're using. But here are some guidelines for the targeting tools to consider: choose the location, gender, age, likes, and interests, relationship status, workplace, and education of your target audience. If you are the admin of a Facebook page, event, or app, you can also target your ad to people who are already connected to you (or exclude your ad if appropriate).

For instance, Facebook describes how a New York wedding planner might identify business prospects (see Figure 5-1):

Audience: 45,200 People

- Who live in the United States

- Who live within 50 miles of New York, NY

- Age 21 and older

- Who are female

- Who are in the category Engaged

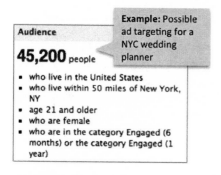

Audience

45,200 people

Example: Possible ad targeting for a NYC wedding planner

- who live in the United States
- who live within 50 miles of New York, NY
- age 21 and older
- who are female
- who are in the category Engaged (6 months) or the category Engaged (1 year)

Figure 5-1. Use Facebook to drill down to your audience. Courtesy of Facebook, Inc.

CPC or CPM?

Whether you choose to pay CPC (cost per click) or CPM (cost per thousand impressions, or views), the cost of Facebook Marketplace ads and Sponsored Stories is set by your maximum bid and the competition for the same (or overlapping) audiences. Generally, you can buy clicks for $0.50–1.50 each, with the average around $0.80. But the cost can vary greatly depending on how lucrative the market is and how voracious the advertisers are. Seasonality plays a role, too: both CPC and CPM prices climb during the holiday season.

CPC bidding generally seems to drive more tangible responses for the dollar (likes, clicks, downloads, and so on). CPM generally drives more overall impressions. So, factor your goals into your bidding strategy—and as mentioned below, for key campaigns you should A/B test the two different bid methods, to see for yourself which one performs best.

Create Facebook Ads That Work

Whatever the ad format, here are seven tactics to ensure that your Facebook ads get results:

1. **Never run a Facebook ad campaign without A/B testing.** Facebook offers strong, intuitive, ad-testing capabilities. Try several different ad headlines, images, offers, and calls to action. You will be stunned by the performance variations between versions. Even veteran marketers are often surprised by which version wins.

2. **Take advantage of audience targeting. Test identical ads on different target audiences.** For instance, try targeting your brand's fans versus friends of fans versus friends of rival brands (with your fans excluded). Brand loyalists and variously qualified prospects will all demonstrate different cost-per-action. And employ highly personalized ads for specific audiences: try geo-targeted regions, gender splits, or zeroing in on a hyper-targeted audience like students at a particular college or employees of a particular business. Facebook's signature strength is the wealth of data it collects on its fans' demographics, likes, and interests. Use it to your benefit as a marketer.

3. **Test identical ads and audiences using the two different bidding methods.** Facebook advertisers can opt to pay CPC or CPM. In my experience, CPM ads offer the best performance when the campaign goal is "likes," leads, or RSVPs. But I have heard anecdotal evidence to the contrary, supporting CPM as a more efficient choice for some advertisers. CPM may be the better model if you care more about brand exposure (impressions) than response (clicks). You won't know until you test.

4. **Make the most of your image.** That 100 x 72 pixels canvas is your Sistine Chapel ceiling. Grab attention with emotional, high-contrast, high-saturation images. Faces work well. It's been shown that smiling, attractive women appeal to users of both genders. Test your logo (especially if it is widely recognized). And try using text as an image, especially with a strong call to action.

5. **Issue a strong call to action.** A very effective Facebook ad campaign tactic is to dangle the prospect of money-saving coupons, free samples, prize giveaways, or other goodies in exchange for the "like." Coffee-mate encourages Facebookers to " 'Like' us to save $1 now," while Nespresso offers a chance to

win a coffee machine. HubSpot offers a free e-book, while Audible.com pitches two free audiobooks. Some advertisers push emotional buttons to elicit a "like": "Click 'like' if you love your kids!" exhorts CafeMom.com. "Click 'like' if you love to ski," reads an ad for a ski resort. Ken Burke, founder and chairman of the MarketLive e-commerce platform, calls this the "'Click Like If' Formula"—and it works.

6. **Change it up.** Facebook audiences get bored easily. Change your ad images every week or even every few days for important campaigns. Refresh the headlines and ad copy, too.

7. **Smaller can be better.** Often, low reach results in higher engagement rate—because Facebook users who see your ad everywhere start to tune it out. Those who see it only occasionally during a Facebook session may be more responsive, not knowing when or if they will see it again. If your daily ad budgets are lower, your targeting more precise, and you use CPC bidding, you may achieve better results for less money.

■ **Note** Facebook's signature strength is the wealth of data it collects on its fans' demographics, likes, and interests. Use it to your advantage as a marketer.

Between the powerful targeting options, frictionless social actions, and huge network reach, Facebook advertising can work for marketers of any size, in any industry. In Facebook ad campaigns I've run, we have consistently been able to turn 70% or more of clicks into "likes." Similarly high percentages opt into becoming e-mail subscribers—and thereby become qualified leads costing around $0.50–1.00 apiece. Enough of these leads become paying customers to make the Facebook platform a credible rival to other online ad platforms—and on Facebook, that formula can scale massively.

While the platform has yet to challenge Google, Yahoo, or Bing search ads on a strict direct-response ROI basis, Facebook ads are a compelling option every online marketer should be testing and optimizing.

Local Businesses: Facebook Offers

Facebook Offers is a feature initially available to "a small number of local businesses" but now in wide release. At first available free to select accounts, Facebook Offers are now a paid promotion, costing a minimum of $5 per offer. Facebook Offers also require an additional promotional commitment through Sponsored Stories.

With Facebook Offers, eligible bricks-and-mortar shops can create a 90-character headline, like "Buy one pair of socks, get another pair free," then enter other criteria to support special deals to be shared in the newsfeeds of their followers.

The offer details and link will appear below a friend's profile picture, with a headline like "Angie White and 5 others claimed an offer at Macy's."

To see if you're eligible, log into your Facebook admin account and visit your brand page. If you are eligible to make an offer, the sharing tool at the top of your page's timeline will show "Offer, Event +" in addition to other post types like Status, Photo/Video, etc.

To claim the offer, all your fans need to do is click "Get Offer" from the story anywhere they see it on Facebook. As an added bonus, the action is shared with their friends. Facebook will send your fan an email, which the fan will either print or display on his mobile phone when he visits your business to redeem the discount.

Here's how to post your offer:

1. Type a 90-character headline describing your offer and making a strong call to action.

2. Upload a photo that will stand out in thumbnail size.

3. Choose how many offers you will honor—either a set maximum number, or "unlimited."

4. Set an expiration date for your offer.

5. Add terms and conditions.

6. Click *Preview* to see what your offer will look like, then click *Post*.

You'll also be prompted to create a Sponsored Story ad to support your offer. When you have finished the set-up process and launched your ad, you'll see a running tally of how many times your offer has been "claimed."

■ **Note**   "Claiming" an offer on Facebook provides the user access to a coupon code and creates a story in the news feed. But it doesn't mean the user has actually bought anything yet. You'll get lots of claims, but perhaps only half will visit your website, and fewer still will complete a purchase.

Facebook Sponsored Search Results

Search Results is another piece of Facebook real estate that recently went up for sale. Now, you can pay to promote any Facebook page, app, or other entity, within the "type-ahead" results on Facebook search.

But if you're picturing keyword-targeted ads modeled on Google AdWords, think again.

Instead of paying to appear in response to particular search queries, with Facebook Sponsored Results you're paying for more visibility and control within the type-ahead results as they would normally be generated. Plus, you can bid for any Facebook entity—including those of your competitors. My own explorations on the site revealed some clever strategies:

- Searched for "Obama" and a Sponsored Result for Mitt Romney appeared

- Searched for "Nike" and a Sponsored Result of EA's John Madden NFL Football game app was displayed

- Searched for "Fidelity" and Scottrade appeared

According to Facebook, "Your ad will appear when the targeted entity appears in the search results." The ad appears under a "Sponsored" banner. You can write up to 70 characters of ad copy, and you can also customize your landing destination somewhat, such as specifying a particular tab on your page.

Sponsored Results ads can employ all the audience targeting and bid management available to Facebook Marketplace and Sponsored Stories ads. Pricing is CPC or CPM.

How do you create a Sponsored Results ad?

Currently, you cannot create Sponsored Results ads in the Ads Manager interface. You must use either Power Editor or the Ads API. Using the API data feed, you pass an ad *type* field of 31 to identify an ad as a Sponsored Result.

Here are the steps for using Power Editor:[5]

1. Create your campaign and your ad

2. Select the Facebook entity you want to promote. It can be an app, page, place, group, event, or other

3. Select "Facebook Ads"

---

[5] Facebook, "Creating an Ad or Sponsored Story," www.facebook.com/help/326113794144384/.

4. Select "Sponsored Result" as the story type

5. Enter a message of up to 70 characters

6. Add your audience targeting and pricing strategy

7. Upload and activate your ad

■ **Tip** To manage Sponsored Results and other Facebook ads in bulk, use Power Editor. Get the documentation and how-to at http://ads.ak.facebook.com/ads/FacebookAds/Power_Editor_2012. pdf.

Sponsored Results is an appealing placement, because Facebook handles hundreds of millions of searches per month—and the search field is front and center of the Facebook user experience (UX).

However, the inability to employ search keywords for ad targeting is a big miss. A prominent Sponsored Results campaign promoting an app for dating site Match.com appeared where you might expect it ("match," "singles," "dating") but also under a huge variety of unrelated searches ("jazz," "sky," "circle") as well as one- and two-letter type-ahead results. This campaign likely employed optimized CPM bidding, so perhaps Match.com achieved its ROAS goals. But in the process, the user experience for Facebookers was worsened by irrelevant search results. The impressions Match.com bought didn't seem very thoughtful or brand-positive to me. I've been happily married for 18 years, and I saw the Match.com ad a *lot*—enough to make me feel Facebook was utilizing its targeting capabilities poorly.

But certainly, Sponsored Results are an intriguing way to draw high attention to your Facebook community. These ads stand out, even when they bear no relationship to the search. For instance, Match.com's ad copy, "Meet local singles and see pics for FREE. Get started now!" makes an impression.

Facebook ad software provider Nanigans released a client study showing that Sponsored Results ads generated 23 times the click-through rates of Sponsored Stories and cost 78% less per click.[6] In one app promotion campaign, Sponsored Results ads resulted in 14 times more app installs compared with Marketplace ads.

"Our early results show users find these placements very engaging," says Nanigans CEO Ric Calvillo.

---

[6] Mark Walsh, "Early Results Promising For Facebook's Sponsored Results," *Online Media Daily*, MediaPost, August 30, 2012, www.mediapost.com/publications/article/181894/ early-results-promising-for-facebooks-sponsored-r.html.

Other companies have reported Sponsored Results click-through rates (CTRs) ranging from 0.5% to over 3%.

As with any of Facebook's new advertising offerings, we can expect enhancements and improvements.

"It's just an initial alpha right now, with a set of marketers... It's still too early to see where it takes us," says Gokul Rajaram, Facebook advertising products director. "[L]ike everything else, we are going to move fast and, as we get learnings, we'll evolve the product."[7]

Paired with other targeting (excluding existing fans and targeting friends of fans, say), Sponsored Results could be useful for recruiting new fans or leads. It is worth testing.

Remarketing with Facebook Exchange

Another important new arrow in Facebook's advertising quiver is its 2012 launch of Facebook Exchange, or FBX, as it's been nicknamed. Its two big elements for marketers are (1) remarketing ads and (2) real-time bidding.

Remarketing, also known as retargeting, is already a much-used advertising practice on the web, where site owners install scripts to cookie their visitors and later display banner ads to them on third-party ad networks throughout the Internet. The goal is to reel in past website visitors for repeat purchases or to recover abandoned shopping carts.

With cookie-driven Facebook Exchange ads, you can target your website abandoners later, on Facebook, with sidebar ads. (Sponsored Stories are not available in this program.)

Picture a visitor to your website who browsed a few products, performed a couple of searches, added an item to her shopping cart, but left your website without checking out. These visitors are identified by cookies, which are used later by third-party websites (news and entertainment sites, blogs, you name it) to trigger relevant display ads.

How pertinent are these banners to your marketing efforts? Depending on the information harvested by your website, your remarketing banner ads can display the exact items that a particular consumer searched, viewed, or abandoned in the cart. Personalized ads like these have been shown to produce a 20%-plus lift in sales conversion over traditional ads.

---

[7] Zach Rodgers, "Inside the World of Gokul Rajaram, Facebook's Ad Architect," AdExchanger, September 5, 2012, www.adexchanger.com/social-media/inside-the-world-of-gokul-rajaram-facebooks-ad-architect/.

While it might seem counterintuitive to pay good money to target your ads at people who've already visited and abandoned your site, it can make great business sense.

Google's Display Network, for instance, reaches 83% of Internet users worldwide. Remarketing ads are shown only to qualified prospects (identified by cookies as people who already "raised their hands" by visiting your website).

▓ **Note**   Facebook Exchange remarketing ads bring Facebook closer than ever to identifying the customer "purchase intent" that all marketers covet. Direct-response marketers are reporting good results from these new ad units.

Even when consumers don't click the ads, the impressions can inspire purchases later. A/B tests, with holdout groups consisting of users who are shown public service announcements rather than ads, have demonstrated purchase incrementality of 15–20%. These influenced purchases are called "view-through" (as opposed to click-through) conversions.

Facebook is now able to use remarketing cookies to trigger ads. "For example," explains Facebook, "a travel site may be interested in reaching a person who searched for a flight but did not complete the purchase. With Facebook Exchange, this travel website can show that person a related ad on Facebook."[8]

FBX ads are facilitated by demand-side platforms, or DSPs, which are ad-management networks that harvest the cookie data, then use it to execute online media buys and manage bids for their clients. The initial DSP partners are AdRoll, AppNexus, Criteo, DataXu, MediaMath, Nanigans, Optimal, Rocket Fuel, TellApart, The Trade Desk, Triggit, Turn, Xaxis, and [x+1]. Cookies dropped by these DSPs contain data on audience segmentation, product information, and so on, in order to drive more precisely targeted ad buys.

These ad buys are executed on Facebook, using a real-time bidding platform (or RTB, in the acronym-happy world of Facebook).

As with any remarketing ad buy, the available impressions are directly proportional to your "cookie pool"—how many unique visitors came to your website and triggered the cookie-dropping code for Facebook Exchange. Recommended ad budgets can run from $25,000 to $50,000 per one million unique users.

---

[8] Stephanie Mlot, "Facebook readying new cookie-based feature for advertisers," June, 15, 2012, www.itproportal.com/2012/06/15/facebook-readying-new-cookie-based-feature-for-advertisers/

Another appeal of the FBX ads is real-time bid management. Because the cookie tracking code is universal, many merchants will be vying for the same "cookied" audience. Say Jane visited the websites of Banana Republic, Chevy, and the Miami Heat. Whether the Heat just won the NBA Finals, or whether Chevy is having a Labor Day sale, might determine which advertiser will bid the most to reach Jane at the moment she logs into Facebook.

Facebook Exchange shows promise for direct-response merchants hoping to achieve positive ROAS. Early advertisers included Orbitz and Nordstrom, and the initial results look attractive[9]—although, since they were reported by the DSP partners, we might take them with a grain of salt. Early results included:

- 4x click-through rate compared with traditional Facebook campaigns

- 10–20x return on investment

- 300% better return on a cost-per-lead basis

- One-fifth the cost per order acquisition (CPA)

- 18–30% conversion rate lift, compared with a holdout group who did not see FBX ads

Google AdWords has long enjoyed the advantage of being closer than any other ad platform to the *purchase intent* of customers—as indicated by the specific items for which they're searching. But with Exchange, Facebook moves much closer to purchase intent than ever before. That's a direction that seems promising indeed for early Facebook Exchange advertisers.

Custom Audiences

If you like the idea of FBX remarketing (which means paying Facebook to target your own website visitors when they're on Facebook), you'll love the new Facebook Custom Audiences. With Custom Audiences, you actually *upload your own in-house customer database to Facebook*, and then use that audience as a target for Facebook ad campaigns.

With Custom Audiences, unique identifiers from your customer lists are used to match your customers to their Facebook accounts in order to advertise to those customers through Facebook. These unique IDs may be e-mail

---

[9] Brittany Darwell, "Ad partners see early promise as Facebook brings FBX retargeting system out of beta," September 13, 2012, Inside Facebook, http://www.insidefacebook.com/2012/09/13/ad-partners-see-early-promise-as-facebook-brings-fbx-retargeting-system-out-of-beta/.

addresses, phone numbers, or (if you're a Facebook app developer who has access to them) Facebook user IDs.

First question: why the heck would any business want to trust Facebook with its customer database?

Second question: why would you pay Facebook for the privilege to advertise to your own customers—people you already have mailing list and e-mail permission to contact directly?

I'm not a hundred percent sure you do want to go down this path. It's a brand-new opportunity you'll need to subject to due diligence. It seems fraught with potential risks, but as I'll explain, Facebook has taken pains to mitigate privacy risks and ensure security.

Here are some arguments in favor of Custom Audiences:

- Facebook "anonymizes" the data you upload and assures you it cannot and will not steal your proprietary customer database or sell it to your rivals.

- You may reap significant business benefits by finding and engaging more of your customers on Facebook and turning them into fans of your brand page. Your online community will grow faster. Your network reach to friends of fans will grow exponentially.

- By strategically building different Custom Audiences on Facebook, you can add yet another channel to your multichannel campaigns: reaching groups with offers and messages that are segmented, consistent, and synchronized with other marketing channels.

Before you resort to Custom Audiences to grow your Facebook fan base, be sure you use your promotional access to your house list in order to e-mail or send direct mail exhorting your customers and prospects to "like" your Facebook page.

But after you've covered those promotional bases, consider testing Custom Audiences.

As Facebook puts it, "Audiences let marketers find their offline audiences among Facebook users. Using email addresses, phone numbers or Facebook user IDs to make the match, you can now find the exact people you want to talk to, in custom audiences that are defined by what you already know."[10]

---

[10] "Custom Audiences," Facebook, www.facebook.com/help/?page=273730399409300

Here's how it works:

- **Audience definition:** Segment your customer base into groups you want to target with specific messages or campaigns. Each audience is represented by a list of e-mails, phone numbers, or Facebook user IDs (UIDs).

- **Hashing:** When you upload your list into Power Editor, the list's contents are hashed, or encoded. According to Facebook, your list of e-mails or phone numbers is not uploaded to Facebook's servers—only the hashes are uploaded.

- **Matching:** Your hashed list is compared with hashed records in the Facebook system.

- **Audience creation:** UIDs of matched Facebook users will be added to a Custom Audience you created in Power Editor. At the end of the process, matched and unmatched hashes are discarded. Repeat for as many segments as you wish to define.

- **Ad targeting:** Your custom audiences are stored in your account to be used in ad targeting (or exclusion). Power Editor displays the size of your matched audience, along with a reach estimate for any ad targeting you choose.

Custom Audiences are available only to managed advertisers who are using the Power Editor interface. You can upload comma-separated values (CSV) or text (TXT) files to Facebook, which will hash the data to anonymize user information (see Figure 5-2).

If you find the idea of uploading your customer e-mail list or phone list to Facebook rather frightening, I don't blame you. However, the company has provided detailed specifics about its hashing process and privacy policies, including assurances that, for instance, no Custom Audiences you upload will be shared with any other companies.

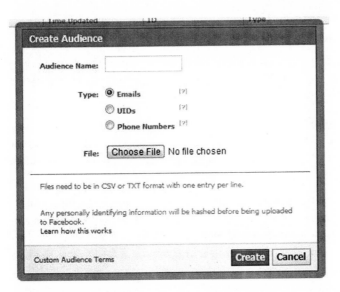

Figure 5-2. Custom Audiences uses Power Editor to match your customers with their Facebook accounts based on e-mail address, phone number, or Facebook user ID. Courtesy of Facebook, Inc.

When Facebook has connected the dots between your customers and its database, you will then be able to target specific Marketplace ads or Sponsored Stories to your existing customers who are not already fans of your brand, urging them to "like" your page on Facebook in exchange, say, for a member–exclusive discount.

You could also target specific events, promotions, or other Facebook campaigns to particular segments within your customer base.

Action Spec Targeting

In January 2012, Facebook launched Open Graph "action spec targeting," made possible by a network of over 60 partner applications linking popular websites and mobile apps with the Facebook timeline. Facebook also published action spec developer tools so that additional third-party app developers could join the party.

The interactions that drive action spec targeting are essentially the same as, or very similar to, the actions on Facebook.com that drive Sponsored Stories. The difference is that these take place outside Facebook and are conveyed back to Facebook through the Open Graph.

Action spec targeting allows Facebook advertisers to extend their reach beyond audience targeting, which is limited to self-reported demographics and interests. Using action spec targeting, advertisers can now target observed behaviors—also known as "behavioral targeting."

For example, if a user listens to a Rihanna tune on Spotify and later visits Facebook, action spec ad targeting could trigger a Facebook ad for the latest Rihanna concert tour.

If this all sounds reminiscent of Facebook's notorious Beacon advertising effort, well, it is. Beacon was launched in 2007, then scuttled less than a year later after a chorus of privacy complaints and legal saber-rattling. A chastened Mark Zuckerberg called the program "a mistake."

What changed between Beacon and Open Graph action spec? The disclosures, permissions, and opt-outs seen by Facebook users are a bit more obvious this time around. But mostly what changed were the times: our cultural comfort level with Facebook advertising has come a long way in a few years. We're a lot more nonchalant.

Advertisers can use action spec to do one of two things: (1) target users who have performed a particular action or (2) create Sponsored Stories ads about the action.

Sponsored Stories may be created only for actions that originate from a page, application, or website (via social plug-ins) and would normally be eligible to appear in the newsfeed.

Advertisers can use action spec to target ads or Sponsored Stories at users (or friends of users) who have listened to music on a particular music player, read a particular article or recipe, or commented on a specific page post. A wide variety of popular apps already support action spec, including entertainment, food, shopping, news, games, and others (see Table 5-1). This network of applications is what makes action spec targeting such a powerful audience- and behavior-targeting tool.

Table 5-1. Examples of Apps Available for Action Spec Ad Targeting[11]

Books	**Food**	**Mashable**
Goodreads	Foodspotting	The Guardian
	Urbanspoon	The Independent
Business		The Onion
BranchOut	**Games**	Today
	Castleville	USAToday
Entertainment	Words With Friends	Washington Post
Dailymotion		WSJ Online
Fandango	**Giving**	Yahoo! News
GetGlue	Causes	
Hulu	FundRazr	**Shopping**
Rotten Tomatoes	JustGiving	Fab
SoundCloud		LivingSocial
StubHub	**Music**	Payvment
Ticketfly	Jelli	Pinterest
Ticketmaster	Rhapsody	ShoeDazzle
USTREAM	Songza	Shopkick
VEVO	Spotify	Vogue
Viddy	Turntable	
		Travel
Fitness	**News**	Airbnb
Endomondo	CBS News	Foursquare
MapMyFitness	Digg	TripAdvisor
Runkeeper	Le Monde	Where I've Been

Facebook Premium Ads

For managed accounts working with a rep or through the Ads API, Premium placements are a way to "go big" with home-page and logout placements. These units have been employed by movie studios, automakers, and other advertisers wanting to reach a mass audience. Generally, they cost around $10 per thousand impressions, and require a minimum spend of $10,000 a month.

Premium placements include home-page placement in the right-hand column (for nonfans), or within the home page and mobile newsfeeds (for fans), as well as large banner ads displayed after logout. Premium ads are now social, so interactions with them appear as "stories" in the newsfeeds of friends of fans. Therefore, Facebook calculates that for every 500,000 fans, marketers have access to 40 million friends of fans.

---

[11] Josh Constine, "Pinterest and 60 Others Demo Open Graph Sites + Apps That Auto-Publish To Facebook," January 18, 2012, Tech Crunch, Aol Tech, http://techcrunch.com/2012/01/18/open-graph-websites/.

Other than the logout banner, Premium ads don't physically differ much from Marketplace ads, Promoted Posts, or Sponsored Stories. They do feature a bigger image, as well as a prominent "social context" element ("Jane Doe and 14 others liked this"). These details, plus the greater reach afforded by home-page placement, set them apart.

According to Facebook, the combination of Premium placement and the new format and social reach yields maximum impact: [12]

1. New Premium ads and Sponsored Stories on the right-hand side are 40% more engaging and 80% more likely to be remembered than previous Facebook ad offerings

2. Premium ads show a 16% increase in fan rate

3. Campaigns that leverage social reach can drive ROI of 3x or greater

Going Mobile

Over 450 million people a month access Facebook from a mobile device, and the rate of mobile use is outpacing desktop use by a factor of two to one. Facebook reaches 80% of the total mobile audience, and the Facebook app is the third most popular of all mobile apps.

Despite all that, Facebook has been criticized (and has publicly criticized itself) for being late to the mobile game—especially from an ad-serving perspective. In 2012, it claimed less than 3% of mobile ad spending, distantly trailing Google, Pandora, Twitter, and others.

However, Facebook has hastened to answer its critics and get up to speed on mobile advertising options. Sponsored Stories and Marketplace ads are now fully distributed on the mobile-optimized website and Facebook mobile app.

Facebook has also announced it is testing a mobile ad network, allowing advertisers to place ads on the mobile applications of third parties. [13]

---

[12] Facebook internal studies, July and August 2011, www.facebook.com/business/fmc/guides/premium.

[13] Brian Womack, "Facebook Gains on Mobile Ads for Other Apps," September 19, 2012, BloombergBusinessweek, www.businessweek.com/news/2012-09-18/facebook-tests-mobile-advertising-on-third-party-applications.

The New Stuff

You'll constantly hear rumors about beta tests and limited releases of new Facebook advertising options: new mobile ad units, newsfeed ads targeting nonfans, paid ads from other websites that are shareable on Facebook via integration with the Open Graph API—the list goes on. As I mentioned earlier, to stay up to date you'll need to do all of the following:

1. Frequently visit the leading blogs

2. Book a regular call with your Facebook ad rep

3. Set up a Google Alert for "Facebook ad"

Do Facebook Ads Really Work?

So how do you make sense of this flurry of new ad units? Do Facebook users love them or hate them—ignore them or respond to them?

Facebook itself reports that a variety of third-party studies of over 60 ad campaigns on Facebook have found that 70% achieved a return of 3x or better on ad spend. Of those, 49% achieved a return of 5x or better.

Not everyone is confident that Facebook advertising is effective. On the very eve of Facebook's public offering, automaker General Motors pulled its Facebook advertising—a hefty $10 million a year media buy. "We currently do not plan to continue with [Facebook] advertising," said GM at the time. *Forbes* magazine reported that even after meeting with Facebook to air their concerns, GM execs "remained unconvinced that advertising on the site made sense."[14]

Since then, GM has dipped a toe back in—and Facebook has done much to improve the landscape for advertisers. Yet it's a far different landscape from the ones you're familiar with from using paid search on Google AdWords, or doing banner advertising campaigns. Facebook and other social networks suffer as advertising venues because (1) users are on the site primarily for entertainment and interaction with friends, not for commercial transactions, and (2) even when they're willing to consider brands and their products, they don't want to leave Facebook to shop.

---

[14] Joann Muller, "GM Says Facebook Ads Don't Work, Pulls $10 Million Account," *Forbes*, May 15, 2012, www.forbes.com/sites/joannmuller/2012/05/15/gm-says-facebook-ads-dont-work-pulls-10-million-account/

However, things are changing remarkably fast. Consumer acceptance of ads in social media is growing. Social networks are delivering powerful and innovative new advertising options that should be very exciting to any marketer.

Social media platforms are unsurpassed in the wealth of personal and demographic information they maintain for each member. But as much as they know about their users (including gender, age, education, interests, alma mater, industry or employer, and so on), social networks have little insight into when a consumer is most leaning toward buying from a business. Search engines, by contrast, know exactly what your customers are looking for when they're searching for it.

Facebook has moved closer to the end of the purchase funnel by offering Facebook Exchange remarketing ads. Facebook is eager to demonstrate that its demographic info—plus exciting other integrations with outside applications and cookies from sites like yours—will capture just as much "user intent" to buy from customers as any search query can capture.

More important, by building ads into the organic fabric of "stories" on the site, and by enabling targeting options from outside its walls, Facebook offers advertisers something new and valuable: the ability to identify customers in a noncommercial setting and engage with them in fun and creative ways. That allows businesses to cultivate a deeper relationship with them in the long term—and be in the front of their minds when that Facebooker is ready to buy.

Summary

I've been spending online ad dollars ever since GoTo launched for pennies a click in the late 1990s (yeah, okay grandpa, keep talking...). I have seen great ad platforms delivering high ROI—and I've seen many ludicrous ways to pour perfectly good money down the drain.

Social media advertising is as new today as CPC search ads were back then. We're already witnessing hits and misses and a rapid-fire pace of change. The cost and value of a social media click or impression are still proving themselves; in coming years they will come nearer to equilibrium. That said, I'm impressed with Facebook's initial ad offerings for three main reasons:

- Sheer audience size: Facebook offers huge numbers, plus passionate engagement.

- Especially with Sponsored Stories, the company offers highly targeted ads that are unobtrusively knit into the fabric of the user experience.

- Thanks to Facebook's technical savvy and ambition, it's not just about Facebook.com. With Facebook Exchange remarketing ads, custom audiences, Open Graph, and action spec targeting, the platform's reach now literally spans the entire Internet.

Facebook is the clear leader in paid social media placements. But as I'll discuss in Chapter 6, the other major platforms now offer noteworthy advertising options of their own. Twitter, YouTube, LinkedIn, and others are definitely worth a look. In some cases, what they lack in size, they more than make up for in targeting capabilities, uniqueness of ad formats, and pure value for the dollar.

Advertising on Twitter and Other Networks

Making the Platforms Work Together

While Facebook offers the dominant market share and greatest variety of ad units, the other social platforms have rolled out compelling opportunities you can't afford to ignore. If you leverage multiple platforms for their unique strengths, you can build a comprehensive social media marketing plan that reaches the widest possible audience, with the fullest spectrum of media types. You'll echo and reinforce your message across multiple social networks, and by dropping remarketing cookies, you'll extend your reach 360 degrees.

Here's a snapshot of how the other platforms can round out your Facebook ad presence and work in concert:

- **Twitter:** If you're a publisher, blogger, or thought leader, use promoted tweets, trends, or accounts to help build a "subscriber base." If you're a retailer, amplify your news, campaigns, and offers from other channels with a timely and efficient promoted newsfeed.

- **YouTube:** With pre-roll ads and featured videos, bring to life the sights and sounds of active, visual products and services. As a bonus, amass a remarketing cookie pool of qualified leads, to be shown banner ads across the Google Display Network.

- **Google+:** The Google+ ad play is not advertising on the social network, but bringing *social proof* into your Google AdWords paid search and online advertising program. It can be powerful.

- **LinkedIn:** Even B2C businesses live in a B2B world much of the time. Ad targeting on LinkedIn can help you zero in on the vendors, business partners, PR audiences, and other professionals who will be part of your company's social media success.

- **Smaller niche players:** In addition to those larger platforms, your paid media strategy could extend to some of the smaller niche players like *Yelp*, *StumbleUpon*, and *TripAdvisor*.

- **Foursquare:** If you're a bricks-and-mortar retailer, Foursquare will be an important element of your coordinated social media promotional strategy. The other social networks can drive awareness and engagement, but only Foursquare can regularly deliver a community of friends into a local business. Foursquare doesn't currently offer paid ads, but if you're a retailer with a physical presence, don't overlook the free promotions I covered in Chapter 3.

Let's look at each of these options in turn to see how they might best fit your advertising needs.

Twitter

Twitter has been slower and more measured than most big social networks in rolling out advertising options. In fact, it was third parties who first sprang up with unauthorized paid-Tweet programs. Eventually, though, Twitter stepped up with three offerings:

- Promoted Tweets
- Promoted Trends
- Promoted Accounts

Lately, Twitter has announced a flurry of user-interest-targeting enhancements to these ad units—and slashed the minimum cost per click (CPC) from $0.50 to a mere penny. It is clear that Twitter intends to be a player in the social media ad market. I think the site is worthy of consideration to augment your Facebook media buy.

Promoted Accounts, Tweets, and Trends

With *Promoted Accounts,* you pay to have your account featured on the left column or within relevant search results. The extra exposure helps you attract new followers. Promoted Accounts appear on the left-hand column under the headline "Who to Follow"—and you may find yourself in pretty good company. A recent promoted account for Smart Mom (8,000 followers) appeared above Bill Gates (six million followers) and His Holiness the Dalai Lama (four million followers).

Promoted Accounts are identified by an orange arrow badge and link to the account profile. They also feature social signals, which will display if the Promoted Account is followed by any @usernames that you already follow.

The added exposure of *Promoted Tweets* also helps attract followers. Assuming you choose your content shrewdly, you can also generate plenty of retweets. But try not to come right out and ask for it by saying something like "RT if you love your kids!"

Promoted Trends bring attention to a trending hashtag, the account that sponsored it, and all the accounts tweeting about it.

Promoted Tweets and Promoted Accounts are sold auction style on a cost per engagement (CPE) model. In other words, you pay only when users click, retweet, comment upon, or favorite your tweet. Promoted Trends, on the other hand, are the "Boardwalk" and "Park Place" of Twitter real estate, costing advertisers upward of $100,000 a day.

A fourth option of passing interest to businesses is *Enhanced Profile Pages.* While these richer, more professional-looking pages are a nice touch for brand image, they're not available to the public and are doled out by Twitter to its big advertisers. If that's you, great! Otherwise, you can make do by customizing your Twitter background and color scheme (see http://support. twitter.com/articles/15357).

Advertisers using any of the three Twitter promotions types have access to analytics dashboards that show the key campaign metrics—impressions, retweets, clicks, replies, and follows—in real time.

The Followers dashboard provides insights about who your followers are (see Figure 6-1). One of the most valuable dimensions is *interest:* Twitter displays a ranking of top interests among your followers (not self-reported; Twitter constructs this algorithmically). Interests tracked by Twitter include food, fashion, health, social causes or charities, parenting, and more.

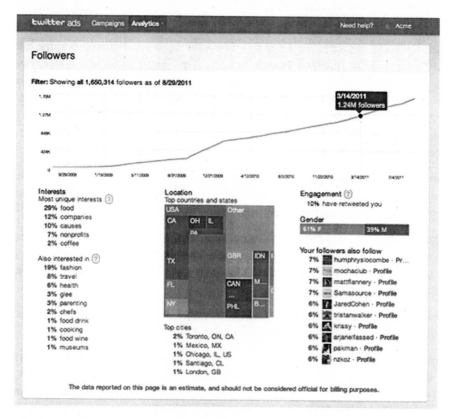

Figure 6-1. Twitter advertisers can drill into the demographic makeup and interests of their audience by using the Followers dashboard. Courtesy of Twitter.

You can also see how you gained followers over time and drill into your audience composition by geography, gender, and engagement rate (i.e., what percentage of your followers have retweeted you). (Speaking of interests, as I'll discuss below, Twitter has now released interest-targeting for its ads, which is an exciting development.)

Twitter promotions tend to engage a smaller audience than similar promotions on Facebook, in part because the promotion presentations are fairly subtle—although they are identified as "sponsored" and they sit at the top of the tweet stream, they don't otherwise stand out as dramatically different from other tweets and trends.

However, that smaller reach is nicely balanced by a true community ethos. Whereas Facebook is a network of overlapping social circles of private profiles, Twitter is more of a public square. The advertisers that have used Promoted Tweets and Trends have generally focused on a strategy of encouraging some critical mass of retweets or use of a trend hashtag to support a good cause or "unlock" a promotion, sale, or giveaway. You can also welcome your new followers with a Twitter-exclusive deal or freebie.

Cirque du Soleil uses Promoted Accounts and Promoted Tweets to engage with followers who have attended its circus performances and to retweet audience responses. American Airlines promoted a "Tweet to win 30K miles" campaign. The United Nations Refugee Agency held a "tweetathon" fundraiser culminating on World Refugee Day.

In other examples, Virgin America airline partnered with Stand Up To Cancer on a one-day flash sale exclusively on Twitter. The "Fly Forward, Give Back" campaign offered fares starting at just $49, with $5 of each fare going to the cancer charity, up to a total of $50,000. The campaign was publicized via Promoted Tweets and a Promoted Trend, #FlyFwdGiveBack.

For Promoted Tweets, Trends, or Accounts, Twitter requires a minimum spend of $5,000 per month and a three-month commitment from its advertisers. You must have an established Twitter presence with at least 50 tweets under your belt. The Twitter team also looks for previous experience running self-serve campaigns (through AdWords or Facebook, for example) and a willingness to provide lots of feedback.

The old $0.50 CPC floor seemed unrealistically high for an unproven medium, so the new one-penny minimum is a welcome move. It should bring Twitter's CPC prices down overall and open the platform to new advertisers. The auction-style dynamics of Promoted Tweets ensure that most campaigns will rise above the $0.01 minimum bid in order to get any meaningful impressions and drive real results. But the price cut is a bold move guaranteed to boost Twitter's attractiveness in the contest for advertiser dollars.

"It will definitely raise the interest among small and mid-size businesses that may not have considered Twitter advertising in the past," says eMarketer analyst Debra Williamson. "Anytime you see one cent, that will juice you to want to try it out."[1]

Interest-Targeting on Twitter

The most compelling change at Twitter is the enhanced interest-targeting, which brings it up to par with Facebook or even leapfrogs its rival (see Figure 6-2). With interest-targeting, Twitter advertisers select from a list of 375 topics and subtopics. Twitter identifies a user's interests algorithmically, by analyzing the contents of his or her tweets and retweets and the handles the

[1] Sarah Mitroff, "Like Baking? Baseball? Twitter Has an Ad for You," *Wired*, August 31, 2012, www.wired.com/business/2012/08/like-baking-baseball-twitter-has-an-ad-for-you/.

user follows. (On Facebook, by contrast, user interests are self-reported and are also revealed by their "likes" as they use the site.)

"For broader reach, you can target more than 350 interest categories, ranging from education to home and garden to investing to soccer," writes Kevin Weil, Twitter's director of product management, on the company's blog. "If you were promoting a new animated film about dogs, you could select animation (under movies and television), cartoons (under hobbies and interests), and dogs (under pets)."[2]

To target more precisely, you can even create custom segments by zeroing in on specific Twitter handles that are relevant to your brand, product, or event. "Custom segments let you reach users with similar interests to that @ username's followers," adds Weil. "They do not let you specifically target the followers of that @username."

This new targeting feature is exciting, as it should enable advertisers to focus with laser-beam efficiency on the leading Twitter handles in the markets they serve. "If you're promoting your indie band's next tour, you can create a custom audience by adding @usernames of related bands," writes Weil, "thus targeting users with the same taste in music."

I'm already seeing good examples of interest-based targeting in action on Twitter. Search for Pandora, for example, and you'll see the Promoted Account of Spotify.

---

[2] Kevin Weil, "Interest targeting: Broaden your reach, reach the right audience," Twitter advertising blog, August 30, 2012, http://advertising.twitter.com/2012/08/interest-targeting-broaden-your-reach.html.

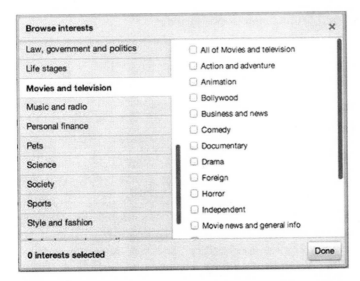

Figure 6-2. With Twitter's new interest-targeting, advertisers can aim their Promoted Tweets, Trends, or Accounts at users fitting any of 375 interest categories. Courtesy of Twitter.

According to Wired.com, "Advertisers can also isolate a specific Twitter handle to create custom interest categories. 'You can give our system a username, we'll look at the follower base of that username and discern interests that are most prominent,' says Twitter's head of product marketing Guy Yalif. 'Then we'll help connect the message to people on Twitter that have those interests.'[3]

Typically, between 1% and 3% of users who see a Promoted Tweet engage with the tweet in some way. But word has it the engagement rate of Promoted Tweets has now risen, thanks to Twitter's new interest-targeting approach.

Bottom line: with these expanded targeting options and one-penny minimum bids, Twitter deserves consideration from any advertiser who can muster the $15,000 table stakes for a three-month test.

YouTube

YouTube, the second most visited of all social media websites, offers a wealth of powerful new advertising options, including integration across the advertising network of its parent company, Google.

---

[3] Sarah Mitroff, Ibid.

YouTube advertising and promotion options include:

- Promoted Videos
- TrueView instream pre-roll ads
- Remarketing across the Google Display Network
- Brand channels
- Home-page and display advertising

Promoted Videos are ordinary YouTube videos, of any length, uploaded to your YouTube account. These videos can appear as relevant search results (driven by keywords, as on the AdWords platform) or alongside contextually related video content on YouTube, along the top and right-hand side of the page. Merchants like Vera Bradley and Pottery Barn Teen have run back-to-school promotions on YouTube, creating themed channels and buying TrueView ads targeted to back-to-school searches and related content.

TrueView "instream" (pre-roll and mid-roll) ads are shorter videos, generally 15 or 30 seconds long, which play before a selected YouTube video loads. TrueView instream video ads are can be skipped after five seconds—and to ensure advertisers pay only for engaged viewers, YouTube doesn't charge for views of 5 seconds or less.

As YouTube puts it, "You're guaranteed at least five seconds of brand exposure, free of charge."

You can also serve text overlay ads, from your Google AdWords account, on top of relevant videos or to relevant audiences, including remarketing audiences.

Whether Promoted Video or TrueView advertising drives your YouTube video views—or whether they're purely organic—each viewer can be collected into a cookie pool that you can market to later, on the Google Display Network. So a YouTube promotional campaign can get attention both today and tomorrow.

▓ **Tip** With YouTube TrueView ads, users can skip an ad after five seconds. Advertisers pay only if a prospect watches past the five-second mark or clicks on the video. That means you'll receive many brand impressions free—while paying only for the most qualified, interested viewers.

Do YouTube's advertising options work for merchants? The evidence suggests they do:

- TRX fitness equipment drove 7% of its online sales from TrueView video ads. Cost-per-conversion was just $14, or about 65% less than its typical acquisition cost. "I was delighted to see an immediate lift in awareness as well as conversions stemming directly from YouTube," says TRX's John Packowski. TRX also used remarketing ads, with the result that heavy holiday traffic produced an expanded cookie pool of candidates to be shown display ads during the "New Year's resolution" season—a critical sales window for fitness gear.[4]

- Richard Petty Driving Experience records customer testimonials on video after drivers' final lap around the racetrack. A 30-day promotion employing TrueView instream ads resulted in a 700% increase in viewership of its videos. In addition, the campaign captured remarketing cookies, allowing Richard Petty Driving Experience to target ad banners to qualified leads. "Remarketing is one of the most cost-effective strategies out there. It can have a profound impact on a business model and help formulate what you want to sell when," says Elliot Antal, e-marketing manager.[5]

- The Nassau Paradise Island Promotion Board used TrueView ads to drive website traffic up 68%. "Analytics show it can cost as little as 15 cents to get a qualified lead living in an important key market like Boston to engage with an entire 30 second video," says Frank Vertolli of the board's agency, Net Conversion. Kim Andersen, the board's VP of marketing, points out that YouTube videos share well across multiple social networks. They generate comments and influence vacation decisions, which in turn often results in user-submitted Nassau vacation videos being uploaded to social media sites. "Video is a cornerstone across all of our touch points," says Andersen.[6]

---

[4] YouTube, "YouTube ads slash average cost-per conversion 65% and drive 7% of online sales for TRX," http://static.googleusercontent.com/external_content/untrusted_dlcp/www.youtube.com/en/us/yt/advertise/medias/pdfs/your-objectives-product-launch-trx-en.pdf.

[5] YouTube, "Richard Petty Driving Experience increases fan engagement 700% with YouTube," http://static.googleusercontent.com/external_content/untrusted_dlcp/www.youtube.com/en/us/yt/advertise/medias/pdfs/resources-success-stories-richard-petty-en.pdf.

[6] Greg Jarboe, "Nassau Paradise Island Promotion Board Reaches Vacationers With YouTube," ReelSEO.com, www.reelseo.com/nassau-paradise-island-promotion-board-youtube/.

In my experience, using TrueView for Promoted Video or pre-roll advertising or to drive a remarketing display ad campaign, these ads deliver qualified traffic at a great cost per view, cost per click, or, in the case of remarketing, cost per order. Another plus is that YouTube stats can reveal fascinating things about the demographics of your channel subscribers and video viewers (see Figure 6-3). Engagement metrics and the "Hot Spots" feature track bounce rates and rewind rates to tell you which parts of your video are most engaging and which cause users to drop off.

In the case of Green Mountain Coffee Roasters, when we ran a tutorial video campaign to introduce Brew Over Ice beverages (iced teas and iced coffees) for the Keurig coffeemaker, we were delighted to see that the most engaging part of the video was the specific moment demonstrating the selection of the six- or eight-ounce setting. Understanding how strong to brew was key to enhancing consumer enjoyment of the new product, and the video campaign proved successful at communicating that small but critical detail.

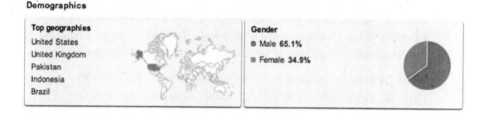

Figure 6-3. YouTube Analytics tracks gender, geographical location, and other demographics of your video viewers and tabulates likes, comments, views, and other interactions with each video. Courtesy of Google.

YouTube Video Remarketing

The Google Display Network encompasses literally millions of websites, reaching 83% of unique Internet users around the world, according to Google. That includes people speaking more than 30 languages in over 100 countries. Websites include Gmail, YouTube, and other high-profile Google-owned properties and partners like About.com.

The ads you display can be any of the types supported for a Display Network campaign—from simple text ads to small or large banners, half banners, buttons, skyscrapers, and leaderboards, among others. You can add this remarketing list to an ad group with standard text ads or display ads created in Display Ad Builder. These campaigns may use either CPC or CPM (cost per thousand views) pricing.

To begin remarketing to your YouTube viewers, step one is to link your business YouTube account to your AdWords account.

Step two is to establish video remarketing audiences in AdWords. The granularity of audience targeting with YouTube and AdWords, based on interaction with your content, is quite powerful. When building a remarketing list, you can include (or exclude) anyone who:

- Viewed any video from your channel
- Visited a channel page (without necessarily viewing the video)
- Viewed any of your videos as an ad
- Liked any of your videos
- Disliked any of your videos
- Commented
- Shared
- Subscribed to your channel
- Unsubscribed
- Viewed a certain video or videos (from a channel other than yours)
- Viewed certain videos as ads
- Liked certain videos
- Disliked certain videos
- Commented or shared certain videos

You'll manage video remarketing lists from the *Targets* tab in AdWords for video. When your remarketing list has gained interactions from at least 100 YouTube viewers, you can add it to a targeting group. Once you have created your audiences, you can select them for any new campaign by expanding *Video remarketing* list to view all available lists.

AdWords reporting offers full visibility into your ad placement and performance, which allows you to adjust your campaigns and bids based on results, or exclude network sites that aren't working for you.

■ **Tip** Be careful using multiple types of targeting. If you use more than one targeting method at a time, Google will apply them all. For example, if you target a specific keyword, age, and channel, your ads will be shown only when all those methods match your ad at the same time. This can restrict your impressions significantly.

Brand Channels

Anyone uploading video to YouTube has a channel, but all the channels have the same layout, the same slate-gray background, and the YouTube logo. YouTube's brand channels allow you to showcase your brand, customizing your YouTube presence to prominently display your brand logo and reflect your color scheme and general look-and-feel. Brand channel content can be syndicated onto any third-party web page (off YouTube) with the inclusion of a line of code.

Gadgets (Google-speak for what most of us think of as widgets) can be coded using APIs to add custom functionality to your channel.

My favorite brand channels combine a strong, on-brand look with superb video that begs to be shared. These channels also demonstrate active community management that keeps the comments, likes, subscriptions, and video responses coming. Check out these best-in-class examples:

- Orabrush (www.youtube.com/Orabrush)
- Victoria's Secret (www.youtube.com/victoriassecret)
- National Hockey League (www.youtube.com/NHLVideo)
- Disney Parks (www.youtube.com/DisneyParks)
- Red Bull (www.youtube.com/redbull)

Customized brand channels don't cost anything, but they're reserved for Google AdWords and YouTube advertisers in the United States and Canada who make regular and significant ad buys on the platform. If you fit the bill, ask your Google rep to hook you up with a custom channel.

Home-Page and Display Advertising

YouTube offers traditional CPM display advertising options in various sizes and rich-media formats, including home-page "takeover" ads for national brands looking to make an enormous splash and sparing no expense. Because these ad placements don't especially tie into the *social* aspects of YouTube or a brand's channel, and aren't much different from high-profile display ad buys on the major portals and other big ad-supported sites, I won't cover them here.

LinkedIn

LinkedIn offers a variety of specialized advertising options unique to its identity as a professional networking site. Chief among them are help-wanted job advertising services and recruiting packages.

The site also offers custom options, like display advertising, sponsorships of specific LinkedIn groups, and dedicated e-mail marketing campaigns. For instance, before my 20th college reunion recently, my alma mater, Middlebury College, sent a highly personalized e-mail pitch to remind me to register to attend the reunion. The e-mail pictured all the people in my professional network on LinkedIn who also happened to have been classmates of mine in the Middlebury class of 1987.

The execution of this email, and the technology that drove it, were pretty impressive and high impact. What better engagement technique for getting a person to read and react to an e-mail than to display profile head shots of the reader's friends? Sure enough, I opened it, scanned the faces with interest, read the e-mail, and felt nostalgic and inspired enough to register for the event then and there.

One eye-opening aspect of the experience was that I don't think of a college as a B2B player, per se—yet the LinkedIn e-mail was a smart, targeted way to reach alums.

These ad units cannot be purchased online—you must reach out to the LinkedIn advertising sales team using the following online form: http://marketing.linkedin.com/contact.

LinkedIn also sells premium subscriptions to individual users who want to transcend the standard membership limits on whom you can see and connect with on the site. With a premium subscription, you are able to direct-message anyone on the site, appear in more search results on the site, and see everyone who has looked at your profile.

LinkedIn supports business pages, modeled somewhat on Facebook pages, but less robust. These are no-cost, and they are worth setting up to familiarize yourself more with the platform, to stake out your territory, and to create a destination page should you want to kick the tires on advertising.

Self-service advertising is driven by a simple web browser admin that lets you create ads with headlines, 75-character blurbs, uploaded images, and targeting choices. Ads can be associated with the current business (or businesses) in your LinkedIn profile, or with you personally, or with any company or organization in the LinkedIn database.

Below I offer some statistics about LinkedIn and its reach.[7]

LinkedIn boasts:

- 175 million members worldwide
- 40 million members in the United States

Through LinkedIn, you can target:

- 7.9 million business decision-makers
- 5.5 million high-tech managers
- 1.3 million small business owners
- 4.2 million corporate executives

The targeting capabilities of LinkedIn are a dream come true for B2B marketers and salespeople. You can aim at a hyperspecific audience demographic based on these criteria:

- Location (continent, country, state, major metro region)
- Company (by name or category)
- Job title
- Job function and/or seniority
- School attended
- Skills (enter a specific skill to target members of that group)
- Group membership

---

[7] "Worldwide Membership," LinkedIn, www.press.linkedin.com/content/default. aspx?NewsAreaId=29.

- Gender

- Age

Like Facebook, LinkedIn does an admirable job of demonstrating, in real time and with specific numbers, how your audience grows smaller as you refine your targeting.

For instance, if you're looking to promote a local event in Los Angeles for members of the pharmaceutical industry, you could refine the audience as follows:

- 175 million global members

- 69.3 million US members

- 2.8 million members in Greater Los Angeles

- 13,273 members in the pharmaceutical industry in Greater Los Angeles

As an advertising venue, LinkedIn works best for business-to-business lead generation. I have been a member of the site for many years and have used it effectively for all sorts of networking: vendor selection, recruiting, business development, research, finding conference speaking opportunities, and seeking interview subjects for this and my prior books. Especially during the four years I worked in marketing and business development for the e-commerce agency Timberline Interactive, I found LinkedIn to be a vital tool for connecting to business prospects and potential vendors.

But frankly, although I love the LinkedIn network, I'm not yet a confirmed fan of the advertising opportunities. As elements of the typical LinkedIn user's experience, self-service ads don't seem to have a high enough profile—I don't think they get the exposure, attention, or response that most advertisers are looking for. Depending on their need to scale, I believe most B2B professionals will get as many results from the excellent free networking and communications features of LinkedIn and may not have to resort to advertising.

Google+

The Google+ play is not about bringing ads to the social network—it's about bringing social media to the world's biggest ad platform.

By linking your Google+ page to your Google AdWords account, you harness the social endorsements of your fans to boost the exposure of your AdWords ads and turbocharge their click-through rate (CTR).

If you're an AdWords advertiser, personalized, social ads are a big development.

When you link your Google+ page to your ads, Google can show more endorsements for your business from your customers and supporters. This raises social awareness of your business and increases its relevance.

With Google+, people can endorse web content wherever they see a +1 button, just as Facebook users employ the *Like* button. This can include Google search results, any Google+ page, or any post including videos, articles, comments, or photos. Google calls +1's "social annotations."

To maximize social annotations in Google+, you should display +1 buttons on your site and connect your website with its Google+ page. When your site links to its Google+ page, and vice versa, a checkmark appears after your website URL on any Google+ page. For it to work, the primary link of your Google+ page must be the URL of your website, and the <head> tag of your website must contain a link-back to Google+ in the format:

```
<link href="https://plus.google.com/{+PageId}" rel="publisher" />
```

Linking your Google+ page and your website is valuable because:

- It helps you connect with friends, fans, and customers
- It boosts the relevance of your site when your fans and their friends perform queries on Google Search
- Your site becomes eligible for Google+ Direct Connect

Google+ Direct Connect is a new feature on Google Search, which allows users to quickly navigate to a Google+ page (and even add that page to their Circles), directly from the search box on Google.com or Google Toolbar, by using a "plus" sign and keyword.

For example, if you search for "+youtube," "+mcdonalds," "+mlb," or "+pepsi," you're immediately taken to the Google+ pages of YouTube, McDonald's, Major League Baseball, or Pepsi, respectively, and given the option to add the page to your Circles.

The power of Google +1 social annotations is that they influence the rank and click-through rate of both ads and organic search results alike.

"We are seeing 5 to 10 percent click-through-rate uplift on any ad that has a social annotation on our own web sites," says Google senior vice president of engineering Vic Gundotra. "We have been in this business for a long time, and there are very few things that give you a 5 to 10 percent increase on ad engagement."[8]

Enabling social extensions in Google AdWords is simple:

1. Verify your Google+ page (visit http://support.google.com/plus/bin/answer.py?hl=en&answer=1713826 for details).

2. Create a social extension in a new AdWords campaign:

    a. Check the box next to Ad extensions > Social.

    b. Enter the URL of your verified Google+ page.

    c. Click *Save* and continue building ads.

Social extensions don't change the AdWords pricing model: you'll be charged only for standard clicks on your text ads that take users to visit your site. You will not be charged when a user +1's your ad, or clicks a link in a +1 annotation.

▣ **Note** Social annotations must be managed in the AdWords browser interface. They are not yet configurable via AdWords Editor or the AdWords API.

Once you have social-annotated ads running in your account, you can apply the "+1 Annotations" segment to your AdWords reporting, which will display your ads' social reach across three categories:

- Impressions with personal annotations (impressions that displayed a friend or contact of the user who had +1'd your page)

- Impressions with basic annotations (impressions that displayed an anonymous count of people who +1'd your page)

- Impressions without any social annotations

StumbleUpon

Although the site isn't talked about in the same breath as the big boys, the StumbleUpon bookmarking network has been around a long time—and was

---

[8] Nick Bilton, "Countering the Google Plus Image Problem," *The New York Times*, March 6, 2012, http://bits.blogs.nytimes.com/2012/03/06/google-defending-google-plus-shares-usage-numbers/.

one of the first social media properties to come to the table with a paid advertising offering.

StumbleUpon offers an ad unit called Paid Discovery, in which advertisers pay for the visibility of their website within the stream of organic, user-shared content.

Advertisers can determine who sees their page by specifying the content category, user interests, and demographic data.

Paid Discovery is available for two budget levels:

- Standard, $0.10 per engaged visitor
- Premium, $0.25 per engaged visitor

These promoted "Stumbles" receive "priority serving in content streams," and they can be targeted by interest, location, and demographics, as well as by device (web or mobile). StumbleUpon provides detailed analytics about campaign virality and engagement; the system can also integrate with Google Analytics.

Personal finance site Mint.com used StumbleUpon Paid Discovery ads to reach new members by targeting the "Financial Planning" category, as well as "Self Improvement," "University/College," and "Internet Tools" interests. Mint.com split its campaign into male and female demographics. It even promoted its "Wedding Budget Checklist" page within StumbleUpon's "Weddings" category.

Stew Langille, vice president of marketing at Mint.com, was pleased with the results, calling StumbleUpon Paid Discovery "the most cost-effective form of advertising that we have used, including pay-per-click advertising on a popular social networking site."[9]

The campaign drove 180,000 average monthly visits to Mint.com from StumbleUpon—only 44% of which were paid clicks.

Paid StumbleUpon campaigns seem to encourage viral transmission, including unpaid traffic from users sharing Paid Stumbles. For example, a cheese-marketing campaign from the Wisconsin Milk Marketing Board got a boost of 60% more free traffic thanks to organic sharing of its initial Paid Stumbles. These kinds of results are due, in part, to StumbleUpon's focus on engagement—the top-tier ads are targeted at the most engaged users in the network, based on factors including time spent, page interaction and activity, share rate, and other criteria.

---

[9] "Case Studies," StumbleUpon, www.stumbleupon.com/pd.

Given the low cost per click, I believe StumbleUpon Paid Discovery is a worthwhile test-and-learn investment. Try it next time you launch a campaign that needs to generate buzz.

Yelp

In Chapter 3, I talked at length about Foursquare as a means to promote a local bricks-and-mortar business. Yelp is another great resource for local operations. Best known for its restaurant reviews, in fact the site boasts more listings for shopping destinations than for eateries. Some 73 million people visited the site in the first quarter of 2012 to sift through local business reviews and ratings.

But whereas Foursquare has no paid advertising offerings to speak of, Yelp has a few worth considering.

Yelp local business advertising packages typically range from $300 to $1,000 per month. Each package includes a dashboard to track your results in the program.

Yelp Deals are similar to Groupon or LivingSocial promotions—you offer consumers a substantial discount on your Yelp Business page, and Yelp gets a 30% cut of the revenue.

If you can make some margin on that, more power to you.

Your Deal will be showcased prominently near the top of your Yelp Business page. In addition to the Deal price, the regular price and discount percentage will also be displayed, so potential customers know what a great Deal you are offering.

Here are three other ad units or targeting angles to consider on Yelp:

1. **Advertise on Yelp Search.** Yelp Ads are placed on search result pages, so that users searching for your category of business in your area will see your business above Yelp's natural search results.

2. **Advertise on Related Businesses.** Want to cut into your competition's market share? You can place ads on the Yelp business pages of your rivals—nearby businesses in your category.

3. **Removal of Competitor Ads.** By the same token, when you advertise, Yelp will remove competitor ads from your Yelp business page, allowing you to keep the purchasing focus on your business.

Yelp's approach to competitor ads is a bit eyebrow-raising. The newly public firm is still losing millions of dollars, and it is locked in an ad-revenue fight with much bigger rivals Google and Facebook. So I expect we will see many more innovative advertising options from the San Francisco-based company.

TripAdvisor

TripAdvisor is the world's largest travel site, with more than 60 million unique monthly visitors and over 75 million reviews and opinions.

TripAdvisor's specialty is ratings and reviews of lodging, attractions, and destinations, along with travel advice, all from real travelers. The site also integrates travel planning and booking tools, making it an attractive platform for hotels, tour companies, and travel and tourism businesses. The TripAdvisor for Business division provides access to those millions of TripAdvisor visitors.

Airlines, travel agencies, tour operators, credit card companies, and lifestyle brands will likely find the TripAdvisor audience attractive. Banner advertising options include traditional "run of site" media buys and home-page takeovers, as well as more targeted campaigns to reach users researching a specific city, state, country, or island. You can also target audience types, such as business, family, or luxury travelers.

Sponsorships are available for two weekly e-mails: TripWatch, a destination-specific newsletter with deals and information on whatever destination the TripAdvisor member is "watching"; and "Member Update," featuring general travel deals and news.

For hotels, restaurants, and attractions, establishing a business account on TripAdvisor is free. Doing so enables you to "claim" your location on the site, update and optimize your business details, and upload photos. Receive e-mail alerts when your business garners new guest reviews—and you'll be able to respond officially to those reviews. You can also get free TripAdvisor widgets and badges to display on your own website or blog.

The centerpiece ad offering, called Business Listings, is aimed at accommodations as small as a B&B or as large as a luxury resort hotel. Business Listings is powered by an appealing, easy-to-use online ad platform, and the flat-fee pricing is very attractive: just $75 a month or so for a small property, up to around $1,000 a month for big hotel properties of several hundred rooms.

Business Listings enables hoteliers to increase a property's exposure by adding direct contact information—a website link, e-mail address, and phone number—to their property pages on TripAdvisor.com. The effectiveness and ROI of these ads can be substantial.

Vancouver's L'Hermitage Hotel reportedly produced $64 in incremental bookings for every dollar spent on its TripAdvisor Business Listing. A study conducted by Forrester Research on behalf of TripAdvisor projects that the 60-room boutique property will receive over $327,000 in incremental bookings over a three-year period on a $7,500 investment.[10]

"Our Business Listings subscription costs us approximately $200 per month, and it more than pays for itself in one day," says Glenn Eleiter, general manager of L'Hermitage. "Payback is very quick."

Other Platforms

Facebook owns a 95% share of the social media market, in terms of time spent engaging with the platform. It's no surprise Facebook is taking up most of the oxygen in the room when it comes to advertising market share. YouTube, Twitter, LinkedIn, and the other options discussed here are distant followers.

Still, beyond these sites, almost every other social platform would be delighted to sell you an ad. Group deal sites like Groupon and LivingSocial can really move the needle, although we often hear cautionary tales of unsustainable discounts and one-night-stand customers.

Zynga will sell you traditional banners and interstitials—or would you prefer to sponsor a nice "in-game, branded virtual item"?

MySpace and Flickr offer an array of banners. Digg allows users to "digg" popular ads—or bury unpopular ones. Reddit has a self-serve ad platform. The opportunities to spend your social advertising dollars are endless.

But as I said in Chapter 4, stick to a budget that reserves the lion's share for the leading platforms and allocates a small test-and-learn budget for others that seem promising.

---

[10] Yahoo! Finance, "Independent Study Finds TripAdvisor Business Listings Generates $64 for Every Dollar Spent," September 5, 2012, http://finance.yahoo.com/news/independent-study-finds-tripadvisor-business-150100932.html.

Summary

While no other social platform offers quite the advertising muscle of Facebook, it's important to recognize the unique benefits of the other networks. Twitter offers reach, simplicity, and value for the dollar, and it should be part of the toolkit for any news, culture, information, or media-oriented business. YouTube is perfect for visual markets, and it has an unmatched ability to build a cookie pool for display advertising across the broader Internet. Google+ is all about boosting the impact of your Google AdWords program.

With a firm grasp of the advertising options, as well as best practices for community management, the next step is to tackle operations management and analytics—how you will execute your programs and measure their impact.

The landscape is rapidly changing. Spend your time and money wisely—but it's okay if you feel a little giddy. Not since 2000, when Google introduced AdWords, have we seen such rapid "creative disruption" of the media markets. We're living through one of the most exciting times in advertising history.

Operations

Running the Farm

Social media advertising campaigns get all the attention—but it's the behind-the-scenes *operations management* of your program that will really set you up for success. This field is a complex intersection point of technology, marketing, and customer relations management, or CRM. Making a positive impact requires financial and personnel resources, planning, and crisp execution.

Having a positive impact also requires savvy operations that can avoid or quickly defuse the public relations disasters that so frequently hit brands today and that can whip through social media, spreading like a virus.

Who Owns Social Media?

Social media is not a channel so much as a tool set. So, asking the organizational question, "Who in our enterprise owns social media?" is not a hundred percent on the mark. Many departments in your organization (market research, customer service, legal, PR, investor relations, marketing) may use social media as a research or listening tool. Or they may leverage social channels to amplify the public communications they send out as a function of their jobs.

So you will certainly have many stakeholders in social media. But you do need to have one overarching "owner" of social, to serve several functions:

- To establish company-wide rules, certification, and processes for publishing to, and interacting in, social channels

- To develop and execute overall social strategy and tactics

- To coordinate messaging and liaison between various stakeholders

- To report holistically on overall social media program performance

- To oversee adherence to the rules and to escalate issues if needed

In most businesses, the social media team lives in the marketing department, with dotted lines to customer service and legal. Where I work, we maintain online communities for each major brand. Marketing brand managers set the strategic and creative direction for their brand communities. Public relations specialists oversee the process—ensuring coordination among the players, encouraging cross promotion, and enforcing the rules of the road.

Another organizational consideration is to leverage the relevant digital skill sets that already exist within your organization. That's generally the province of the e-commerce or digital team, which is usually under marketing.

"Bring the three facets of digital—paid, owned and social—under one roof," advises Shiv Singh, global head of digital for PepsiCo Beverages. "That's extremely important. I'm lucky in that PepsiCo recognized the importance of having all facets of digital in one place... I believe the only way to drive maximum value is to look at digital holistically."[1]

Because social media offer such powerful communications platforms, they have many stakeholders across an enterprise. The most natural home for social media is within the digital team of your marketing department. But there must be strong "dotted lines" to legal and customer service teams, as well as robust processes for internal communication, approval, and escalation of crisis response across departments.

Planning Your Social Media Program

In Chapter 2, I talked about the need for a formal charter document for your social media program—something between a marketing plan and a full-blown business plan. You'll also need more tactical daily and seasonal plans.

High-impact social media campaigns involve many moving parts, both within the social media landscape and in traditional media. Such campaigns call upon players in your marketing, legal, customer service, and operations departments. They require technology development and a number of weeks or months of lead time.

As a result, a social media program requires disciplined advance planning. You'll need to include some of the following:

---

[1] Brandon Gutman, "How PepsiCo's Shiv Singh Is Making a Splash in Digital," *Forbes*, January 13, 2011, www.forbes.com/sites/marketshare/2011/01/13/pepsi-on-refreshing-digital/.

- Daily community management staffing plan
- Monthly publishing schedules
- Research, survey, and customer insights projects
- Promotions and campaign strategy briefs
- Creative design briefs
- Technology requirements: writing, vendor selection or in-house development, user-experience testing, and debugging
- Budgeting and reporting

While I urge you to write planning documents, we're not asking for the Magna Carta here. Creative ad campaign briefs can be a couple of pages long, describing the goals, outlining the offer or promotion, and noting the milestones and moving parts needed to bring it to life.

Your monthly content calendar is no more than a couple of pages of bulleted ideas for posts. Most successful online communities fall into something of a regular routine, with traditions like "Fan Exclusive Deal of the Week" falling on a Tuesday, say, followed by recipes on Wednesday, then "Fan Follow Friday" to shine the spotlight on someone in your fan base. Also natural for your social media publishing plan are holidays, including relevant "Hallmark holidays" that fit your market and key anniversary dates for your business, as well as commercial events like Black Friday and Cyber Monday.

Scheduling and execution of social media campaigns can be done comfortably with whatever project management tool you already use, whether it's Basecamp, Excel, or something else—as long as it's not the back of an envelope.

Budget Accurately

What does it cost to run a social media program? Is such a program a bootstrap operation? Or is it one that has the funds to deliver on its promise to the brand and its fans, with sufficient staff, technology, and promotional dollars to make an impact?

Based on my experience, I'd propose that the social media budget should be in the neighborhood of 5–10% of the entire marketing budget. Within that, paid social media advertising ought to receive 5–10% of the overall online ad budget.

Public data on social media budgets is very scarce. Many studies confirm that companies plan to increase spending on social in general and social advertising in particular. But they say nothing about specific dollar figures.

As one reference point, Rilla Delorier, chief marketing officer of SunTrust Bank, was quoted in *Ad Age* as saying, "The great thing is less than 5% of my total spend is in social media. We've reached over a million customers this year through that mechanism. It's a very efficient way to get feedback on what's working and what's not."[2]

John Bell, who runs Social@Ogilvy, the social media practice at Ogilvy & Mather, constructed a matrix of suggested budget allocations for social media as a percentage of total marketing budget. Delorier's comment factored into Bell's thinking. At the low end, Bell places "obligatory experimenters," spending just 1%. As a business progresses through "questing" to a "well-integrated" program, and from "adoption" to a "go big" mindset, Bell sees the budget allocation for social rising to 5%, then 7%, then 12% and ultimately as high as 17%. He cautions, though, that by the time an enterprise reaches the high end, social has become so well integrated into the overall budget that you can't clearly connect dollars solely to social.[3]

I've created a hypothetical budget to get you thinking about your likely expense categories (see Figure 7-1):

- **Personnel:** Whether dedicated in-house staff, outsourced agency, or combination of the two, this will be the biggest slice of the pie.

- **Social media advertising:** The money you spend on Facebook, Foursquare, Twitter, and so on.

- **Software:** Used for monitoring, publishing, campaign management, and analytics.

- **Campaign design and development:** Includes promotions, sweepstakes, games, and apps to support free sample giveaways.

---

[2] Jennifer Rooney, "How SunTrust Bank Worked to Build Trust Among Distrustful Consumers," *Ad Age*, August 26, 2010, http://adage.com/article/cmo-interviews/marketing-suntrust-cmo-rilla-delorier-social-media-outreach/145598/.

[3] John Bell, "How Much Should Brands Budget for Social Media?" The Digital Image Mapping Project, August 30, 2012, http://johnbell.typepad.com/weblog/2010/08/how-much-should-brands-budget-for-social-media.html.

- **Prizes or free samples:** Like it or not, these are key engines for brands to drive engagement in social media. You need to fund these programs.

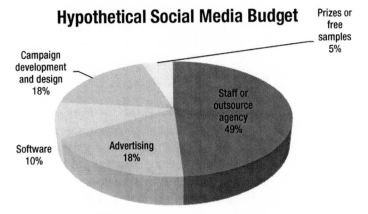

Figure 7-1. To adequately fund your social media spending, parcel out your budget across personnel, software, creative design, and paid advertising—and don't forget prizes or free samples.

Social Media Certification

In the Green Mountain Coffee Roasters specialty coffee business, we have a remarkable social media diva and cat-herder named Kristen Mercure. Kristen, a senior public relations specialist, is responsible for overseeing and coordinating the social media efforts of all our brand managers and their outside agencies. She also serves as liaison between these dozens of people and the stakeholders in public relations, legal, customer service, and other departments.

It is no small task, which is why Kristen manages several formal, full-day social media certification classes per year, attended by anyone who will be involved in social media campaigns, content posting, or interaction with our online communities.

Social media certification is also vitally important. The legal department, for example, has drafted a social media use policy for all employees to sign, as well as a specific policy document for social media certified representatives.

During the certification course, we talk about what constitutes ideal behavior (authenticity, responsiveness, fun, friendliness, knowledgeable answers, and so on). We brainstorm about potential social media disasters—how to deal with customer complaints that go ballistic, how not to divulge sensitive information, and so forth. We discuss scenarios that we can resolve ourselves, as social media reps, and which ones require an escalated response.

After the training, all participants take an online test to demonstrate that they have learned the rules of the road. Only when they complete the course and pass the test do we give them the go-ahead to publish posts or responses on behalf of the company, on the company blog or in any online community.

Basic Documents You Need

I know that many businesses, especially smaller ones, shoot from the hip. Blogs are easy to set up; anybody can create a Facebook page and start posting immediately. But don't let the ease of use of these platforms encourage you to act impulsively. Even if you've already been running your corporate social media program for months or even years without formal guidance and policy documents, stop and take a deep breath. Invest the time to craft basic written documents for your social media team members to read, discuss in a training session, understand, and sign.

I recommend that your employees get to know the following documents inside out and, where relevant, sign them:

- **Mission documents and FAQs:** These are not legal documents for signature, but they're important for tone setting and orientation. They describe the company's brand tenets as they relate to the social media space, express the main goals of the program, and list all the social media URLs maintained by the company.

- **Social media use policy:** Governs how (and when) all employees will use social networks and social media. This policy statement is often part of a larger document on employee computer, network, and Internet use.

- **Social media representative policy:** Governs the conduct of employees certified to represent the company in social media as part of their job function. Covers content and language guidelines, nondisclosure rules, escalation paths for specific issues, maintenance of passwords, and more.

■ **Tip** For policy help, visit the Social Media Governance database, which contains the social media policies of over 200 companies and organizations, including Apple, Nordstrom, Razorfish, and others: http://socialmediagovernance.com/policies.php.

Publishing Management

Sitting at the helm of a corporate social media program, you must view yourself as a *publisher*. Your team is always just one button click from an audience of millions. The social media certification process ensures that your team knows and follows the overall brand mission, rules of engagement, and escalation paths before they start publishing posts and interacting with fans.

Whether you use a third-party social media publishing platform, or post directly from each of the social networks, you must observe the quality-control processes of a "real" publisher:

- Create a monthly content calendar, in advance, and subject it to editorial review and approval, legal review, and proofreading.

- Before publishing, subject each post to another spell check and have it approved by a manager or "second pair of eyes" to catch any errors, typos, or any circumstance that has changed since initial approval of the content calendar.

- Before publishing, be one hundred percent certain you're logged into the right account (see the tip below).

- When linking to content on your website, test that all links are functioning and are tagged for web analytics; promoted products are in stock; any promoted discounts are being correctly applied; any sign-up forms or other functionality on the target page are working properly.

- By their nature, wall interactions with fans are more spontaneous. But you still must spell check, speak in the brand voice, and observe your established CRM rules of engagement. Daily or weekly, a manager should review all posts and provide specific feedback to team members on any posts that missed the mark in tone, helpfulness, accuracy, or response time.

- Whatever you publish, invest the time and focused attention to reread it the moment it goes live. Review takes mere seconds. It is simple to edit or delete a post. I'm amazed at how often typos make it onto some brand fan pages and how long they can persist before anyone fixes them.

■ **Tip**   Many embarrassing moments occur when Facebook page admins accidentally post their personal content to the brand fan page, or vice versa, or to the wrong brand (see the section on "Damage Control" later in this chapter). Before posting, always check the top of your Facebook screen for a notification like "You are posting, commenting, and liking as Jane Doe..." and change accounts if necessary.

INTERVIEW: CHRIS BOUDREAUX, ACCENTURE, SOCIAL POLICY MAKER

In 2009, the San Francisco-based social media consultant Chris Boudreaux created an online database of social media policies. His studies of social media have been referenced by corporations, governments, industry analysts, and nonprofits worldwide.

At the social media agency Converseon, Boudreaux served clients including IBM, Ford, Univision, and Walmart. In 2011, he coauthored *The Social Media Management Handbook* at Accenture, where he led business transformation programs at Fortune 500 clients including Boeing and Microsoft. He regularly codes web apps to stay abreast of current technologies.

Most people would say corporate social media policies are pretty dry stuff. What interests you about them?

Boudreaux: While it is true that the legal aspects of social media policies may feel a bit burdensome to some folks, policies are critical to any organization using social media, for the following reasons: one, laws in the space are evolving, and organizations need to help their employees comply with relevant regulations, which vary by industry and jurisdiction; two, companies should help employees understand how to protect themselves in social media, in addition to protecting the company; and three, companies should guide employee use of social media such that they are able to support the goals of the brand, to the extent it makes sense for the brand.

The Federal Trade Commission (FTC) took a stance on social media that could have big implications for businesses. What's your take on it?

Boudreaux: The FTC is simply applying rules that have always existed for celebrity endorsers, to people in social media. The spirit and terms of the FTC guidance are pretty straightforward. However, compliance at scale does require thoughtful implementation of business process and technology, which does require a bit of effort for some brands to work through. Also, the FTC has only really pursued *brands* when violations have occurred, and not the *endorsers* of the brands.

How have social media changed CRM? Can you recommend processes and software tools to help organizations manage this new communications channel?

Boudreaux: This is a big question. I typically include sales, marketing, and customer service in CRM. Within those areas, social media data are now being used to better understand customers and prospects. Salespeople use social media data when calling on their customers. In those cases, the key change is that brands are accessing conversations that do not necessarily involve them. That is, a brand can listen to what you say to other people, and use that to better understand you. The impacts are similar to companies like Google watching everything you do on the web (which sites you visit, which buttons you click), to understand you and your interests.

Also, social channels are used for customer service delivery, in plain, public view. This is a big change from interacting in email or phone, which were never accessible by the public.

What social media topic are you tackling next?

Boudreaux: I'm helping brands with broader implications and requirements for governing social media operations in large organizations, including analytics and strategy capabilities—beyond policies and compliance.

Building Your Social Media Dream Team

I hope I've sold you on the merits of the social media certification process. But now, who are you going to certify? Gone are the days when you could entrust your organization's social media program to a computer-savvy intern (if those days ever really existed). "I spend a ton of time on Facebook and Twitter!" is not a qualification. Today you need motivated professionals who view social media management as a career.

Sure, enthusiasm for the platforms is a must. Your candidates must embrace the different cultures of Twitter, Facebook, or YouTube—whatever platforms are your priority. The ideal candidate will also be customer-centric and brand obsessed, display a clear vision for an effective social media campaign strategy, and serve as a reliable compass for how to comport oneself online. Fluency with web-based tools and attention to detail are also key. Remember, your social media representatives are just one "publish" button away from the eyes of the entire world.

Titles and job descriptions? They are changing like a kaleidoscope. Here are a few possibilities:

- Social media director

- Social media manager
- Community manager
- Blogger in chief
- Brand evangelist
- Social media strategist
- Social media specialist
- Online community specialist
- Social media coordinator
- Social media campaign manager
- Social media representative
- Social media admin

In addition to hiring a core staff, you may find that social media demands extra bodies from time to time to support seasonal campaign events. A lot of exciting promotions are being done by different brands employing college campus reps, "street teams," guerrilla marketers, brand ambassadors, blogger networks and more—online and offline. I'll talk about some of them in Chapter 9.

Choosing a Social Media Agency

If your business is new to the social space or constrained by personnel resources, a specialty agency can be a great support to add bandwidth, get you started, enhance your strategy, and help you avoid common mistakes. Just be sure you trust the people you're working with. Request references as well as case studies of brands like yours. Check out agencies' work online—the campaigns of their clients, social ads (these will usually emerge after you "like" a brand on Facebook), daily postings, and community management interactions. Interview the firm's references; in addition, dig a bit into current and past clients who may not be provided to you as references. Reach out to these folks on LinkedIn to ask if they'll share their experiences with you.

Cost can be a big consideration. You can engage freelancers and consultants for a few hundred dollars a month. Specialty social media firms capable of managing your daily postings and helping drive overall strategy start at a few thousand dollars a month, and—in the case of big-name social media agencies or the digital arms of top ad agencies—they can run into tens of thousands a month. To some degree, you get what you pay for, but I'd caution you that there's something of a gold-rush mentality among digital firms staking out social media "practices." Be sure you and the agency agree on what the specific deliverables will be: how much content posting, what's the service-level agreement for turnaround time for community management interactions, how many hours of strategic consulting will the agency provide, and how will it be delivered (a session, a presentation, or a printed report)? How many campaigns and supporting applications will be designed and run, and what will be their scope?

Note Before outsourcing your social media needs to an agency, get a written agreement on what the agency will do, how it will report, how quickly it will move (and during what hours of operation—nights? weekends?), and what the outcomes should be.

Most important, when you hear an agency pitch and interview its team, you should feel confident the agency is a good cultural fit. The ideal agency knows the social space inside and out. Its team "gets" your brand, can connect personally with your consumers, and can speak in your brand voice, with authenticity, authority, and passion. The agency wants a *long-term relationship* with your company, its brands, and its fans. It is humble enough to know that your brand—not the agency—is what makes the community.

16 QUESTIONS TO ASK A PROSPECTIVE SOCIAL MEDIA AGENCY

Here are some important things to ask before you engage a social media expert or agency (and yes, some of these questions are a little provocative).

1. What makes my brand a good fit for social media?
2. How did you come to specialize in social media—what's your professional background?
3. What's the biggest crisis or screw-up you've been involved in, and how did you control the damage?
4. What was your biggest accomplishment as a social media manager?
5. Can you describe the team that will be working on our account and what their typical day will look like?
6. How many people-hours will you spend on my account each month?
7. What would you recommend as our top strategic goals?
8. How will we measure our progress toward those goals?

9. What software tools do you use for brand monitoring, publishing, and analytics?

10. What level of access would we have to these tools?

11. If we expressed dissatisfaction with the team or the results, how would you respond?

12. Can you give us two or three creative campaign ideas that would appeal to our customers or prospects?

13. What platforms or tactics would you recommend we avoid?

14. What will you do to drive our fan and follower growth?

15. What can your firm do for me that a smart, hungry, entry-level staffer couldn't?

16. In addition to what we would pay you, how much should we budget to support social media campaigns and activity?

Technology Infrastructure

The good news is, you probably don't have to buy any servers.

Hardware

Social media and Web 2.0 technologies go hand in hand, so virtually everything you need to support your social media program from a technology and database perspective will live in the cloud.

That's a good thing for speed to market, low investment, and robustness. Establishing a presence on the major social networks is free, for the most part. It's stunning to think how quickly and inexpensively you can be amassing an audience of hundreds of thousands, communicating with them, and publishing and promoting to them.

Software

You will probably make technology investments in cloud software tools to help you do the following:

- Monitor your brand reputation, industry, and rivals

- Efficiently publish to several social networks

- Perform customer relationship management

- Launch sweepstakes, games, group deals, and other specialized campaigns

- Track and report analytics

You'll also task developers with enabling social features on your own website. Adding widgets and social plug-ins from Facebook, Twitter, YouTube, LinkedIn, and other platforms requires little to no developer resources. Custom integration with the social networks requires programming, HTML, JavaScript, API, and other skills. I'll explore the topic in more depth in Chapter 10, but for now, it's important just to know that the social media program will have to budget for in-house or outsourced developers.

▓ **Tip** What kind of developers do you need? (1) To integrate your website with Facebook, you need a developer who is proficient on your website platform and can work with XFBML, JavaScript SDK, and APIs. (2) To integrate your mobile app or mobile website with Facebook, you need an iOS, Android, or web developer. (3) To develop apps for Facebook, you can use any language that supports web programming, such as PHP, Python, Java, or C#.

The downside of public networks and cloud computing is that an unprecedented amount of your brand equity has migrated to platforms you don't control, with member databases you don't own. Yes, you could try to construct a "walled garden"—and I'll talk about proprietary social networks next in Chapter 10—but my preference is to engage with the big public networks in a way that seeks to bring much of the relationship, intellectual property, and SEO benefit back to the proprietary site.

Monitoring Tools

As I mentioned in Chapter 2 on best practices, it's vital to approach the social media landscape first as a *listening* post, not as a speaking platform. Social media represent the new public square, and they are an ideal place to hear the conversations of your target consumers as they talk about your brand, the marketplace (what they like, what they hate, what they need), and your competitors. Listening is not just the first step in developing a strategy for how you'll approach social media. It's also an ongoing, everyday responsibility—a modern-day discipline your company needs to practice, to ensure that you are able to:

- Resolve consumer problems and complaints wherever they emerge on the web

- Detect cultural trends, memes, fads—and potential scandals—early

- Monitor the volume and sentiment of mentions of your brand (and your competitors' brands)

To be a good listener, you'll need *social media brand-monitoring tools*. There are decent free utilities out there to alert you when your brand is mentioned in the press, for instance. But to reliably track, report, and act on brand mentions throughout the various social media platforms, you'll need to invest in one of the leading software packages, such as HootSuite, Sprout Social, or Radian6.

The best social media software combines all three of the key requirements:

- Brand monitoring

- Publishing management

- Social analytics and reporting

Publishing and Management Tools

Shoutlet, Vocus, HootSuite, and TweetDeck are just a few of the leading applications for publishing posts and managing conversations across multiple social media networks (see Figure 7-2).

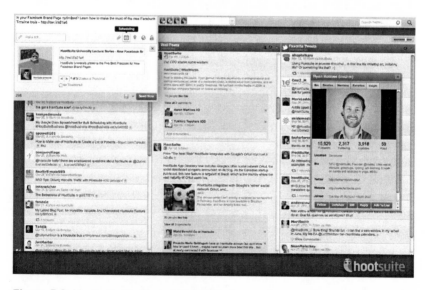

Figure 7-2. Hootsuite Dashboard. HootSuite is one of many software tools to help you manage your social media efforts. Courtesy of Hootsuite.

Ad-Management Tools

Most businesses will not require custom software to manage their advertising on social media platforms. But for organizations running large and complex ad buys across several social networks, or testing a huge variety of different ad versions or microtargeting audiences by location or other criteria, there are management tools worth considering.

For instance, BuyBuddy from Buddy Media allows you to manage your social media ad buys from one central console and lets you measure performance against an impressive array of performance goals (see Figure 7-3):

- People talking about this
- Page "likes"
- Post "likes"
- Comments
- Shares
- Twitter @ mentions
- Check-ins
- Photo tags
- Offers shared
- Offers claimed
- App installs
- App uses
- Credit spending in an app
- RSVPs

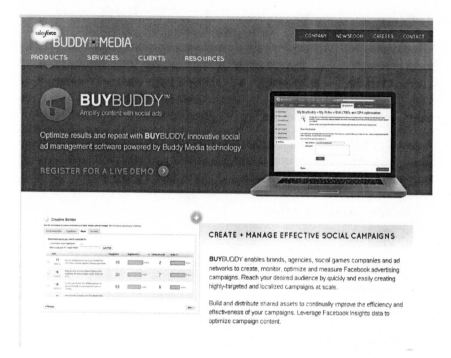

Figure 7-3. BuyBuddy, now part of Salesforce Marketing Cloud, lets you track the results of your social media ad campaigns and optimize their performance. Courtesy salesforce.com.

Because social media advertising targets actions that are so different from the paid search-and-display ad model, social ads deserve their own management software. I advise you, though, to first manage your social media ads directly, in each ad platform's administrative interface. Until you're personally familiar with the different platforms, and some of the inefficiencies there, it's premature to invest in a third-party ad-management tool.

Campaign Platforms

Whether you want to run a refer-a-friend promotion, launch a sweepstakes, a poll, or a photo contest, unlock a group deal when you get 10,000 new Facebook fans, or make an exclusive offer to new Twitter followers, you'll need to do some app building or use a special technology platform designed for social media campaigns. You may need more than one! I'll delve into these in Chapter 9.

Analytics Platforms

All the major web analytics, including Google Analytics, Coremetrics, and Omniture, offer reporting suites devoted to social media as a source of traffic to your website. But a new crop of analytics tools specifically for social media metrics has emerged, which I'll cover in Chapter 8.

Damage Control

Throughout this book, I've focused on the positive impact your social media program can have on your fans and on the company's image. We've explored best practices and sought to learn from some of the most inspiring examples and case studies across different industries.

But when talking about social media operations, we can't neglect *disaster preparedness*. It's one of the unpleasant but vital responsibilities of a social media team: you must anticipate the worst and know how to respond to it to defuse a situation and prevent it from worsening.

Quite simply, your team must respond quickly to any developments in your online community and in social media at large. And when you identify the earliest beginnings of a scandal or public relations disaster, you must quickly escalate it to more senior folks in the company—with recommendations for how to resolve it.

To get you in the right frame of mind, here are a few examples of brand-bludgeoning social media screw-ups—some of which were nipped in the bud, some of which were mishandled and went viral.

- **KitchenAid Disses Obama's Dead Grandma:** When Barack Obama, in the opening debate of the 2012 election, remarked that his grandmother never lived to see him elected, a snarky tweet from the mixer manufacturer KitchenAid joked, "Obamas gma even knew it was going 2 b bad! She died 3 days b4 he became president!" The tasteless and partisan tweet set up a firestorm of angry retweets and coverage from Mashable, CNN, *USA Today*, and others. The offensive tweet was actually from a KitchenAid social media rep accidentally tweeting under the corporate account rather than a personal one. Although KitchenAid promptly deleted the tweet and tried to explain it away, the reputational damage was done. Senior brand manager Cynthia Soledad was forced to take the reins in the middle of the night, apologizing for the mistake and reaching out to journalists to tell KitchenAid's side of the story.

- **"No one here knows how to f#*!ing drive":** In a similar story in 2011, an update appeared on the Chrysler Twitter account that inflamed both consumers and Chrysler alike. The tweet read, "I find it ironic that Detroit is known as #motorcity and yet no one here knows how to f#*!ing drive." Chrysler responded quickly by deleting the tweet, posting an apology and explaining that its account had been compromised. What had happened was that an employee of New Media Strategies, Chrysler's social agency, inadvertently tweeted under the @ChryslerAutos account instead of his personal account. The employee was fired, and Chrysler did not renew its contract with New Media Strategies.

- **Red Cross #gettngslizzerd:** The American Red Cross posted this embarrassing message to its Twitter account: "Ryan found two more 4 bottle packs of Dogfish Head's Midas touch beer.... when we drink we do it right #gettngslizzerd." Soon it was being retweeted, and within an hour the Red Cross social media director had gotten wind of it. She promptly deleted the errant post and defused the incident by sending this humorous Tweet: "We've deleted the rogue tweet but rest assured the Red Cross is sober and we've confiscated the keys." The speedy and good-natured response saved the day.

- **#McDStories:** McDonald's attempt at promoting the fast food chain via a promoted hashtag campaign on Twitter backfired when users coopted the tag to post 140-character tweets sharing horror stories and blasting the food. *Forbes* covered the story with the headline "When a Hashtag Becomes a Bashtag." Rick Wion, McDonald's social media director, admitted: "Within an hour, we saw that it wasn't going as planned. It was negative enough that we set about a change of course."

- **Dub the Dew:** Mountain Dew built a website and turned to crowd-source voting to name its new green-apple soda. Problem was, tech-savvy users of the online bulletin board 4chan.org took control and pushed to the top such offensive and brand-damaging suggestions as "Diabeetus" and "Hitler did nothing wrong." Mountain Dew was forced to take down the site and scuttle the entire promotion.

- **United Breaks Guitars:** In 2008, professional musician Dave Carroll sat in a United Airlines jet on the tarmac preparing to leave Chicago O'Hare, when he and fellow passengers noticed baggage handlers roughly throwing luggage—including Carroll's $3,500 Taylor guitar. When he landed, Carroll found his guitar had been destroyed. He spent the next year fighting fruitlessly to get United to pay for his guitar. Then he gave up and resorted to YouTube, uploading a series of funny music videos entitled "United Breaks Guitars." The videos went viral, reaching over 16 million views, and even resulted in a book and speaking tour for Carroll. United finally apologized and donated $3,000 to a charity of Carroll's choice. But by then, much damage to the airline's public image (and probably its business) had already been done.

Corporate social media disaster tales run the spectrum, but I see just a handful of root causes:

1. **Operational sloppiness:** Lack of quality control, preparedness, oversight, systematic processes, or structure. The ease and speed of publishing to social media is both a blessing and a curse. Adopting strong editorial systems and CRM processes and controls will minimize the likelihood of all-too-public mistakes.

2. **Failure to move at Internet speed:** The social media environment is fast-moving and consumer controlled. Globally, social delivers trillions of impressions and intercommunications every second; in 2012, for example, the NFL Superbowl alone inspired over 10,000 tweets a second. Inaction can turn a relatively unremarkable complaint into a viral fiasco. Monitor your brand constantly. React speedily to any trending crisis. Never assume "it will just go away." Be ready to apologize and provide honest explanations or remedies. Be humble, personal, authentic, and don't be afraid to be funny if the situation warrants it.

3. **Tone deafness:** The landscape of social media is emotional. Fan pages of cherished brands, large or small, can feel like a lovefest. But some brands and industries are polarizing, as in the McDonald's example above. Sometimes they're downright hated—think Wall Street investment banks, oil companies, cable companies, cell phone carriers. Whether planning a major campaign or executing daily wall-management, hope for the best but *prepare for the worst*. Not everyone loves you. Haters are gonna hate. Be attuned to public sentiment and to the cultural vibe of each social media platform. Be a good listener—be open to hearing problems and issues from your consumers and resolving them publicly. Don't be passive. Help shape the tone of the conversation playing out in your fan communities. Prepare

and post "house rules" as a tab on your Facebook page, and delete posts that are profane, hateful, abusive, or otherwise violate your rules. Completely sanitizing the conversation in social media would be unwise (and impossible). But it's your right and responsibility to keep your company's social media communities on topic and brand supportive.

The bottom line: bad things can happen to good brands out there. Be alert, be prepared, take responsibility, respond quickly. Don't hesitate to show your humanity or lighten a tense situation with a little humor.

Your Social Media Command Center

You've planned, budgeted, and staffed your social media operation. You've invested in and mastered powerful social media software. You know what you need now.

A social media command center, or SMCC.

Of course!

The digital marketing geek's version of a "man cave," the social media command center, was hatched in June 2010 by PepsiCo in its Chicago headquarters, for its Gatorade brand. Dubbed the "Gatorade Mission Control Center," it consisted of a centrally located, glass-walled room, glowing with the light of six huge flat-screen monitors displaying social media visualizations from Radian6 and IBM software. From there, command center staffers monitored brand mentions and trending responses to Gatorade commercials and content uploaded to YouTube and USTREAM.

The goal of the project, says Gatorade senior marketing director Carla Hassan, is to "take the largest sports brand in the world and turn it into [the] largest participatory brand in the world."

Gatorade's intense focus translates into blazing-fast responsiveness. When it aired its "Gatorade has evolved" commercials, which featured music by rap artist David Banner, Mission Control quickly noticed the tune was being widely discussed in social media. Within 24 hours, Gatorade had signed Banner to produce a full-length version of the song, which was distributed to Gatorade followers and fans on Twitter and Facebook.[4]

Since Gatorade's pioneering move in 2010, a variety of organizations have employed social media command centers, including Dell, the American Red

---

[4] Adam Ostrow, "Inside Gatorade's Social Media Command Center," Mashable, June 15, 2010, http://mashable.com/2010/06/15/gatorade-social-media-mission-control/.

Cross, Clemson University, Superbowl XLVI, Kansas City for the 2012 MLB All-Star Game, and Edelman public relations.

Dell built its "Ground Control" social media listening center in 2010, and employs it for market research, customer service, and continuous process improvement. Dell's system tracks a stunning 22,000 social media posts about its products every day. "Ground Control is about tracking the largest number of possible conversations across the web and making sure we 'internalize' that feedback, good or bad," says Dell's VP of social media and community, Manish Mehta. "It's also about tracking what you might call the 'long tail'—those smaller matters that might not bubble to the surface today, but are out there, and deserve to be heard."[5]

Event-driven operations like the NFL and the American Red Cross, which recently built social media command centers, are naturals for this approach to social media because of the intensity of focus and the fast pace of change on the ground. Clustered around half a dozen monitors and exchanging hurried perceptions and responses, an SMCC team can identify and defuse rapidly trending issues: parking and traffic problems, a bomb threat. An SMCC team can tap into and stoke social memes inspired by game highlights, TV ads, and half-time shows. At the most basic level, the team can aggressively staff up to the spiking volume of social mentions, so they can respond, "like," retweet, and otherwise amplify the conversation more widely into the social network, in real time, as events are unfolding.

Superbowl XLVI established a 2,800-square-foot command center in downtown Indianapolis, just blocks from the event. The goals were: (1) to extend hospitality to fans and visitors across social media channels; (2) ensure public safety through careful monitoring of any signs of trouble; (3) capture the event for those who couldn't attend in person; and (4) amplify positive sentiment about the event.

"We are known for our friendliness, we wanted to make sure everyone had a great experience at the Super Bowl coming from different parts of the country, whether it was on the airplane, airport, street, cab, or online," said Taulbee Jackson, CEO of Raidious and a member of the Super Bowl XLVI host committee. In the end, the command center and Jackson's efforts were a huge success, in terms of both the volume of interactions handled and the positive sentiment generated.[6]

---

[5] Ekaterina Walter, "How Top Brands Like Gatorade And The Super Bowl Use Social-Media Command Centers," Fast Company, June 22, 2012, www.fastcompany.com/1841131/how-top-brands-gatorade-and-super-bowl-use-social-media-command-centers.

[6] Ibid.

Social media command centers are not inexpensive—they are likely to cost upward of $120K a year. But for an ambitious brand generating a high volume of social mentions, an SMCC could just be the perfect operational vehicle to take the strategy I've been talking about, and the technology, and bring them together for flawless execution that reaches and delights your online community.

Summary

Community interaction, marketing campaigns, and promotions are the exciting aspects of social media—the stuff that happens in the glare of the spotlight. But what makes it all succeed is the unglamorous, backstage work of operations management: solid planning, budgeting, and staffing—and damage control when things go awry.

Social media marketing is no passing fad. It's here to stay. To succeed takes the same discipline, structure, allocation of resources, and cycle of continuous improvement that you apply to other aspects of your business. In fact, operational excellence can separate winning programs from losers. While other businesses may be throwing money and effort pell-mell at social media, you can conduct your program with foresight, strategic thinking, and clear goals in mind.

Of course, establishing goals can be tough in the social media space. Much of what you'll do in social will be quite trackable, as digital media tend to be. But the wealth of measurable activity may still leave you scratching your head as to what you're actually *achieving* for your business. In Chapter 8, I'll address which performance measures really matter—and which ones are merely noise.

Measuring Success

Tracking the Vital Signs and Demonstrating Results

As a results-driven marketer, you'll need to take these steps as part of your social media program:

- Establish priorities and quantifiable goals

- Choose tracking tools

- Report your numbers, growth, progress against plan, and comparison with rivals

Businesses and organizations can no longer expect to kick the tires on social media without opening their wallets. Unpaid interns will not be enough to make an impact. Tacking on social media as a fraction of someone's job description is little better.

You'll need to staff up, with talented in-house people and perhaps with outside agency help. Plus, you'll need to invest real dollars in the technology platforms, advertising support, and promotions that make the best social media programs sing.

With real social media programs now costing real money, the folks in the green eyeshades will inevitably ask the question:

What is the goal, and what is the return on investment?

As a person who has spent most of my career in direct marketing, I'm the first to admit that compared with online ad campaigns, the ROI of social media is still a bit nebulous. It's difficult to track or precisely quantify.

I also firmly believe that social media and online networking are still in their infancy and that their relationship to marketing and business is changing fast. So the real ROI to focus on is the *risk of ignoring*.

Any business or organization must commit to a high-profile presence on the major social networks or be overshadowed by competitors who are quicker and more aggressive.

But that doesn't mean you should rush onto Facebook, Twitter, Pinterest, Google+, YouTube and the like without a plan. You need a strategy, clear and measurable goals for success, and a means to track your progress.

What Are Your Goals?

There are countless brands and businesses out there, each with its own business model and approach. But there are really just four broad goals to aspire to with your social media efforts:

- **Brand engagement, advocacy, and loyalty:** Your best, most loyal customers will be the first to seek you out in the social sphere, and you must be there for them, connecting one to one, cultivating a deeper relationship, rewarding them with "surprise and delight" campaigns or sweepstakes, and furthering their understanding of and enjoyment of your brand. Perhaps you'll associate yourself with the pleasures of music, online games, or real-world events. Ideally, you'll tie your brand to a bigger cause. For instance, PetSmart's social media effort focuses not on cat food and dog collars, but on beloved, adorable pets and the issue of animal welfare. Patagonia's is about surfing, paddling, and climbing—and environmentalism to ensure that those beautiful landscapes are preserved. Pepsi isn't about carbonated sugar water, but about "living for the moment."

- **Customer service:** Questions and complaints no longer obediently queue to your 1-800 number or your customer service e-mail. They come 24/7 to your Facebook or Twitter pages—or they're posted elsewhere in cyberspace, and it's your CS team's job to monitor the web for brand mentions, so they can sniff out and resolve any budding product-quality fiascos or brand blunders, wherever they emerge.

- **Lead generation:** Social is a great place to get your brand in front of good, qualified prospects. Over 80% of consumers report they use the web to research products and services. In a world where consumer attention is fleeting and trust is scarce, businesses must embrace the power of social media. Word-of-mouth endorsements from friends or from "shoppers like me" are the single most trusted buying influence today. Social media platforms allow you to introduce yourself to potential candidates in an atmosphere that is more personal and less overtly commercial than traditional online marketing. This lets your brand loyalists spread the word and do your selling for you.

- **Brand awareness:** Paid social advertising can target prospects by interest, sometimes incredibly precisely. Attract them with product samplings and sweepstakes, or get them into your database to receive your e-mail newsletter. But be sure to offer compelling, real benefits, not just a succession of uninspired promotional spam. Another powerful way to reach new customers is through the friend feeds of your existing fans. Friends share a lot of the same interests, hobbies, style, and tastes. That's what makes them friends! So when your fans are "liking" and commenting on your stuff— or when your website connects to Facebook to let them share their product reviews and other on-site activities with friends—you make an ideal, soft-sell, friend-endorsed impression on their entire friend networks. The same echo is heard when you ask your followers to retweet your messages on Twitter. You can augment the friend feed with Facebook advertising targeted to "friends of fans." This network effect gives you impetus to build your fan base to critical mass. The more fans you have, the more friends of fans, and you'll start to see your fan base grow organically, day by day.

- **Revenue:** Social media efforts drive very real dollars, although not always through a direct conduit. In Chapter 9, I'll explore how businesses are driving sales through group discounts, social coupons, refer-a-friend campaigns, and Facebook e-commerce applications. In this chapter, I'll explain how to establish your foundation for social commerce by showing you how to track revenue from social channels.

Table 8-1 shows some of the tactics you can deploy to meet these four goals.

Table 8-1. Social Media Goals and Tactics to Achieve Them

Social Media Goal	Tactics to Achieve the Goal
Brand Engagement, Advocacy, and Loyalty	Wall posts Community interaction "Surprise and delight" campaigns Contests, sweepstakes, promotions, cause campaigns, games, Twitter trends Social integration of product reviews, e-commerce actions Product sampling Social loyalty points programs Badging and gamification
Customer Service	Community interaction "Surprise and delight" campaigns Brand-mention monitoring
Lead Generation and Brand Awareness	Product giveaways, free samples Sweepstakes and contests Refer-a-friend campaigns E-mail newsletter sign-up
Revenue	Promotional wall posts Social coupons Group deals Groupon, LivingSocial Refer-a-friend campaigns Facebook commerce

You'll note that some tactics support multiple goals. Not all businesses will employ all tactics. And some businesses will have only indirect revenue-driving goals, which might be measured by milestones like event RSVPs or coupon downloads, as opposed to actual dollars. (Again, I'll cover most of these tactics in greater detail in Chapter 9.)

What Is a Facebook Fan Really Worth?

The most accessible measures of progress in your social media program are the raw numbers of fans: Facebook "likes," Twitter followers, YouTube subscribers and so on. But that begs the question: what is the actual value of these fans? A number of mostly small and unscientific studies have sought to quantify the value of a Facebook fan, and they've been all over the map in their methodologies and results.

Vitrue arrived at the underwhelming number of $3.60, by equating the value of brand mentions in the social graph with the cost of having to buy impressions via PR or advertising.

SocialCode compared the cost of advertising and conversion rates of nonfans and fans and came up with a value of $9.56 per fan.

Syncapse observed that fans of a brand on Facebook buy more from a company than nonfans and are 28% more likely to continue as loyal customers. Based on this data, Syncapse concluded that a Facebook fan was worth $161.

One weakness of these studies is the chicken-and-egg question. Which came first, the Facebook fandom or the customer's brand advocacy? People "like" the brands that they actually like. It's not surprising that higher response rates and order values are correlated with being a fan of a brand on Facebook. But correlation does not equal causation.

In my view, the value of a sizeable and thriving Facebook community can be split into two parts. First, there's retention. For your existing best customers, Facebook helps you foster brand loyalty. Facebook didn't create the customer, but it may help you retain the customer and generate more sales per year from him or her. Every business experiences customer attrition, or churn, and for many businesses it's a huge financial drain. The cost to retain an existing consumer—through customer service, engagement, and rewards—is much lower than the cost of advertising to win a brand-new customer.

The other value of an online community is for acquisition. Positive word-of-mouth recommendations, user-generated content, search engine benefit, "earned media" (aka free publicity), and other positive brand awareness helps you turn prospects into leads, and eventually turn those leads into buyers.

The brand-equity building that goes on in the process is also real and tangible—if not perfectly quantifiable. But attitude & usage (A&U) studies and net promoter scores are good ways to track the trends of awareness of your brand and consumers' loyalty to you as they change over time. Net promoter scores are derived from customer surveys like the free Bizrate postpurchase questionnaire, which is used by thousands of retailers to gauge customer satisfaction with the online shopping experience, fulfillment, customer service, and product. Your score on the final question—"How likely are you to recommend this retailer to others?"—is your net promoter score, from 0 (not at all likely) to 10 (extremely likely).

Managing a big and high-impact online community cannot help but burnish your brand's image in the hearts and minds of consumers. If you're making a positive connection on social media, you should be able to track improvements in your net promoter score over time.

Social Media Analytics

What will you measure? How will you measure it? Your goal is to demonstrate that the costs of your social media program are more than offset by the return on that investment. Demonstrating ROI is the end game.

As you write your social media business plan, keep in mind that you'll need to drive toward five big, overarching measures that everyone in your organization will understand. Maintaining your focus on these measures will make it easier to navigate the world of social media analytics.

Here are the big five:

- Leads

- Revenue

- New customers: track leads from social media and their conversion to buyers

- Retention: benchmark the loyalty of a small sample of active members of the online community against your overall customer loyalty

- Net promoter score

And here are some best practices to ensure your social media program is results-oriented, and grounded in sound analytics practices:

- Use platform reporting of the social media networks to track the fans, followers, on-platform reach, and interactivity of your online community

- Consider using monitoring software like HootSuite or Radian6 to listen to the social conversation—tracking your brand impressions and the level of positive sentiment toward your brand

- Use your web analytics software to measure how much traffic, sales, e-newsletter signups, and other benefits are flowing to you from social

- If you add *Like* buttons and other social plug-ins and interactive features to your website, use Facebook Insights reporting to tell you how much activity each button is generating, which of your content stimulates the most comments, and the demographic profile of the people interacting with your site content (see Figure 8-1)

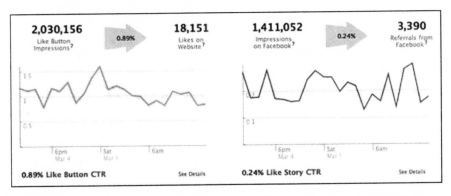

Figure 8-1. You can benefit from Facebook Insights reporting when you create a Facebook app, or if you add *Like* buttons and other Facebook-style interactivity to your website via Social Plugins. Courtesy of Facebook, Inc.

First, track Facebook "likes," Twitter followers, YouTube subscribers, and views. These overall audience measures don't mean a lot, in and of themselves, but they're the easiest data to capture, and they do serve as the pulse and vital signs of your program. Steadily growing fan bases indicate that your promotions are appealing and that they're reaching the right audience. Whether your goal is to connect with loyal customers or reach prospective customers in your "friends of fans" reach—or both—the *size of your online community* really matters.

■ **Tip** Your top-level social media metrics are about the size of your online community—total Facebook fans, Twitter followers, YouTube subscribers—as well as the network reach these fans give you. These are the numbers that indicate your promotions are working and your communications are reaching a big and growing audience. In social media, size does matter.

Tools for Social Media Analytics

Social networks and social media (including interactive tools you add to your website) encompass a very broad landscape. Some of the activity you'll want to track is occurring on your fan pages. Some of it is on your website. And much of it is occurring across the Internet at large—in conversations that advocates and detractors are having on public forums about your brand, products, and industry. Analytics tools exist to track all of these social touch points. To simplify things, with social media analytics, you're trying to capture four perspectives:

- Activity and attitudes on your brand pages
- Brand-related activity and attitudes in the social sphere at large
- Impact on your online business
- Impact on your offline business

Each perspective can be fleshed out with a variety of analytics tools, some more quantitative than others. Let's look at some options in more detail.

Your Online Community

For the heartbeat of your own brand pages, you'll rely on the native statistics from Facebook, Twitter, YouTube, Pinterest, Google+, and whatever other platforms you're active on. These will include measures of audience (fans, followers, and subscribers, plus network reach) as well as interactivity (comments, retweets, re-pins, video views). As a social media manager, you'll find harvesting data from several platforms is an inefficient process, so you'll probably want to use an aggregating tool like HootSuite, Radian6, TweetDeck, or SocialMention (see Figure 8-2). These will bring all the key metrics from the major social networks onto one convenient dashboard.

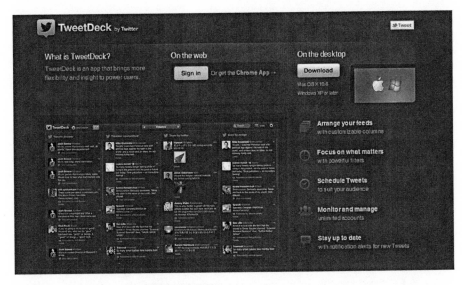

Figure 8-2. Twitter's TweetDeck combines publishing tools for "power users" with smart monitoring and filtering tools that make it easier to keep an eye on your brand and industry. Courtesy of Twitter.

As you report on your progress to others within your enterprise, either you can grant them "reports access" to these analytics platforms, or you can export your reports in PDF, Excel, or other formats.

Radian 6, acquired by the big CRM platform Salesforce.com, is a comprehensive social media listening and engagement tool. Radian6 offers an Engagement Console for viewing and participating in conversations on several social platforms and for managing work flow and publishing your posts to social media. The Insights module takes a powerfully visual approach, rich with bar charts, pie graphs, and word clouds, to reflect trending topics, consumer sentiment, campaign results, and more. The Radian6 dashboard brings it all together, as shown in Figure 8-3.

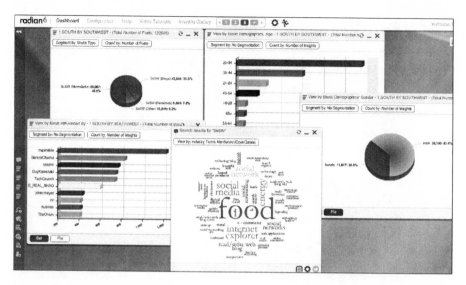

Figure 8-3. A Salesforce Marketing Cloud social media dashboard. (Salesforce.com recently acquired and combined industry leaders Buddy Media and Radian6.) Salesforce Marketing Cloud excels at monitoring trends and brand conversations, and identifying your most active brand loyalists across the internet, whether they're active on your fan pages or not. Image courtesy of Salesforce.com.

You'll also want to augment the mostly quantitative data found in these reports with qualitative and anecdotal material: customer testimonials, complaints resolved, feedback. Be judicious about it—nobody in the C-suite wants to see long threads of back-and-forth Facebook conversations. But a well-chosen example of a new customer won over from a rival, or a big media mention that started as an under-the-radar interaction with a blogger—that stuff is gold. So too are customer insights gleaned about new products, your competitive position, product quality problems, and more.

Our social media and customer-care teams at Green Mountain Coffee Roasters regularly share anecdotal feedback from our online community. Customer care tallies up positive and negative feedback, groups and quantifies it by topic, and shares the highlights.

In our monthly reports, we also include screenshots of important campaigns or promotions we ran in social media.

Facebook Insights

Facebook Insights, the native stats available to any page administrator on Facebook, deliver a host of metrics that are worth reporting within your organization (see Figures 8-4, 8-5, and 8-6). And if you pay attention to them, they'll help you do a more effective job of community management. Let's take a look at them:

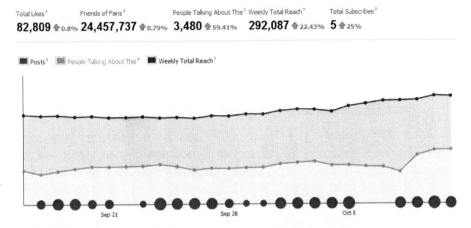

Total Likes? 82,809 ↑0.8% Friends of Fans? 24,457,737 ↑0.79% People Talking About This? 3,480 ↑59.41% Weekly Total Reach? 292,087 ↑22.43% Total Subscribes? 5 ↑25%

■ Posts? ■ People Talking About This? ■ Weekly Total Reach?

Figure 8-4. You can measure progress in terms of "likes," weekly total reach, and comments, graphed in relation to the cadence of your page posts. You can also drill into each post to see which ones generated the most interactivity. Courtesy of Facebook, Inc.

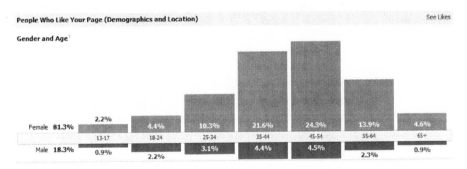

People Who Like Your Page (Demographics and Location)   See Likes

Gender and Age?

	13-17	18-24	25-34	35-44	45-54	55-64	65+
Female 81.3%	2.2%	4.4%	10.3%	21.6%	24.3%	13.9%	4.6%
Male 18.3%	0.9%	2.2%	3.1%	4.4%	4.5%	2.3%	0.9%

Figure 8-5. You can analyze your fan base and the audience you're reaching by age group and gender, shown in this distribution chart, as well as by language spoken, or the city or country in which they live. Courtesy of Facebook, Inc.

- **Likes:** Also known as fans, this is the total number of people who have "liked" your company or brand page.

- **Reach:** In the context of Facebook Insights reports, Reach is an aggregate view of the demographics of all the people you reached with your posts and ads: age, gender, location, language. Reach also shows the attributes of those who *Checked In* to your page and of those who *Talked About* your page.

- *Friends of Fans:* The number of unique friends of everyone who "liked" your page. This audience is hundreds of times bigger than your immediate fan base. The mean number of friends per user is currently around 100 on Facebook, but in my experience, our *Friends of Fans* number is about 140 times the size of our fan base.

- *Total Reach:* The total unique audience—fans (or Likes) plus Friends of Fans—who saw any of your posts, as well as any of your Facebook ads or Sponsored Stories.

Facebook Insights shows you these metrics as summary data for your page and details the interactivity of each and every wall post, photo, video, poll, or other content you put up. This is especially helpful because it enables you to build a more vibrant community of back-and-forth commentary and fans spreading the word to friends. If you conduct major campaigns, like sweepstakes or free sampling events, you'll see steeper, stair-step growth patterns. Also available in Insights are charts comparing new Likes to "unlikes." If you see spikes in "unlikes," it could be a sign your promotions are reaching the wrong audience, or a new direction in your page posts is turning off your fans. The network effect is of no help if your posts are too blah to inspire anyone to share them!

Here is the wall-post data tracked by Facebook Insights:

- *Reach:* A different metric than the "Reach" described above, here it means how many people saw each post. This is a function of how many fans your brand has, plus any interactions with your post that were reposted into the newsfeeds of friends of fans.

- *Engaged Users:* How many clicked on each post, photo, event, or other content.

- *Talking About This:* How many "liked" the post, commented on it, shared it with friends, or RSVPd if it was an event.

- *Virality:* The most powerful metric for comparing posts with each other for their impact on your audience. Of all the people who saw the post, this is the percentage who "talked about it."

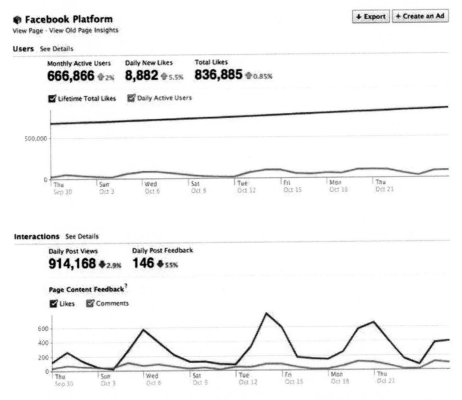

Figure 8-6. The Users chart (top) shows new Likes and cumulative Likes growing steadily. The bottom chart, Interactions, shows a typical "heartbeat" pattern of interactivity and views rising and falling with each post—in this example, weekly bursts of activity. Courtesy of Facebook, Inc.

That last metric, *virality*, is important. The average Facebook user has 359 friends. When a member of your community likes, shares, joins, downloads, comments, or performs other interactions with your brand content, it creates stories in that member's newsfeed—an amplification. In my experience, the typical post generates 1% virality or a bit less. Posts that push people's buttons and generate high response can measure 2.5% virality or even more.

Here are a few rules of thumb:

- On Facebook pages, aim to achieve post virality above 1%.

- Talking About This is another function of virality. I want to see it measuring above 1% of the total fan base.

- To keep a program growing steadily, I want to see each week's New Likes coming in above 0.5% of the total Likes. Obviously, you will see faster growth the smaller and newer your program is.

- If these metrics are healthy, they will translate to strong Reach. A good weekly Reach is about 1x to 3x your total fan base.

- Out of curiosity, I divide Reach by Talking About This, to get a sense of how connected my fanbase is—how many Facebook friends each one has, on average.

Your Brand in the Social Sphere

As I discussed in Chapter 3, monitoring the web for *mentions of your brand* is a critical, core competency of a responsive social media program. HootSuite, MediaVantage, Sprout Social, SocialMention, Seesmic, and similar monitoring tools (including free utilities like TweetDeck will be your antennae to the wider social media world and what people are saying about your industry, your category, your brand, and your rivals.

A free and very easy way to get started monitoring your brand is to set up a Google Alert for your brand name (www.google.com/alerts). This will generate an alert e-mail or text to you any time your brand or company is mentioned in an online news story.

For a more comprehensive dashboard, enter your brand name at SocialMention. com and you'll get a powerful snapshot of your brand's visibility across social media, the rate of mentions of your brand, scores of examples of actual posts mentioning your brand on Facebook and Twitter, and an overall rating of strength, passion, sentiment, and reach.

For instance, among other useful data, SocialMention reports that the Victoria's Secret brand is mentioned on social media *every 25 seconds*. The ratio of positive to negative sentiment is 12:1.

Social media campaigns can have an immediate impact on brand mentions and positive sentiment. Measuring these effects and reporting them across your team or company is critically important, because they will be the first signs you see that your program is working. Sales will come, but they'll be harder to connect directly to your efforts on social.

One key metric you'll pull out of these platforms will be *total brand mentions*. You should expect that your brand's profile will be rising as your social media program progresses. And you'll also want to track positive versus negative sentiment, as well as net sentiment. Scandals are a great way to boost brand mentions, but for brand equity, not so much.

Impact on Your Online Business

The other social media analytics platform is the one you're already using: your web analytics software that captures visits, sales, e-mail sign-ups, and other activity on your website. Whenever you link from social media back to your site, use campaign-tracking links. That way you'll be able to see how many visits, e-mail signups, orders, sales, and other metrics are driven by particular social campaigns, social media platforms, and your social media program as a whole.

Every website analytics software program supports campaign tracking, and most work about the same. Table 8-2 is an example of how I would set up social media tracking codes in the most widely used web stats package, Google Analytics.

Table 8-2. Google Analytics Campaign Tag Protocol for Tracking Visits from Your Social Media Posts

Attribute	Argument	Description	Example
Campaign Source	utm_source	Referring source (where the campaign is being run)	Facebook
Campaign Medium	utm_medium	Marketing channel	social
Attribute	**Argument**	**Description**	**Example**
Campaign Term	utm_term	[optional, usually for search]	
Campaign Content	utm_content	Describes the ad version or content	share-the-love
Campaign Name	utm_campaign	Name of promotion	refer-a-friend

Here's how the campaign example looks as a Google Analytics tracking link:

www.YourDomain.com/?utm_source=facebook&utm_medium=social&utm_content=share-the-love&utm_campaign=refer-a-friend

---

■ **Note** With Google Analytics (and many other web stats packages), campaign tracking is case sensitive, so be consistent or else you'll find the same campaigns and channels spread across different buckets. I use all lowercase words, with hyphens as spaces.

These long and homely tracking URLs wouldn't look presentable on a social media post—nor do they fit comfortably within Twitter's 140-character maximum. So once you've generated a tracking link, use a URL shortener like bit.ly or tinyurl.com to shrink it to manageable size.

The beauty of this tagging protocol is that if you tag consistently, you can slice and dice the results however you like. You can drill down to the most granular level of individual post, offer, or ad version performance. By looking at higher-level attributes, you can see how much activity is being driven by Facebook versus YouTube, for all campaigns, for the trailing 12 months.

You can also track the total impact of your social media links as a channel, or compare unpaid social traffic to paid advertising on the social networks.

■ **Tip** Google Analytics users can easily generate campaign links for posts on social media pages (and other campaigns) by using the URL Builder: http://support.google.com/analytics/bin/answer.py?hl=en&answer=1033867

I also pay a lot of attention to user-generated content, product ratings and reviews, customer surveys, and feedback. Bizrate, Bazaarvoice, ForeSee Results, blog comments—all are vitally important reads on how well you're doing in the eyes of the customer. Because these actions happen on your website rather than on Facebook or Twitter, they may not "feel" like social media, but they are!

Social offer and refer-a-friend platforms like Extole, SocialTwist, and Social Annex can use your trackable links, and they also have their own reports, which can be exported as Excel or PDF documents.

Impact on Your Offline Business

If you operate a bricks-and-mortar presence or distribute your products or services across a distribution network, it's a lot harder to pinpoint the impact that online, social-media-driven buzz has on your brand's sales offline. One elementary way is simply to plot topline social media metrics, like fan base or brand mentions, against an offline sales curve (see Figure 8-7). Chances are the two charts will be strongly correlated. That can be a convincing demonstration to senior management about the worth of your social media marketing efforts.

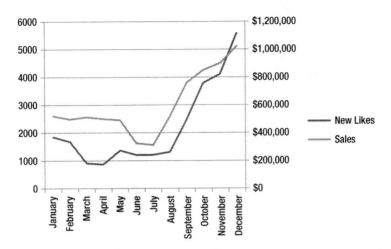

Figure 8-7. It can be compelling to chart the incremental growth of your online community against your monthly sales curve. They'll likely demonstrate similar seasonality, and both will correlate with your marketing and promotional activity.

But correlation is not causation. Strong brands generate strong followings—a truth that is manifested today on Facebook and the other social stamping grounds. If you want to demonstrate a tighter linkage between your online social media work and offline results, use digital coupons—available only when a set number of fans "unlock" a group deal (see Chapter 7). You can do this on your own fan page or via social shopping platforms like Groupon or LivingSocial. These sites have been maligned for delivering razor-thin or money-losing margins to merchants who may never see the repeat purchase behavior they need in order to be successful. On the other hand, social shopping platforms can drive huge volume and sweep new consumers in the door. When Gap kicked off its first national Groupon campaign in 2010, it logged $11 million in sales in its brick-and-mortar stores all over the country and drove so much web traffic that Groupon's network admins had to scurry to prevent a server crash.

Other measurements of offline business impact can be derived from attitude & usage and other surveys. If you have the budget, you can hire a market research firm to conduct a custom A&U study about your brand—consumer awareness of it and what consumers think of it compared with rival brands. But even with a small budget, you can add Bizrate customer satisfaction surveys to your website. Or e-mail a survey to your customers—or ask for candid feedback from your Facebook fans. Overall brand awareness, positive versus negative brand sentiment, volume and sentiment of brand social mentions, and net promoter score ("How likely are you to recommend this brand or product to your friends or family?") are all vital measures of the good that your social media efforts are doing for your brand equity.

Brand Engagement Metrics

Number of posts, impressions, virality, and reach are good measures of activity on a social network. But part of the goal is enticing community members to venture off Facebook and Twitter, visit your website and engage with your brand, sign up for e-mail newsletters, and eventually buy.

Here are some ways to measure the effectiveness of your social media program in improving your brand equity and brand reach and driving activity to your core business:

- E-mail sign-ups

- Sweepstakes sign-ups

- Number of product reviews, average ratings, number of shares, and rate of sharing

- Product samples distributed

- "Surprise and delight" campaigns (unexpected gifts, prizes, or other feel-good gestures for your most loyal fans and followers)

- Tell-a-friend totals and rate

- Tracked sales direct from social media, including tell-a-friend campaigns and group deals

- Lifetime value of customers originating from social media

In addition to internal stats reports from Facebook, Twitter, YouTube, and other platforms, these measures help you get your finger on the pulse of (1) your brand equity across the social sphere and (2) traffic and business coming from social media to your website.

Here are the particular metrics to follow in aggregate, from all social media channels combined, and what they mean:

- ***Reach:*** As with the Facebook example above, this is the total audience reached by all your social media posts—your fans and followers, plus the exponentially magnified impact of any likes, comments, or shares.

- ***Engagement:*** Total number of interactions with your post (likes, comments, shares, retweets, and so forth). This can also be expressed as a percentage (total interactions / total number of fans).

- **Share of voice:** Total number of references to your brand—be they positive, neutral, or negative—divided by total number of references to all brands and companies in your industry.

- **Share of media:** A more granular take on share of voice, this could track your brand's share of all references to your industry on a particular social network (Facebook, say, or Twitter).

- **Share of sentiment:** What fraction of all positive sentiment was devoted to your brand? The same calculation is made for neutral and negative sentiment, for all brands in the category.

- **Net promoter score:** Long before social media emerged as a marketing and CRM channel, customer-centric businesses focused on net promoter score to track the level of customer satisfaction, as measured by customer feedback surveys. The math is simple: where you fall on a scale of zero to ten on the likelihood that your customers would recommend you to others.

- **Net sentiment:** (Positive + neutral conversations—negative conversations) / Total conversations about the brand.

- **Social influence measurement (SIM):** A metric devised by the agency Razorfish, SIM is net sentiment for the brand divided by net sentiment for the industry.

- **Net brand reputation:** Positive sentiment percentage minus negative sentiment percentage, compared against others in the industry.

Although Facebook Insights is good at showing how much response your posts are generating, it's not good at showing whether you're doing your brand credit or harm. When BP was befouling the Gulf of Mexico, or when Rush Limbaugh was sounding off about a certain Georgetown law student, the controversies sent thousands of people to the BP and Rush Facebook pages. In came a tidal wave of mostly critical comments and sharing, and—because you can't comment without "liking" a brand page—tons of new fans. But it's clear all that virality was mostly the bad kind (think bubonic plague).

To truly measure whether you're succeeding in your efforts at building brand equity and attracting new business, you need to measure positive versus negative sentiment.

Social Media Software

Tracking all the metrics I've been discussing has the potential to be enormously time-consuming. Thankfully, a number of software platforms (most of them cloud-based web browser tools) are available to consolidate your key analytics data and more. Several paid software platforms and free utilities have arisen to serve social media program managers in meeting their three most urgent needs:

- **Brand monitoring:** Use social media listening tools to monitor your brands.

- **Engagement management:** Write your posts from one centralized command center and publish them simultaneously to Facebook, Twitter, LinkedIn, blogs, and other platforms.

- **Analytics and reporting:** Track and report on the performance of your social media program—from the impact of each post, to total numbers of fans, followers, reach, and engagement—and the overall impact of social media on your website's sales, leads, and other key performance indicators, or KPIs.

HootSuite

HootSuite is one of the original social media software tools, and it is especially strong as a *publishing management platform*. If you're active on several different social media platforms, it can be time-consuming and inefficient to log into each one to publish your wall posts, or to read and respond to comments. HootSuite and programs like it are streamlined dashboards that offer you one place for writing and scheduling your posts for all the different networks—and for monitoring comments and conducting conversations with fans. You can use HootSuite to collaborate and develop work flows with your social media team, assign tasks, and schedule posts and uploads to Facebook, Twitter, LinkedIn, Google+, YouTube, Flickr, Tumblr and more, all from one dashboard.

If you need to check in on your social media program or post on the go, HootsSuite's management dashboards and reports are available in mobile web and tablet versions and as apps for iPhone, Android, and Blackberry.

One of the best things about HootSuite is that you can run a basic program, of five social media profiles, free. Since each brand and each platform is one profile, you'll eventually want to go with HootSuite Pro, but at the time this book went to press, that cost a mere $9.99 a month. Custom enterprise programs cost more, but they provide features that have become a necessity for bigger companies: unlimited profiles, unlimited team members, and tech support. The team work-flow and publishing management features mentioned above are enterprise features.

PepsiCo, Corbis, McDonald's, and Hard Rock Cafe are among those on the HootSuite client list. Product and support are available in English, Spanish, Portuguese, French, and Japanese. Learn more at www.Hootsuite.com, Twitter @hootsuite.

Radian6

Radian6 was founded in 2006 and purchased by the B2B cloud software company Salesforce in 2011. As a listening tool, Radian6 integrates with Facebook, Twitter, YouTube, LinkedIn, the blogosphere, forums, and mainstream and niche news sites—the company claims "150 million sources" in all. Radian6 dashboards offer very intuitive charts and infographics. Its listening tools are driven by keywords or hashtags you select, associated with your brand or product names, markets you serve, rivals, and more.

Those keywords pull in tens of thousands of conversations. Using simple but powerful filtering tools, Radian6 lets you separate the wheat from the chaff to home in on the most influential people (including their fans and followers, even their Klout Scores), see conversation trends charted over time, analyze the demographics of the people you're reaching—even drill down to their physical location on a map view.

Radian6 offers robust team member access and role management, as well as an engagement suite with modules for publishing to Facebook and Twitter. This software excels at taking a CRM approach to interaction with fans, followers, bloggers, and the rest of the social web. Similar to Salesforce, Radian6 can store the threads of conversations between your team and its fans and stakeholders in the social sphere.

One of the more expensive platforms available today, Radian6 has plenty of powerful and well-executed features to justify the price. If your organization is already using Salesforce, there may be special Radian6 pricing available, plus you'll benefit from handy features such as integration with Salesforce Chatter.

Pricing runs from $600 a month for basic "Business" to a hefty $10K a month for Enterprise.

Other Platforms

HootSuite and Radian6 are just two examples of the kind of functionality you can find in today's social media software. Here's a sampling of other platforms:

- **BuddyMedia:** Publishing, communications, promotions, and social media ad buying. Acquired by Salesforce.com.

- **Shoutlet:** Publishing and scheduling, member profiling, CRM, analytics, and some design tools for building social media profile pages and Facebook tabs.

- **Sprout Social:** Comprehensive publishing management, brand monitoring, and analytics. This is an affordable, up-and-coming platform, and the company offers a free trial.

- **Sysomos:** Marketed as complete social media management software, Sysomos is especially strong in brand monitoring and analytics.

- **TweetDeck:** Twitter's free downloadable app for Mac or Windows, TweetDeck offers columnar views of your feeds, plus filtering and alert functions—Twitter for power users.

- **Vitrue:** Oracle's comprehensive suite of social media management tools.

- **Vocus:** The leading public relations software, now retooled for social media.

- **Wildfire:** Google's entry into the social media software field.

There are hordes of other, more specialized tools out there to tackle particular social media tasks. Ning lets you build your own niche social network site. Disqus bolts interactive commenting and rating onto any website or blog. TurnTo does something similar with its social Q&A functionality. And in Chapter 9, we'll look under the hood of several new social commerce and marketing suites that let you harness the power of word of mouth and the wisdom of the crowd to energize your PR and marketing campaigns.

"KEEPING UP WITH THE JONESES.COM"

One important set of data to track isn't even connected to your program. I'm referring, of course, to your top competitor's metrics. How many fans, followers, and subscribers do rival companies have? What sort of apps have they developed? What promotions and campaigns are they running?

By doing competitive analysis you accomplish several things:

- Benchmark your growth against rivals

- Get some ideas of tactics to try—or avoid

- Gain ammunition if your own social media investments need support from upper management

Keeping up with rivals in the social media space may seem trivial, but it's not. Many people, especially younger ones, perceive a brand's social following as central to its coolness or relevance. To some consumers, it doesn't matter if your sales are twice those of your nearest competitor. If the competition has more fans, they look bigger and more relevant than you. If the party looks "dead," who wants to walk in the door and join?

Any of the brand-monitoring tools I've discussed in this chapter are easily used to gather data about the pace of brand mentions and sentiment surrounding your competitors. You can benchmark yourself against your rivals both in terms of social chatter and in consumer ratings from places like Bizrate.com.

Social networks have launched a number of advertising options you can use to help you keep up with the Joneses—or, to some degree, eat the Joneses' lunch.

Facebook ads, for instance, enable you to target users by their "likes"—which can include your rival's brand name. As I discussed in Chapter 6, Twitter goes a step further, allowing you to target an ad to a specific @username, which can be your rival's Twitter account. Twitter says that doesn't mean your ad will be exposed to all the followers of that @username; instead, the account will be used to identify the *type* of Twitter user you're looking for. But that sounds like splitting hairs to me.

Yelp goes even further, allowing you to place ads on your rival's business page—and pay to block the ads of others from your page.

The good news is that social media still offer relatively inexpensive places to experiment, and they have the potential to disrupt the old order. Social media platforms are a place where smaller, newer brands that "get" social media can forge ahead of bigger but less social-savvy competitors in the race to make an impact on online consumers.

It's Only Anecdotal...

Not all the accomplishments of a successful social media program can be boiled down to numbers. In this field, anecdotal evidence, used responsibly, *is* evidence. Many social media agencies and program managers make a practice of including especially heartwarming wall posts, happily resolved customer service gripes, enthusiastic retweets, or other evidence of viral success in their monthly status reports. These provide a terrific counterpoint to your charts and numbers, and they put a human face on your work.

Sharing anecdotes and highlighting particular fan posts or interactions can be golden when you're seeking to demonstrate to higher-ups that a strong, positive social media presence is boosting your brand identity, turning complaints into praise, winning customers from rivals, or stimulating superfans to advocate your brand and recruit new consumers.

For example, one of our Green Mountain Coffee Roasters brands received an e-mail from the husband of a fan, wanting to surprise her on her birthday. He explained that his wife so loved our brand that she would be thrilled to receive birthday wishes from us on our Facebook page. We went one better. We sent her a surprise birthday gift of a free Keurig brewer and K-Cup coffee, and we created a Facebook wall-post image showing a decorated cupcake with candles and her name on it, wishing her happy birthday.

That entire series of interactions, captured in screenshots of wall posts, fan reactions, and the gratitude of the "superfan," combined to tell an unforgettable story. That story captured the intensity of a customer's devotion to our products and the power of social media to make a strong connection stronger still.

If each of your monthly progress reports contains a gem or two like that, you'll soon find you're creating ardent supporters of your social media program throughout your company.

Anointing Your Influentials

In any online community, the vast bulk of the activity of commenting, liking, uploading, voting, and other interactivity—and we're talking 80-plus percent— is carried out by a tiny minority of hyperengaged fans. They've been dubbed:

- Influentials
- Brand ambassadors
- Superfans

As I'll explore in Chapter 9, these superfans are fantastic for your online reputation. They provide a vital feedback loop for your consumer insights research, they are crucial for the viral spread of any campaign, and they're terrific for your business.

Many of the software platforms I've discussed here offer special features to help you search for, identify, reach out to, and cultivate these influentials. Social monitoring tools use web-crawling techniques to find your most active, most devoted fans, both on your brand pages and on the web at large. You can use them to become aware of who your real brand ambassadors are and then get a direct conversation started.

By monitoring Twitter, Facebook, and the rest of the social web, software can be your best friend—for finding your best friends.

Summary

Measurement is a big topic, and as I've indicated in this chapter, the sources of social media intelligence are scattered all over the place—on your fan pages, your website, and throughout the Internet at large. Thankfully, a number of software tools are now available to consolidate much of that data and enable you to report it within your company as an indicator of the impact of your work.

But numbers alone won't tell the story, because social media are still evolving. As we saw, research firms have come up with wildly divergent numbers to quantify the value of a Facebook fan. Furthermore, you will better communicate some of your impact with a word cloud or a powerful anecdote.

With the array of different measurement tools available, I'm confident that you'll be able to tell a compelling story of how your social media efforts are reaching an exponentially increasing audience, generating business leads, driving direct sales, improving your brand image, raising your public profile, and fostering customer loyalty. In my experience, you'll be able to do all these things at a strikingly low cost, regardless of how you quantify the benefits.

With a measurement and reporting process in place, you'll be ready to tackle two of the most ambitious social media initiatives:

- Comprehensive social media campaigns, and
- Software development projects that feature social "hooks," or integrations with the major social networks

Because these can be expensive, measurement is critical to proving return on investment. But as I'll demonstrate in Chapter 9, they are some of the most powerful, high-impact projects you can undertake.

Advanced Social Media Campaigns
Taking It to the Next Level

Now it's time to distinguish between everyday community management and periodic social media *campaigns*. Posting to the social platforms, interacting with fans, and performing customer service are your daily social media disciplines. They are the routine blocking and tackling—the minimum table stakes of building an online community and steadily growing it.

However, the leading business social media programs do not content themselves with steady, linear growth. Ambitious, integrated social media campaigns are the engine of stair-step growth. They have the dual advantages of attracting new members to your community and generating enthusiasm among your existing fans.

These promotional or charitable campaigns require planning, infrastructure development, and financial investment. But they're clearly what separate the best from the rest.

An integrated social media campaign does the following:

- Begins with sound strategy and specific number goals for success (fan growth, sign-up, votes, coupon redemptions, sample requests, revenue, and so forth).

- Embodies a strong, single campaign theme and message, with a clear call to action.

- Harnesses the power of your existing network and the dynamics of viral social media transmission of your message.

- Centers on an engaging, interactive technology solution for consumer engagement, data capture, and viral spread. Online sweepstakes, games, free-sample distributions, voting or polling, and fundraising campaigns are the tactics that engage and inspire people on social media today. Pulling them off requires robust, specialized technology platforms.

- Benefits from promotion, paid advertising, and buzz-building across every channel. Your postings on all major social platforms, your website, promotional e-mail program, online and social media ads, press releases, print media, and other consumer touch points must all speak in concert in support of the campaign.

- Is complex and time-consuming, requiring financial and technology investment and skillful execution. That may sound discouraging, but it's your secret weapon. Because social media campaigns are complicated, they present a barrier to entry to your rivals, who may not have the know-how or dedicated financial resources to compete with you on the social stage.

How the Network Effect Can Turbocharge Your Marketing

Any marketing campaign you launch today, in any channel, should leverage the power of social media. Whether it's a new product or service, or a special sale or offer, you must *amplify your message* beyond traditional media (TV, catalog, traditional e-mail, and paid search) by asking your fans and followers to spread the word.

The key to campaign planning is *integration* across media channels, online and off.

"My goal is to further push a digital innovation agenda through greater linkages between owned, paid and social media, while also scaling up our mobile marketing efforts," says PepsiCo's Shiv Singh. "In this world, social media is at the heart of everything that we do digitally."[1]

---

[1] Brandon Gutman, "How PepsiCo's Shiv Singh Is Making A Splash In Digital," *Forbes*, January 13, 2011, www.forbes.com/sites/marketshare/2011/01/13/pepsi-on-refreshing-digital/.

To that end, the Pepsi.com website has been completely made over into a social media dashboard, dubbed "Pepsi Pulse," for Pepsi-related tweets including its #LiveForNow promoted hashtag, user commentary on the Pepsi-sponsored reality TV show *The X Factor*, and music and video streams integrated with Pepsi's nine-million-fan Facebook community.

Moving social media to the center of its brand allows Pepsi to place the focus not on the product, but on the personalities, lifestyles, and passions of Pepsi drinkers, which are ultimately a lot more interesting than any fizzy beverage. And the network effect of social media multiplies the impact of all those Pepsi tweets, shares, and brand mentions a few hundredfold.

Advocacy and Social Marketing Platforms

Social campaigns, integrated with other digital and traditional advertising, are some of the most exciting initiatives happening in marketing and business today. Consumers hold the keys to your success, and they've shown they will reward the truly *remarkable* campaign ideas—by responding enthusiastically and endorsing them to friends. And they will punish the unremarkable ideas by responding with a great, big yawn or, worse, by ridiculing them.

Luckily, a stable of new social campaign platforms are ready to serve your business or organization. Many of them are quite affordable.

The emergence and growth of social promotional platforms has recently been as exponential as the expansion of social media itself. Extole, Social Annex, SocialTwist, ShopSocially, Offerpop, Strutta, Votigo, and others operate in the space, offering many overlapping features. No doubt they will be joined by more newcomers. Meanwhile, the three behemoths—Oracle, Salesforce, and Google—have placed their bets by acquiring Vitrue, BuddyMedia, and Wildfire, respectively.

Assuming you have done the basic work of building a decent-sized and engaged online community, you can now get serious ROI by utilizing one of these tool sets.

BuddyMedia

New York–based BuddyMedia was founded in 2007 and bought by Salesforce in 2012. The software is now integrated into the Salesforce "Marketing Cloud" product suite. BuddyMedia is a leading social media marketing platform, and it's an especially compelling choice if your company is already using Salesforce.

BuddyMedia works with a thousand brands, including L'Oréal, Hewlett-Packard, Carnival Cruise Lines, and Virgin Mobile. The platform has five modules, each of which features its own dashboard and analytics:

- **BuyBuddy:** Social ad-management tool

- **ProfileBuddy:** Profile design and content management tool

- **ConversationBuddy:** For publishing wall posts and moderating social conversations

- **ReachBuddy:** For creating web widgets and other online content with embedded "hooks" to the major social networks

- **ConversionBuddy:** For social shopping, with Facebook and Twitter integration

ePrize

ePrize doesn't focus exclusively on social media—its sweet spot is designing and hosting digital and mobile games, sweepstakes, contests, and loyalty-points programs. The company incentivizes consumer behavior across mobile, social, and web for brands including Coca-Cola, Microsoft, Gap, MillerCoors, Yahoo!, Procter & Gamble, and AT&T.

Because games and sweepstakes are so virally popular on the social web today, I urge any brand to consider them as lead-generation and customer engagement tactics.

ePrize can integrate any of its online promotions with the major social platforms. The company also offers social-specific campaigns, including Twitter polls and contests, Facebook apps and games, blogger outreach, and other social campaigns.

Extole

When it came time to launch a refer-a-friend program for the Café Express Savings Club coffee delivery service, I chose Extole, a San Francisco-based company founded in 2009 with offices in New York. The tool set combines website design, Facebook tabs, a "sharing widget," a friend-to-friend e-mail platform, and coupon code management.

Extole powers refer-a-friend programs, social coupons, and other campaigns for Audi, Redbox, CanvasPop, Seamless, Shutterfly, Kate Spade, 24 Hour Fitness, and others. The company demonstrates an impressive commitment not just to the technology that drives social sharing but also to the softer skills that make it truly sing: offer design, graphic presentation, and promotional support. That's valuable, because social promotions are emphatically *not* an "if you build it, they will come" proposition.

In addition to its refer-a-friend platform, Extole offers a suite of social promotions, including shared sweepstakes and group deals that can, for instance, "unlock" a coupon code after 10,000 fans have "liked" a page or opted into an e-mail newsletter. Extole is also developing some exciting new features with Open Graph (Facebook) integration, making it easy to embed social hooks into the product pages or conversion pages of your website to let your customers share their likes, loves, wish lists, purchases, and other "social expressions" across Facebook.

Offerpop

Offerpop is more affordable than some of its rival platforms, and it offers a jaw-dropping variety of modules: refer-a-friend, photo contests, video contests, quizzes, fan faves, group deals, new follower offers, Twitter and Facebook exclusive offers, fundraising campaigns, and more.

The Offerpop platform is simple to use—a web-based admin tool that lets anyone create and launch a custom campaign, with WYSIWYG and HTML options, that ultimately becomes a Facebook tab or Twitter landing page.

The campaign reporting tools are clean, colorful, and easy to distribute to others in your organization.

Offerpop has a variety of pricing options, ranging from a basic pay-per-campaign model to a monthly subscription based on your company's number of fans and followers—starting at just $15 a month for companies with a few hundred fans, up to $2,500 a month for as many as 500,000 fans. And regardless of size, you can start with a free trial, one campaign for 14 days.

Thousands of companies large and small have run Offerpop campaigns—among them such big names as Audi, Pepperidge Farm, American Eagle Outfitters, Disney, Lipton, and Birchbox.

Social Annex

Social Annex bills itself as a "one stop social platform," combining refer-a-friend, social expressions, social discovery, social engagement, contests, sharing, discovery, and loyalty tools.

The Los Angeles–based company serves mostly smaller brands, like 4inkjets, DollarDays, and DeepDiscount.com.

Social Annex charges a flat monthly fee based on your monthly unique visitor traffic, so there's no disincentive to mounting lots of campaigns as there might be with an a la carte pricing model.

SocialTwist

Similar to Extole, SocialTwist's specialty is "social referrals," also known as refer-a-friend or tell-a-friend programs. SocialTwist has a roster of blue-chip clients, including Sara Lee, Intel, Lysol, Barnes & Noble, Peet's Coffee & Tea, and Coca-Cola.

Michael McDowell, manager of shopper marketing at Sara Lee, gives the platform high marks. "With the help of SocialTwist, Sara Lee was able to reach 50 percent of our total campaign goal within the first seven days of the promotion—an incredible feat and unprecedented success."[2]

ShopSocially

ShopSocially is another comprehensive suite of social promotion tools, as shown in Table 9-1.

Table 9-1. ShopSocially Promotional Tools for Marketers

Promotion	How It Works
Viral Offer Sharing	Embeds socially shareable offers into your e-mail, Facebook, or Twitter campaigns.
Share-a-Promotion	To unlock a discount, visitors must first share it with friends.
Get-a-Fan	Enables Facebook fan acquisition on your website by giving your visitors an incentive to become a fan.
Ask-a-Friend	Encourages visitors to ask their friends to weigh in on the buying decision. This will increase visitor engagement and generate referral traffic.
Share-a-Purchase	When shoppers complete a purchase, they are presented with an incentive to share the news with friends on Facebook or Twitter.
Shopping Community	Engages visitors by showing them what other shoppers have bought. Allows shoppers to interact with each other, exchanging product recommendations and reviews.

[2] "Customers," SocialTwist, www://tellafriend.socialtwist.com/customer-testimonials

ShopSocially's "Share-a-Purchase" functionality is similar to Extole's "social expressions," which can be integrated with an e-commerce website. I'll discuss them in Chapter 10, which covers social integrations for your site.

Vitrue

Vitrue calls itself an "SRM" platform (a variation on the trusty CRM acronym), for social relationship management. Vitrue features four main modules: Publisher, Tabs, Shop, and Analytics.

The Publisher suite enables a number of powerful promotions: audience targeting, social promotions, fan exclusives, mobile optimization, and integration with e-commerce websites.

As you might expect of an Oracle-acquired platform, Vitrue boasts a number of very large, global brands in its customer base: McDonald's, Hyundai, LEGO, Smucker's, Frito-Lay, IKEA, Toys "R" Us, MTV, and American Express, among others.

Wildfire

Founded in 2008 in Silicon Valley and acquired in 2012 by Google, Wildfire is not just a social promotions tool. The Wildfire Social Marketing Suite combines promotions, publishing, ad management, and analytics with integration across all the major social networks.

"It's a powerful, easy-to-use tool for social marketing," says Kyle Thorne, social relations manager of Virgin Atlantic, "and we've seen great results."[3]

With over 16,000 customers—including big names like Amazon, EA, KFC, Jamba Juice, Target, Travelocity, and Gap—Wildfire is well positioned to benefit from Google's powerful support. Although Vitrue and BuddyMedia are formidable products, I wouldn't be surprised to see Wildfire emerge as the standard and most ubiquitous social marketing software after the inevitable consolidation hits this still nascent and crowded field.

Pricing is a la carte, ranging from a low of 99 cents a day plus $5 per promotion at the basic level, up to $4.99 a day and $250 per promotion at the premium level. What distinguishes basic from premium are bells and whistles like multiple domain name management, more robust analytics and brand monitoring, custom design services, and so on.

---

[3] "Wildfire Announces New Social Marketing Suite," June 21, 2011, www://blog.wildfireapp.com/2011/06/21/social-marketing-suite/

With Google as its new corporate parent, can Wildfire still be expected to play nice and support integration with rival social networks, or will it steer toward Google+ exclusively? Says Google: "We remain focused on helping brands run and measure their social engagement and ad campaigns across the entire web and across all social services—Facebook, Twitter, YouTube, Google+, Pinterest, LinkedIn and more."[4]

To Discount, or Not to Discount?

What all these platforms have in common is the ability to knit social shopping, sharing, and advocacy into the fabric of your e-commerce business. It's also worth talking about a few of the big "group deals" and "social shopping" platforms with which you can partner. Groupon and LivingSocial are the two largest daily-deal sites, with audiences of millions. They leverage social dynamics to help you sell a lot of your products, at irresistible discounts. Groupons can be "unlocked" when a minimum number of members buy them. Deep discounts can be hard on your margins, but if you can make the math work, either of the deal sites can move the revenue needle for you.

Groupon offers online deals, but it still works best for bricks-and-mortar retailers. Groupon has worked with over 250,000 brands, from the little San Antonio Bagel Shop (Groupon promotions filled the shop, which estimates that 80% of its Groupon redeemers became repeat customers), to Gap, which drove $11 million in one campaign, selling over 440,000 Groupons nationwide.

People-powered commerce can be uncorked at sites like Etsy and CafePress. Companies like Uncommon Goods have launched crowd-sourced product development campaigns. Creative projects, charity, good works, and tech start-ups can attract crowd-funding on Kickstarter and GoFundMe. There's no limit to the innovative ways you can use social media to develop, market, promote, and sell your stuff.

"The number one incentive that drives the 'like' behavior for brands on Facebook is *discounts*, or couponing," says Boulder-based brand marketing expert Erika Napoletano.[5] But Napoletano warns marketers not to cheapen their brands and not to train their customers to wait for a deep discount.

"The like has become currency," says Napoletano. "People *spend* a like, and they expect to get something in return."

---

[4] Wildfire by Google, "Wildfire is Joining Google!" July 31, 2012, http://blog.wildfireapp.com/2012/07/31/wildfire-is-joining-google/.

[5] Erika Napoletano, remarks at National Etailing and Mailing Organization of America (NEMOA) directXchange conference, Groton, Connecticut, September 19, 2012.

That something can be a discount, certainly—but the best discounts are rare, noteworthy, and exclusive. Fan discounts are reserved for your members only, people following you on Twitter, "liking" you on Facebook or otherwise actively engaged with your brand in social media.

Exclusive discounts are a way of rewarding your existing fans and enticing new ones. Establishing a "like gate" on a Facebook tab requires that users must first "like" your brand before seeing the discount code or other exclusive content. While "like gates" for major promotions sometimes cause a rash of "unfriendings" after a promotion has run its course, I've found that if your brand lives up to the expectations of its fans and is delivering fun and valuable content and authentic engagement, such "unfriendings" will be few.

The Yankee Candle Company releases new candle fragrances each season, and as a reward for Facebook fans, the company offered an exclusive scent available only to fans. Similarly, when Heinz introduced its new balsamic-flavored ketchup, it was offered initially as a Facebook fan exclusive. Victoria's Secret frequently offers its Facebook and Twitter communities access to benefits like limited-edition panties, free music downloads, and free perfume, jewelry, and accessories. Kate Spade gives Facebook fans exclusive access to one-day 75%-off "sample sales." In 2011, Ann Taylor offered a four-day, 40% "Friends & Family" special to its fans and followers—and received such a positive response that their servers strained under the load.

Information can be valuable, too. B2B and service businesses can offer free PDFs or e-books, while music and entertainment companies can offer free MP3s or videos.

Whether the currency you employ is discounting or exclusive products, or both, your goal should be to reward loyal customers and generate excitement across the social media platforms—all without cheapening your valuable brand image.

Sweepstakes Promotions

From my earliest social media promotions and Facebook advertising campaigns, I've leaned heavily on sweepstakes and giveaways for lead generation. They are still among the most effective ways to cut through the noise, generate enthusiasm among your existing fans, and attract new fans.

Yes, new fans are always a goal of these promotions, but they're not an end in themselves. They are a means to an end.

For a chance to win prizes, entrants must supply basic contact info such as a valid e-mail address. Three simple rules ensure that your sweepstakes promotions will generate big returns:

- To get to the entry form, people must become fans or followers of your brand. In other words, use a "like gate" on the Facebook tab or external website that supports the sweepstakes, or a "follow gate" on your Twitter account.

- The entry form should feature a prechecked opt-in to your e-mail newsletter program or other permission-based marketing. Give people a clear, easy way to opt out. Assuming your brand is well regarded and your campaign attracts good, qualified prospects, you'll be pleasantly surprised by the high proportion of sweepstakes entrants who will give you permission to send them e-mail or catalogs.

- Keep the prizing and the theme of your promotion true to the products or services you sell, or tightly dialed into the interests of the market you serve. Free products, gift cards, or "shopping sprees" at your store may not seem especially creative, but qualified consumers respond to them. Win or lose, after the sweepstakes has run its course, your entrants are more likely to be qualified, interested prospects. Home-makeover sweepstakes at This Old House.com, or event ticket giveaways by NASCAR, are in the audience's sweet spot. Oprah Winfrey's "Mom's Day Out" sweepstakes is more of a stretch, but the pedicures and shopping sprees it offers are still good fits for Oprah's audience demographic. On the other hand, cash giveaways and all-over-the-map prizes of electronics, cars, and other random goodies simply attract an unqualified, undifferentiated throng of entrants. That's not what you want if your goal is building a lasting, cohesive online community.

Fiat USA's Fiat 500 giveaway is a great example of an effective sweepstakes. Fiat celebrated its "500,000-like" milestone on Facebook by giving ten lucky fans each a free Fiat 500. Now, that was a high-impact promotion! I like the fact that the car's model number ties into the milestone and that Fiat echoed the promotion across several media: Facebook, YouTube, Twitter, and a fun Fiat "Spin to Win" mobile app. The promotion yielded media coverage, new Facebook fans, and enthusiastic buzz about the car.

APP AND TAB DEVELOPMENT

Whether a vendor performs the work for you, or you do it in-house, robust social media promotions require traditional web programming, mobile, and Facebook app and tab development.

The best place to stay current with the Facebook development platform and the Graph API, and to download software development kits (SDKs), is at http:// developers.facebook.com/.

On the mobile applications front, when I wrote this, in 2012, Apple's App Store offered 600,000 apps. There were another 600,000 Android apps, and the newly launched Facebook App Center offered just 600 Facebook-integrated apps (for both web and mobile).

Becoming a successful mobile/social app developer is a huge task demanding specialist knowledge. Here are a few recommended resources:

—*Beginning Facebook Game Apps Development*, by Wayne Graham (Apress, 2012)

—*Facebook Application Development for Dummies*, by Jesse Stay (For Dummies, 2011)

—*App Empire: Make Money, Have a Life, and Let Technology Work for You*, by Chad Mureta (Wiley, 2012)

—*Cracking iPhone and Android Native Development: Cross-Platform Mobile Apps Without the Kludge*, by Matthew Baxter-Reynolds (Apress, 2010)

—*Pro Smartphone Cross-Platform Development: iPhone, Blackberry, Windows Mobile and Android Development and Distribution*, by Sarah Allen, Vidal Graupera, and Lee Lundrigan (Apress, 2010)

Contests and Voting

Many brands have had great success with contests. But contests do have their minuses as well as pluses. On the plus side, requiring your entrants to submit something—a video, a piece of artwork, an essay—engages them creatively and emotionally with your brand and underscores the cause or purpose of your promotion.

On the downside, many brands and agencies will tell you that the extra consumer effort required in a contest always depresses response. Assuming you do sufficient promotion and have some fan base to start with, you might reasonably expect 30,000 entries to a simple, random-winner sweepstakes. If you require submission of creative work or some other time-consuming contest application, expect to depress response tenfold.

Or, be willing to seriously upgrade the prizes you're offering.

Big, impressive prizes can inspire candidates to create ambitious application essays, videos, or other entry projects. Take the "Best Job in the World." This 2009 contest offered a six-month tropical island caretaker job along Australia's Great Barrier Reef. Tourism Queensland gave applicants the chance for a six-figure "job" serving as an ambassador for Australia tourism.

These promotions work best when you leverage a smaller universe of applicants (who invest the time to create compelling applications) with a larger but less engaged community of advocates who will spread the buzz and vote for finalists and winners.

For instance, when the 2010 Pepsi "Refresh Project" stepped up to the table to give away $20 million to worthy causes, it attracted so much attention that it chose to cap applications at 1,000 per month. Even so, compare the relatively few entries to the much larger social reach of voting, commentary, and media buzz inspired by those entries:

- 352 ideas funded
- 12,000 funding ideas submitted
- 1,600,000 comments
- 80,000,000 votes
- 3,390,000,000 impressions

The best formula for prizing is to offer:

- One remarkable grand prize to generate buzz and attract applicants
- Several second and third prizes related more directly to the products you sell or the markets you serve
- Modest daily or weekly or "instant win" prizes to keep people coming back during the promotional period

For example, Intel's "A Momentary Lapse" slow-motion and time-lapse video contest was a way to bring attention to the video capabilities—and blazing speed—of Intel-powered Dell Ultrabook laptops. The contest offered $50,000 in prizes consisting of Ultrabooks, video software, and cameras. From weekly prizes to a grand prize, there were many ways to win during the 30-day promotion.

While it's easier to judge your contest and select winners internally, if you chose that route, you'd miss out on an important way to do some social buzz-building: public voting. The voting dynamic is a central benefit of contest promotions. Pepsi's "Refresh Project," or Boden's Diamond Jubilee contest, are great examples of social voting done right.

■ **Tip**   Because contests attract relatively few entrants but can generate many votes, consider adding a "like gate" and an e-mail opt-in or other marketing permission to your online voting form.

Gamification

Everybody loves a game. That's especially true online, where "casual games"—fun but not overly complicated game experiences—have skyrocketed in popularity. When the addictive nature of online games meets social sharing, the result is vastly improved virality, or spread.

You can add game dynamics to energize your social media and digital campaigns. For example, with its "Fan Fun" application, Chiquita "gamified" banana-buying and tapped into the enthusiasm of the baseball-loving Little Leaguers in its core audience. Chiquita's mobile and tablet apps feature a geo-location tool that allows grocery shoppers to check into stores selling Chiquita bananas. There's a "cardmaker" feature for young sluggers to transform their photos into baseball trading cards. There's also a trivia game, as well as a sweepstakes to win game tickets, sporting goods, and—you guessed it—bananas.

■ **Tip**   For inspiration about adding game dynamics to your digital experiences, watch Seth Priebatsch, founder of SCVNGR, in his TED keynote speech, "Building a Game Layer on Top of the World," www.ted.com/talks/seth_priebatsch_the_game_layer_on_top_of_the_world.html.

Tab Development

Facebook app development and tab development lie at the very heart of successful social media campaign strategy (see sidebar above). Custom tabs enable marketers to engage their audiences with interactive games, sweepstakes, contests, and more. Tabs also provide the platform for collecting fan data (such as sweepstakes sign-ups, e-mail newsletter opt-ins, and inquiries), which allows you to maintain a direct relationship—and ultimately convert leads to customers.

Facebook's platform offers a suite of programming and formatting tools enabling your developers (or outside specialist firms) to customize and add interactivity to your brand's Facebook presence. Utilizing Facebook query language and the Facebook Graph API, here's an illustration of what you can offer visitors to your fan page:

- E-mail newsletter or mail-order catalog sign-up forms

- Interactive games

- Sweepstakes, polls, and contests

- User-generated content, including video, images, recipes, reviews, you name it

- Integration with Twitter feeds, job posts, weather information—any API-accessible data sources

- E-commerce functionality integrated with your online store

In 2012, the proprietary Facebook Markup Language (FBML) was discontinued in favor of more open web standards. One welcome development for tab developers is that Facebook now supports iframe applications: you can design and develop on your own web platform—external to Facebook—and use a simple iframe to embed your external web page content in a tab within your brand's Facebook page.

Facebook iframe applications use HTML, CSS, JavaScript, and other web standards and can be powered by any web programming language. You'll have to host the web page, images, data, style sheets, and other resources on a secure HTTPS server. For your iframe app to interact with Facebook content, you need to use the Facebook software development kit and employ eXtended Facebook Markup Language (XFBML) tags, which Facebook continues to support.

Whether you plan to support your campaign with a simple sign-up form or an ambitious interactive game, the place to start is Facebook's documentation: http://developers.facebook.com/docs/guides/canvas/.

Charitable Campaigns

Many brands have found that charitable causes, "cause marketing," and other good works are natural fits for social media. Corporate social responsibility campaigns represent the heart and personal face of your organization—and they're designed to appeal to your like-minded fans who support the same causes.

While studies show that most people who "like" a brand on social media are looking for exclusive discounts, once consumers become part of your online community, there are significant benefits to educating them about your social responsibility and the causes you support:

- 75% of consumers believe social responsibility is important

- 70% are willing to pay more to buy from socially responsible companies

- 55% would choose a product that supports a good cause over one that doesn't[6]

The tools of social media are perfectly suited to organizing, disseminating, and amplifying—exponentially—an activist or charitable cause. Of course, activists have long used Twitter and other platforms to spread the word in social and political grassroots movements worldwide. For years, the social web has amplified anti-World Trade Organization protests, Wikileaks news, Arab Spring uprisings, Occupy Wall Street, and fund-raising campaigns for any cause you can name. But it's a newer phenomenon to see businesses building charitable campaigns into their social media planning calendars.

What does this mean for your company? Two things:

- Your social media efforts resonate more with people when you associate your brand with a big idea or cause.

- The causes you support speak volumes about what kind of company you are. Education, health care, women's issues, environmental conservation, promotion of arts and culture? All are valuable causes, but whatever your company embraces should align with its market and the values of its consumers. Your company's charitable priorities will differ depending on whether you are, say, Scholastic, Johnson & Johnson, Athleta, Patagonia, or Dick Blick Art Materials.

---

[6] Elena Malykhina, "Social Responsibility Boosts Brand Perception," *Adweek*, March 31, 2010, http://adweek.com/news/advertising-branding/social-responsibility-boosts-brand-perception-101965.

The personal networks of your fans are vitally important for the spread of your charitable campaign. Some 84% of people say the most appropriate form of solicitation for charity is friend-to-friend.[7]

The general social media concepts and tactics we've explored thus far give you a lot to work with to conduct a successful cause-marketing campaign. Now let's turn our attention to a few examples of brands that have carried out successful charitable efforts in social media.

Subaru of America's "Share the Love" campaign is a socially conscious twist on the typical rebate-oriented sales event. For every new Subaru vehicle sold or leased in December, Subaru donates $250 to the owner's choice of five charities. In 2012, to help select the charities, Subaru's passionate Facebook fans cast nearly 200,000 votes, tapping the Alzheimer's Association and USO to join ASPCA, Make-A-Wish Foundation, and Meals On Wheels. Over the past four years, Subaru has donated nearly $20 million to charity through "Share the Love."

"The charitable stuff we do and the sponsorships translated really well to social," observes Michael McHale, director of corporate communications at Subaru of America. "Our buyers tend to like good causes. Subaru buyers tend to be nice people."[8]

Tyson Foods focuses its philanthropic energy on hunger relief. Since 2000, the company has donated more than 80 million pounds of food to hundreds of US food banks and relief agencies. Tyson partners with hunger-relief organization Share Our Strength and maintains a dedicated campaign website, blog, and presences on Facebook and Twitter. On Twitter, Tyson has mounted local food pantry campaigns in Austin, Boston, New York, and San Francisco, pledging to donate 100 pounds of food for every blog comment or retweet. In Austin, Tyson generated 350 comments—enough to fill its 35,000-pound truckload—in just four hours.

"Shine the spotlight on the cause and what others are doing, rather than yourself," advises Ed Nicholson, Tyson Foods director of community and public relations. "It will generally reflect favorably back on you. Pound-for-pound, authentic engagement trumps cash. And you probably have resources the cause needs desperately, even if it isn't money."[9]

---

[7] Convio, "The Next Generation of American Giving," March 2010, www.convio.com/files/next-gen-whitepaper.pdf.

[8] Telephone interview by the author, October 5, 2012.

[9] Kate Olsen and Geoff Livingston, "Cause Marketing through Social Media: 5 Steps to Successful Online Campaign," Network for Good and Zoetica, www1.networkforgood.org/ckfinder/userfiles/files/CauseMarketingThroughSocialMedia.pdf.

Spanish-language broadcaster Univision supports Ya Es Hora ("now is the time") to promote Latino civic engagement, citizenship, voter engagement, census enumeration, college education, and other community issues.

Other examples—from Target, Kraft, and American Express (all discussed later in this chapter)—provide ample evidence for how broad the spectrum of cause marketing can be. Certainly, there's a relevant cause to energize and add meaning to your own organization's social media program.

▧ **Tip**   Need help to strategize and execute a charitable campaign in social media? Download the free document "Cause Marketing through Social Media: 5 Steps to Successful Online Campaigns," www1.networkforgood.org/ckfinder/userfiles/files/ CauseMarketingThroughSocialMedia.pdf.

Buzz: Word of Mouth, Promotion, and Going Viral

Key to the success of social media campaigns is that they appeal to your core "superfans" and that they're easy to spread by word of mouth, from these influential customers throughout the social sphere at large.

The invention of word-of-mouth marketing, or WOM, was inevitable, once marketers realized consumers were tuning out traditional ads and turning their attention instead to the recommendations of strangers on the Internet. For it to be effective, WOM must remain unpaid, authentic, and people-powered. The work of a marketer is not to control the message, but to create a favorable environment for people to receive it and pass it along.

The five pillars of successful WOM are:

- Develop a true and catchy "story" about your brand, product, or service

- Identify and cultivate the *influentials*—well-connected people in your market, who are inclined to spread the word and effective at doing it

- Find fun and clever ways to seed the story, especially among influentials

- Create tools that make it easy to spread the story

- Interact with your community, so the sharing impulse becomes an ongoing conversation

Ted Wright is the owner of Fizz, a leading word-of-mouth marketing agency based outside Atlanta, Georgia. Fizz has led memorable viral campaigns for Pabst Blue Ribbon and other brands. Are you curious whether your brand is a good candidate for a word-of-mouth campaign? To Wright, the answer is easy: "Do you have a good brand story that once people learn it, they will want to share it with others? If you answered 'yes,' then influencer marketing will work for your brand."[10]

This litmus test is very simple—yet it's remarkable how many of the products that marketers aspire to squeeze into a word-of-mouth strategy will fail that simple test. Most products, brands, and campaigns lack any real story worthy of retelling to a friend or relative.

To develop a good story, think of the startup entrepreneur honing his elevator pitch for the VC. Brainstorm with your team and explore what makes your product, service, company culture, cause, style, or campaign noteworthy, interesting, and special.

Identify the people most likely to embrace the story and spread it around. These may be your best, most loyal customers, or brand advocates active in the blogosphere. Perhaps they haven't yet discovered you, but they're bigwigs in a specialized market you're targeting.

In *The Tipping Point* (Little, Brown and Company, 2000), Malcolm Gladwell introduced three distinct personality types responsible for driving an idea or phenomenon to the point that it "tips" and becomes viral—as a hot fashion trend, a revolutionary product, or a popular social cause.

- **Connectors:** Profoundly social, these folks seem to know everybody and take special delight in making good introductions, bringing like-minded people together, and linking people to opportunities.

- **Mavens:** Passionate experts and enthusiasts whom we trust. They have their ears to the ground, they have done their homework, and they love to share their knowledge.

- **Salespeople:** Charismatic persuaders, they are the tastemakers. When they get behind something, they have the power, influence, and personality to make it cool.

---

[10] Deepak Gupta, "Word of Mouth Marketing by Ted Wright," Marketing by Deepak, June 27, 2010, www.marketingbydeepak.com/word-of-mouth-marketing-by-ted-wright/.

Influencers

Ted Wright identifies people he describes as the *influencers*: "You know them: The person who always has the best recommendation for restaurants, new drinks, music, books; whatever they are passionate about. They have a lot of information that is valuable to their friends. In short, Influencers are a personality type; not a person."[11]

Call them influentials, evangelists, superfans, brand ambassadors, mavens, or connectors. Whatever the label, these people play disproportionate roles in turning your product story into a viral buzz.

Wright estimates that influencers represent about 15% of the North American population. They love to search for new things. They share with friends and acquaintances by telling stories. Their tastes and recommendations are trusted. Their discoveries save their friends time and effort.

Strong brands enjoy good access to their customers—access that has become more direct and more personal than ever, thanks to social media. With focus, you can identify and cultivate the best and most influential among those customers. And if you want help with fan identification and buzz-building, Fizz and others manage networks of potential brand advocates.

Fizz has built a relatively small network of influencers—people with the personality traits described above and with a record of connecting with others online and in person and making authentic, passionate, trusted recommendations. BzzAgent, which maintains a very large network of 850,000 influencers, says, "We put products in the hands of hundreds of thousands of real consumers and help them share their opinions about them with friends and family via reviews, Facebook posts, photos and videos, blog posts and more."

Smiley360 has a network of 300,000 consumers, who, it says, "provide valuable feedback about popular brands, and that feedback can actually collectively drive the market."

Brand Influencers, a social media and guerrilla marketing agency, has assembled custom influencer groups for a broad range of campaigns—including a Congressional election, teen fashions, and a gambling casino.

Fans and Superfans

Even if you don't intend to run an organized word-of-mouth campaign, it pays to identify your superfans. These elite few are your best customers, who

---

[11] Deepak Gupta, Ibid.

happen to be superactive in social media and aren't shy about recommending you, beating the drum, spreading the word. They are not only loyal buyers, they're also natural tastemakers, with big networks of actual and virtual friends and followers.

Your online community manager should know them by name. A superfan, or brand advocate, devotes long hours to online posting and passionate, real interaction with online friends. A superfan has done her research, knows the competitive advantage of your stuff, and is bursting with eagerness to share it. A superfan is someone who:

- Writes glowing reviews, testimonials, or recommendations about your products

- Touts your customer service and adores your brand

- Enjoys a large audience of Twitter followers, blog readers, Facebook friends, LinkedIn connections

- Is liberal with his or her opinions—discusses your brand freely, online and off (if you have a bumper sticker, it is on her car)

- Actively promotes your products and your brand to friends, acquaintances—even total strangers

Identifying and cultivating brand advocates like these can be one of the most powerful accomplishments of your social program. Like a Vegas casino pampering its high rollers, a neighborhood pub greeting its regulars, or a Hollywood agent catering to the A-list, you should go out of your way to provide VIP treatment for your superfans. They're worth it. Remember that retaining an existing customer is always cheaper than acquiring a brand-new one.

And the extra benefit of superfans is that they don't just continue as customers—they actively promote and advocate for your brand, bringing new customers into the fold.

So when you see signs that someone is a superfan, surprise and delight them with free gifts, heartfelt behind-the-scenes thank yous, and other authentic gestures of gratitude.

Create a formal ambassador program built around a limited number of superfans. Creative Playthings launched a program for "mommy bloggers," devoted to educational toys. Finnish scissors-maker Fiskars runs a scrapbooking community with a dozen carefully recruited ambassadors at the helm. My employer, Green Mountain Coffee Roasters, has identified influential coffee bloggers and keeps them supplied with new products to review and special offers to share with their passionate readers.

Get to know your superfans. Meet them in person, if possible. Let them know how important they are to you and your brand. They will become a core audience that is especially receptive to your social media campaigns and disproportionately key to making them successful.

Case Studies

There's no better way to recognize the breadth of possibilities for social media marketing than to drill into a few case studies. These examples from real businesses exemplify innovative thinking, crisp execution, multichannel marketing support, and smart leveraging of the network effect.

Whether you're supporting a good cause, generating buzz, or trying to drive more business, these best-of-breed social media campaigns offer a useful template.

■ **Tip**   Each year, the Multichannel Merchant Awards recognize brands for executing superior multichannel marketing campaigns. Check out the winners for valuable lessons on employing social in your media mix: www.multichannelmerchant.com/2012-mcm-awards-winners/.

Target: Rallying to a Good Cause

Target kicked off back-to-school season 2012 with a charitable campaign aimed straight for the hearts of America's moms. "Help us give up to $2.5 million in support of schools," exhorted Target's Facebook page to its 16 million fans.

The message was clear and compelling, leveraging a good cause and making a direct call for social sharing and engagement through online voting: "Together we're giving K-12 schools up to $10,000 each in Target GiftCards for books or any supplies they need. You can help by voting for a school each week. Rally your friends because for every 25 votes a school receives, Target will send a $25 gift card. Vote now."

The "Give With Target" campaign attracted thousands of votes for the most active schools and helped Target select the recipients of the $2.5 million ahead of schedule. The social-powered campaign exhibited several best practices:

- **Charitable cause:** Support for education through free school supplies resonated perfectly with the audience (moms) and the season (back to school).

- **Strong calls to action:** Classic direct-marketing rules of thumb still apply in the social space. To cut through the clutter and elicit response, Target's designs were clean and bold. Text was simple and brief. Target used a single prominent and engaging image; people's faces work especially well in social media. The company made explicit calls to action, like "find a school" and "vote now."

- **Fan engagement:** A robust Facebook application called up a database of thousands of K-12 schools nationwide. When users found their local elementary school, they could vote for it, then connect to their Facebook friend network to exhort their friends to vote. The $25 gift card is an appealing incentive, and the 25-vote threshold feels attainable. Most of us know 25 fellow parents who would support our school. That's essential. Consumers who are too jaded to e-mail their friends for a one-in-a-million sweepstakes may be more responsive to a smaller reward that's more realistic to attain.

- **Gamification:** By ranking the top vote-getting schools in real time, as well as displaying all recent votes in a scrolling activity feed, the Target campaign added elements of a game. That encouraged more referrals ("We've got to get to the top!"), as well as repeat visits to check status.

- **Multichannel:** While Facebook was the main touch point for the campaign, Target supported it with the Twitter hashtag #givewithtarget, traditional press releases, YouTube videos, a cross-country Target bus tour with actress/singer Bridgit Mendler, and more.

- **Repeatable:** This particular charitable campaign was part of a larger $1 billion for education campaign that Target is pursuing over multiple years. The advantages of this approach are threefold: (1) it demonstrates the brand's continued loyalty to an important cause, (2) it aims for a bigger, higher-impact overall goal, and (3) it enables the company to reuse the same channels, tactics, and technology platforms, so Target isn't constantly reinventing the wheel.

- **Trackable:** This application was nicely designed with a lot of trackable metrics to gauge impact: new fans, likes, shares, nominated schools, referrals, votes, and awarded gift cards. Do all those figures add up to a tangible ROI number? No— but they are meaningful measures of brand engagement and positive brand impressions, which are bound to stimulate more loyalty and drive new consumers into the stores.

Kraft Foods: "Huddle to Fight Hunger"

Kraft Foods is a $50 billion consumer packaged-goods company with scores of brands including Oreo, Nabisco, Maxwell House, and Cadbury. Kraft maintains several Facebook and Twitter presences for its various brands, as well as campaign-focused communities like its football-themed 2011 charitable "Huddle to Fight Hunger."

Hunger, nutrition, and related issues are natural causes for food companies like Kraft or Tyson. They're critically important societal issues we can all agree on—and they are especially important to the moms who make up the bulk of Kraft's online communities.

The mission statement of "Huddle to Fight Hunger" is a textbook example of how to synthesize your core values in one brief statement: "We're a community that blends what Americans are passionate about—football, food, and helping others."

"Huddle to Fight Hunger" set a goal of giving away 20 million meals to local food shelves through its partner charity, Feeding America.

"During tough times, consumers want to help others who are less fortunate," comments Valerie Moens, senior manager of corporate affairs at Kraft Foods. "Our research tells us that 65% of consumers say they experience an emotional reward when they give."[12]

For each consumer who entered his or her name and e-mail address on the campaign website, Kraft donated a meal to Feeding America. Entering a zip code allowed the donation to be directed to a local food shelf in the consumer's community.

The company also used donations as an incentive to encourage Facebook "likes" and to drive grocery coupon redemptions for brands including Oscar Mayer and Maxwell House.

The campaign employed gamification to engage fans with its "2-Minute Trivia Drill" and offered a sweepstakes to win a trip to the "Kraft Fight Hunger

---

[12] Shahnaz Mahmud, "Kraft Foods 'Huddle to Fight Hunger' campaign supports charitable giving," August 25, 2010, www.dmnews.com/kraft-foods-huddle-to-fight-hunger-campaign-supports-charitable-giving/article/177514/

Bowl," the college football game of which Kraft became title sponsor. The "Huddle to Fight Hunger" campaign was a truly multichannel effort, combining mobile, online, print, and retail store elements. Retired hall-of-fame quarterback Joe Montana lent his endorsement, as did celebrity chefs and sports journalists.

American Express: "Link, Like, Love"

American Express has been at the vanguard of social media campaigning on two fronts: with consumer-facing promotions and with B2B campaigns aimed at the network of merchant companies that accept the Amex charge card.

In 2011, American Express launched "Link, Like, Love," a Facebook app that delivers deals based on cardmember likes and interests. With it, Amex cardmembers can sync their cards with their Facebook, Twitter, or Foursquare accounts, then claim deals that will be reflected as a credit on their card statement.

For instance, cardmembers spending $20 on-site at the U.S. Open tennis tournament earned $10 back on their statements. Those who spent $200 at Best Buy received $20 back. Other brands offering "Link, Like, Love" promotions include Travelocity, Tommy Hilfiger, 20th Century Fox, Dunkin' Donuts, Whole Foods Market, and 1-800-FLOWERS.

The deals, which appear on a cardmember's personal "dashboard" within the application, are driven by Facebook likes, interests, check-ins, and other social signals. As Amex explains, a cardmember who likes Whole Foods Market on Facebook or who checks into their local Whole Foods on Facebook Places may receive a Whole Foods Market deal. If the show *Glee* is among her interests on Facebook, she may see a Fox offer for *Glee: The 3D Concert Movie*. Naturally, the deals are shareable on the Facebook social graph.

"American Express has created innovative programs on Facebook that continue to put people at the center of their business," says David Fischer, vice president of advertising and global operations at Facebook. "[Like, Link, Love] takes advantage of the power of the social graph to create value for people and drive meaningful business results."[13]

American Express has done a stellar job of building a big network across all the major social platforms. In addition to its 2.5 million Facebook fans and 19 million views of its YouTube videos, Amex connects to half a million Twitter followers. The Amex Twitter account nicely observes the Twitter ethos by

---

[13] "American Express Launches 'Link, Like, Love' on Facebook," July 19, 2011, about. americanexpress.com/news/pr/2011/link.aspx.

feeling a bit more personal, a bit less corporate—for instance, crediting by name the real people behind its tweets: Amex employees Mona Hamouly, Matt Burton, and Amy Tokarski.

Over 70,000 Facebook users have downloaded the "Link, Like, Love" app. Amex supports the initiative with Sponsored Stories advertising—so when one of your friends downloads the app, you're very likely to see an ad proclaiming that fact.

Helping Businesses Go Social

I like how Amex works both sides of the aisle, excelling in consumer promotions at the same time it bolsters its connection to merchants.

To power the "Link, Like, Love" network with strong offers, American Express supports a self-serve, online "Go Social" offer tool (www.gosocial. americanexpress.com), enabling bricks-and-mortar businesses to distribute location-based cardmember deals on Facebook Places, Foursquare, and other digital platforms. The platform also supports e-commerce offers for merchants without a bricks-and-mortar presence. Once your promotion is live, you can view performance stats, including total redemptions, sales, and average order value (AOV).

Amex also partnered with Facebook with its Open Forum, www.facebook. com/open, to support small businesses with social media promotion. In its "Big Break for Small Business" contest, American Express recently awarded five small businesses grand prizes of $25,000 each, plus one-on-one strategy sessions with Facebook to develop a social media plan and put it to use. Over 12,000 businesses entered, and winners were determined by fan voting.

The grand prizes weren't the only payoff: all entries stood to win $50 to $100 credits for Facebook advertising.

"Small businesses' number-one need is to get new customers," says Laura Fink, vice president of social media at American Express. "And increasingly we're seeing that social media is helping to level the playing field for small businesses."[14]

In 2011, Amex was a founding partner of Small Business Saturday, a promotion declaring the Saturday between Black Friday and Cyber Monday as an occasion to celebrate small enterprise by shopping at locally owned businesses. Small

---

[14] Tara Lynn Wagner, "Amex, Facebook Hold Contest That Lets Small Biz Owners Harness Power of Social Media," NY1 News, August 23, 2012, www.ny1.com/content/ny1_living/money_matters/167384/amex--facebook-hold-contest-that-lets-small-biz-owners-harness-power-of-social-media.

Business Saturday has attracted almost three million fans on Facebook and garnered coverage in *Forbes, USA Today,* and other media. The dedicated www. smallbusinesssaturday.com website and its Facebook fan page offer an array of free advertising and promotional tools, with an emphasis on social media and online business:

- $100 of free Twitter advertising
- Free downloadable "Come In and Shop Small" retail store signage
- Page-building tools from Facebook and Pagemodo
- Website building tools from Yola
- Offer-creating wizard for Amex's "Go Social" platform

Amex also partnered with Google to sponsor a "My Business Story" channel on YouTube, http://www.youtube.com/user/mybusinessstory, which has attracted three million views, gaining attention for the participating small businesses and momentum for the Small Business Saturday promotion as a whole.

Altogether, Amex has made an impressive commitment to helping its merchants succeed with social media marketing. My impression is that for any organization, Amex could make a good partner for navigating this space.

■ **Tip**   Could you use $50 to $100 in Facebook advertising credit (or as much as $25,000 in funding for your small business)? Check out American Express Company's "Big Break for Small Business" on Facebook: www.facebook.com/Open.

The Membership Effect

Echoing the "network effect" well known to computer scientists, Amex has registered the service mark "The Membership Effect" and uses it prominently in commercials online and in traditional media.

The concept underpins the company's approach to social media. Amex is about more than financial transactions. It is about the network of merchants and members and the emotions behind those transactions. Or, as the company puts it on their fan pages: "Explore the community of people, products, and ideas powered by American Express."

Clif Bar: Grassroots Style

Clif Bar & Company of Emeryville, California, is a friendly, quirky, and socially conscious business that makes organic energy bars. Its guiding principles, or "five aspirations," are all related to sustainability: to sustain the planet, the community, its people, its business, and its brands.

Clif Bar has a passionate social media community, centered on outdoor adventure, active lifestyle, health, fitness, sustainability, and conservation. Clif doesn't pour a ton of money into social media. It conducts clever promotions that are true to its core principles and that connect directly to its fans. Each year, Clif Bar executes a number of Facebook and Twitter giveaways celebrating outdoor adventure, distributing up to 5,000 bars each time.

"Clif Bar's approach to social media is unique," says Michelle Ferguson, executive vice president of marketing at Clif Bar & Company. Ferguson comments that the company started with a "very grassroots philosophy," personally connecting with customers at active sports and outdoor events. "We view our online conversations in the same spirit as the conversations we have in person—we're just using technology to have them."[15]

Clif Bar sponsors teams in triathlon, cycling, paddling, and other sports. Company owners and husband-and-wife duo Kit Crawford and Gary Erickson log plenty of miles in their custom biodiesel RV, handing out Clif Bars and Luna Bars at expos and sporting events nationwide. These activities are colorfully documented on the Clif Bar social media accounts and in the company blog.

The company ran a 2012 Labor Day weekend Twitter promotion and sweepstakes to launch its Clif Mojo trail-mix energy bar, challenging its 100,000+ Twitter followers to "show your mojo" by tweeting what outdoor activity they were engaged in, and where.

Each geo-located tweet earned a coupon for a free Clif Mojo bar, as well as an entry into a sweepstakes. Prizes included a Garmin Forerunner GPS, Clif products, and other goodies.

Campaign elements consisted of a dedicated contest landing page, a YouTube video, a dedicated Twitter account (@CLIFMojoGo), and outreach to Twitter followers. The campaign garnered several hundred retweets and sweepstakes entries—kindling enthusiasm and press coverage for the new product in the process.

---

[15] Patricia Odell, "Clif Bar Gets People Geo-tweeting for a Coupon," August 15, 2012, *Chief Marketer*, www.chiefmarketer.com/promotional-marketing/clif-bar-gets-people-geo-tweeting-coupon.

As you might expect, Clif Bar & Company also exhibits a fondness for cause marketing. Struck by the fact that 40% of urban travel is two miles or less—and that 90% of those trips are by car—Clif Bar employees decided to try to change their behavior and that of their larger community. "It's why Clif Bar employees came up with the idea for a game to encourage more bike trips instead of cars," noted the company blog. "We called it the Two Mile Challenge, not because riding a bike two miles is that difficult of a task for anyone—but rather that we tend to get comfortable in our cars and it's a challenge to rethink the drive."[16]

Clif Bar is committed to supporting and promoting bicycling. The company donates $100,000 a year to bike nonprofits. Each month, the 2 Mile Challenge community directs donations to a different organization that is building a more bike-friendly America.

Whether spreading the promotional word via Twitter, raising consciousness and funds for worthy causes, or showing up in person at outdoor events, Clif Bar & Company demonstrates the value of true, grassroots community engagement. It doesn't take a ton of money—but it does take a ton of passion and authenticity.

Love: It's What Makes a Subaru a Subaru

In this book, I've drawn examples from a broad spectrum of brands and markets, some of which I have a personal affinity for, and others less so. But Subaru is truly close to my heart. I live in rural Vermont, where it's said we have four seasons: foliage, winter, mud, and July. Thanks to its surefootedness on all that snow, mud, and dirt roads, the all-wheel-drive Subaru is practically the official state car. The Outback model is perennially the best-selling vehicle in Vermont.

Over the decades, my wife and I have owned five Subarus: the DL, GL, Impreza, Legacy, and an Outback. Although I'm not in the high-performance, expert "car guy" category, I probably rank among the most devoted enthusiasts of the Subaru brand.

It's no wonder I've been attentive to how Subaru of America manages its social media campaigns. And the closer I look, the more impressed I am with the way the brand really "gets" social media and is running a program that harmonizes everyday community management with major social media campaigns and applications.

---

[16] Clif Bar and Company, "Motivation," 2 Mile Challenge Blog, August 2012, www.2milechallenge.com/blog/2012/08/motivation/.

The Subaru Facebook page generates a great deal of interactivity from fans. Subaru owners upload favorite photos of their cars in action, or at rest in the great outdoors. They add favorite travel destinations to the interactive map of the "Subaru Guide to Everything." In the "Love All You Can Do" app, Subaru drivers can upload events all over the country that embody the "adventure" pillar of the Subaru brand—be they triathlons, arts festivals, rally races, or whitewater paddles.

The goal of all this sharing is to create personal engagement, not necessarily for it to go viral. "Your first-car experience is shareable, but it's not multi-shareable," notes Michael McHale, director of corporate communications for Subaru of America.[17] An individual car owner can connect with the Subaru brand and fellow Subaru owners by sharing a memory with the community. A car shopper can configure her ideal vehicle on www.Subaru.com, then share it with Facebook trends and ask, "What do you think?"

People don't spread this kind of sharing further, so it doesn't go viral like cute kitten pictures, say, or videos of a polar bear getting stuck in the ice. But it is a strong positive for the brand, it fosters a connection between Subaru and its fans, and it lets friends of fans see how engaged their friends are with Subaru.

"We approach social as a conversation," says McHale. "The voice of the company, any company, has changed enormously. Before social, we spoke to the media, then the media put their own spin on it and they spoke to the customer. Now, we speak directly to customers. And now they can speak back to you in a way that everyone else can see. Before social, the approach was to sell them a product and go on your way. But now you're conducting a conversation, and that conversation and relationship can go on for a long time. The car-buying cycle is seven years."

Despite his focus on conversation, McHale's interest is facilitating conversations between fans—not necessarily being part of the conversation himself.

"When you're a fan of a sports team, you love the team. Do you love the management? Not always. They may love your product—they certainly love their car. They love to talk to fellow owners. But they may not love or always want to talk with the company."

Enthusiasts' forums, like the Impreza owners group www.NASIOC.com, are a case in point. "We change the wheels from a four-bolt to a five-bolt pattern, and those forums just light up." But the unique chemistry and energy of a chat room full of passionate car enthusiasts can be altered when a company representative enters the room and introduces himself. "Do they really want to talk with you?" McHale asks rhetorically. "We know that there are times

---

[17] Personal interview, October 5, 2012.

that they will, and so we facilitate that conversation. But we know there are times when they just want to talk between themselves. Sometimes the conversation gets limited by what we can and can't say in public. We can't, for example, answer when they ask when the next car is coming out. That has a strict launch cadence that we can't break on Facebook."

Enthusiast communities devote a lot of energy to in-depth online conversations. But don't expect that kind of high engagement from the general social media audience. As McHale notes, "Most people don't get into a conversation. They say 'boo,' or 'yay,' and they're gone. It's an issue of time for them—they're busy."

When your brand covers a lot of ground and appeals to distinct customer types, developing content for social media can be a challenge. For McHale, that could mean, "Make sure the performance guy gets enough motor sports, and make sure the lady who owns a Forester gets enough gardening tips."

At the end of the day, what's the impact of all this customer engagement? Subaru performs some post-purchase customer surveys to try to determine how many of their new car buyers engaged with the company in social media before buying their new car. But McHale points out that it can be a mistake to put too much stock in quantifying the benefits of social media. Like publicity and other aspects of brand marketing, the benefits can be elusive—but they are real.

"Digital's the death of us all," McHale exaggerates to make a point, "because it's all so trackable, so measurable. It's stopping us creating art, because it's all science. Before digital, a marketer came up with an idea for a campaign because it felt right, in his gut. It's becoming harder to do art. But really, Facebook is still an art. There aren't metrics to prove you're doing it right. You just have to know in your gut that it's good for the brand. When we get our car on the cover of an automotive magazine, we know it's good. We don't know exactly how good, we just know it's good. It's the same with social."

With almost a million Facebook fans, the brand's social media program clearly has reached an enviable critical mass. Each Subaru of America wall post inspires from 1,000 to as many as 10,000 "likes," plus dozens of comments and hundreds of shares. "Social is not limited to Facebook," McHale acknowledges. "But Facebook is the huge gorilla in the room."

In addition to Facebook, Subaru boasts a robust Twitter following of 65,000, and it is also active on Pinterest and Foursquare. "Foursquare is good for us," says McHale, "because we go to events, so it works for us to say, 'We're at Master the Mountain, come visit us,' at such and such ski resort." For local events like this, Subaru's field team will message their Facebook fans and Foursquare followers with opportunities to win prizes, receive giveaways, get free coffee or hot chocolate, or get VIP parking at the resort for Subaru drivers.

It is valuable to note that this very large online community comprises many segments and factions. Some members are so devoted they'll invest significant time and creativity generating content for apps like the Guide to Everything. Others are just passing through with that quick "boo" or "yay." Considering that the car-buying cycle stretches across seven years, Subaru of America is smart to engage with both audiences on their own terms, to support the relationship in an ongoing way, to be patient, and to be ready to step up the conversation and deepen the relationship when the time comes for a customer to buy a new car.

INTERVIEW: MICHAEL MCHALE, SUBARU OF AMERICA, DIRECTOR OF CORPORATE COMMUNICATIONS

What's the overarching story or theme of Subaru of America's social media presence?

We start with the brand, and under that, the brand pillars are about adventure, longevity, safety, and reliability.

How can you encourage positive word of mouth?

Much of what we are doing is digital or viral, but not necessarily social. If you're talking to everyone, but they're not talking to one another, it's not social.

People say, "If only you can get customers engaged in a conversation in social, they'll do your marketing." It's not true. The customer is not going to shill for you unless you give them something worth their while—great, engaging content they want to share on their own terms.

What are some favorite themes for wall posts?

We do a "Throwback Thursday" and "Fan Follow Friday"—those both work well, especially among the performance guys, the enthusiasts. Each Friday, we recognize one fan who takes a spectacular photo that we love. We make the image our Facebook cover photo for the day.

Do you have any advice for brands trying to stand out and adapt their message to resonate on social media?

When does a brand stop being a brand? When it works so hard to reflect the customer that it loses its own identity. At some point you have to stop reflecting the customer, and just be who you are. Here's the side of our brand you like, but it's still a side of our brand. If we were to tailor everything to what we think a customer wants us to be, we'd lose our identity.

Let's Get Physical: From Virtual to Actual—Tweetups, Meet-Ups, and More

Up to this point, I've focused almost exclusively on the online world—how social media and networks play out on the Internet and via mobile phones. Most social media books (and most social media marketers) never get beyond that frame of reference. But what's especially exciting about social media is how effectively it reaches into people's daily lives and engages them personally in something. That something—be it a cause, a product, a service, a relationship, or entertainment—has the power to leap out of the laptop or smartphone and come to life in living, breathing, bricks-and-mortar 3D.

How? Take the concept of Tweetups. Twitter has always excelled as a news aggregator and messaging platform; it's largely a new, socialized, public-facing instant-messaging and e-mail platform. Twitter users found early on it was ideal for planning group get-togethers, whether a spontaneous TGIF at a local watering hole or an informal breakout session at an industry conference.

One salient fact about Tweetups is that they sprang naturally from the personal bonds developed among Twitter users following one another and being inspired by similar topics and trends, generating real friendships and personal exchanges—people who got to know and like each other through Twitter or LinkedIn.

Twitter itself is a great platform for promoting a Tweetup and dealing with logistics, but as an event planner, you'll need to support your Tweetups and meet-ups with some RSVP event tools, like Eventbrite, LinkedIn, Facebook events, or Meetup.com. That way you'll be able to invite and remind attendees, maintain a socially visible list of who's attending, publish an agenda, give the event location, and mention a dress code or other details if needed.

"Whenever possible, meet your fans and followers face to face," suggests Lauren Parajon, social media manager at Standing Dog Interactive, in Dallas. "Host fan-appreciation parties or fan-only events. Create opportunities for physical high-fives."[18]

Social media can be an organizing platform for flash mobs—those spontaneous-seeming public performances that are actually carefully planned and choreographed in advance. Urban "street teams" of guerrilla marketers, free-sample distributors, word-of-mouth advocates, or performance artists are

---

[18] Lauren Parajon, "Turning Brand Advocates Into Superfans with High-Fives," Social Media Today, March 27, 2012, http://socialmediatoday.com/lauren-parajon/478018/turning-brand-advocates-superfans-high-fives.

now frequently part of multichannel campaigns in which social media play a vital role.

If your brand is connecting with its fans on social media but wondering what is the next step, consider real, person-to-person interaction.

In May 2012, the fashion brand Express staged a live, outdoor fashion show at Chicago's Millennium Park. The brand leveraged social, mobile, and in-person touch points to make a splash on the streets of Chicago and in the media. The event was a fantastic example of multimedia social marketing.

Express supported the event with coordinated campaigns in geo-targeted e-mail and via Facebook, Twitter, Instagram, Foursquare, store signage, street teams, YouTube, print media, local online and print media, and local fashion blogs.

Photo-sharing site Instagram was a natural fit for the fashion show. Express took it one step further, partnering with Instaprint, a wireless onsite printing technology, to enable attendees to actually print their photos in real time.

Express offered its fans behind-the-scenes looks at the preshow setup, the event, and the after-party. All the photos and video taken at the show served as the foundation for Express's fall print, digital, television, and in-store marketing campaigns.

Twitter and Foursquare were ideal for driving real-time mobile interaction. On Twitter, Express leveraged the #EXPRunway hashtag in all posts. Foursquare featured tips at landmark Chicago check-ins, including Navy Pier, Wrigley Field, and O'Hare Airport, as well as Express store locations.

To get the word out locally, Express activated its Chicago-area customers, media, and street teams, including:

- Express-branded ice cream trucks handing out treats wrapped in event invites

- Geo-targeted e-mail invitations

- Print and online ads in local style and entertainment outlets

- Signage, handouts, and bag stuffers in Chicago-area stores

- Brand ambassadors in high-traffic areas on the day of the show

- Personal invites to influential Chicago fashion and style bloggers

The results exceeded the Express team's hopes: the fashion show attracted over 3,000 attendees and received over 725,000 earned digital impressions. It's an impressive example of the power of coordinated multichannel marketing, with social media—in other words, *people*—at the very heart of it.

Summary

The campaigns I've explored here run the spectrum—from grassroots efforts to big-budget extravaganzas, from charitable campaigns to sales efforts. What they have in common is that they're tailored to the emotions, priorities, and situations of the ordinary folks who make up our social media fan bases. Whether your fans are motivated by exclusive discounts, a lavish prize, an addictive game, or the chance to do some good in the world, the campaign strategy is much the same.

Facebook tabs and Facebook apps support your campaigns in the social media space. In Chapter 10, I'll discuss how to build integrations between your company's website and the social networks. Your goal is to create robust, engaging brand experiences on Facebook and Twitter—and to activate rich social connections from your website back to those social networks. Doing this will bring you closer to a 360-degree view, where social and commerce come full circle.

Power Up Your Platform

Integrating Social into Your Website

Most of my focus in this book has been on how to optimize your presence on Facebook, Twitter, YouTube, and other social networks. Building a thriving online community requires investment in your page and development of tabs, posts, videos, and more—a seemingly endless stream of content. All that activity pays off in leads, new customers, and increased customer loyalty. But it can be unsettling to invest so many content assets in a platform you don't own or fully control.

Now, you can add social interactivity to something you do control—your own website. You can hook your website into the social graph—and benefit your business in three ways:

- You'll improve customer engagement and conversion rate on your website, thanks to the *social proof* of friends who bought or recommended certain items

- You'll generate positive word of mouth when your customer activity is posted to the Facebook and Twitter newsfeeds

- You'll gain valuable data on the likes, interests, education, jobs, friends, and countless other data points of your customers—data that you'd never see were it not for Facebook integration

Let's start with the easiest ways to connect your web properties with the social media universe and then work our way through increasingly ambitious and powerful approaches.

Your Website 2.0: Integrating with Social Networks

Your business can leverage the power of the people by taking some of the following steps (in increasing order of complexity):

- Participating (as a hosted community and as an advertiser) on the main social networks

- Pasting simple widget code into your site, employing Facebook, Twitter, YouTube, LinkedIn, and other widgets to add basic social content to the web experience you offer

- Using AddThis, ShareThis, FriendFeed, or more robust integrations via Facebook Connect

- Installing product reviews and ratings software

- Enabling social sign-in—utilizing the login credentials of users' Facebook or Twitter accounts

- Building your own social features on your website from scratch

The advantage of using third-party platforms is that it's quick and easy, you'll reach an enormous installed base of members, and those platforms are continuously expanding, improving, and adding new features.

Widgets, or Social Plug-ins

Basic integrations with your social media presence are available as widgets, so you can display them on your website with a simple cut-and-paste of the widget code.

The benefit of widgets is their ease of use—they're a fast, simple way to enlarge the footprint of your online community and disseminate what its members are saying. But widgets do have shortcomings. They aren't customizable beyond a few tweaks to fonts, colors, and size. And they can't be personalized to individual visitors to your site. Instead, all visitors will see the same thing (the latest Twitter posts in your stream, or the latest comments from members in the Facebook activity feed, for instance). That can pique the interest of some visitors to consider joining, and it might cast a certain halo of social proof around your brand if the newsfeed is active and enthusiastic about your products. But widgets are not as powerful and interactive as some of the integrations I'll get to later.

The first wave of social media integration on websites took the form of the now ubiquitous footer icons, displaying Facebook, Twitter, and other logos and linking to your community to join or follow. Wave two, employing active "like and "follow" widgets, makes it easier to get the desired outcome with a single click, without your visitors ever having to leave your site.

Facebook Social Plug-ins

Facebook offers 11 widgets to add Facebook interactivity to your website:

- *Like* button: Shares directly to Facebook in one click

- *Send* button: Shares content with friends

- *Subscribe* button: Allows users to subscribe to (follow) other users

- *Comments*: Enables comments on any piece of content on your site

- *Activity Feed*: Shows users what their friends are liking and commenting upon on your site

- *Recommendations* box: Delivers users' personalized suggestions for pages on your site they might like

- *Recommendations* bar: Lets users "like" content, receive recommendations, and share their product recommendations with friends

- *Like* Box: A combined activity stream and *Like* button

- *Login* button: Login link accompanied by pictures of the users' friends who have already joined the site

- *Registration*: Also known as social sign-in—allows users to log into your site using their Facebook credentials

- *Facepile*: Displays a grid of profile photos of users who have liked your page or registered for it

▧ **Tip**   For documentation on all 11 Facebook social plug-ins, visit http://developers.facebook.com/docs/plugins/.

Twitter Widgets and APIs

As might be expected, Twitter's widget offerings are few, clean, and simple:

- **Embedded Tweets:** They allow you to cut and paste any tweet into your website. Embedded Tweets are displayed with functional retweet, reply, favorite, and follow buttons.

- **Twitter cards:** These are embeddable content for your website that look, frankly, a lot like a Facebook wall post. They partner a tweet that links to your content, with a screenshot and link to the content itself.

- **Embeddable timelines:** These are the most useful format. Any public Twitter timeline can be syndicated to your website with one line of code. Once it's embedded, new posts appear automatically within the scrollable timeline. *Retweet, Follow,* and other buttons are functional.

In addition to cut-and-paste widgets, Twitter offers a full API and development environment so you can build web applications that interact with the four types of Twitter objects:

- Tweets
- Users (people)
- Entities (specific things contained in tweets, such as URLs, hashtags, and so on)
- Places

■ **Tip** Find the *Like* button widget at http://developers.facebook.com/docs/reference/plugins/ like/. Get Twitter *Share a link, Follow, Mention,* and *Hashtag* buttons at www.twitter.com/about/ resources/buttons.

Product Ratings and Reviews

For e-commerce companies, user-submitted product ratings and reviews are a vital ingredient for earning trust from online shoppers. Virtually everyone today either shops online or researches purchases online. Saturated by a flood of advertising messages, consumers have learned to tune out most commercial messages. They have grown skeptical of the claims of marketers, instead placing their trust in the advice of friends and family.

In the Web 2.0 world, the definition of "friends and family" has blurred, with consumers placing similar levels of trust in the product recommendations of their friend networks and those of strangers who are fellow online community members or "shoppers like me."

Social media endorsements from ordinary people feel more trustworthy and less biased than commercial messages from marketers. Among these cues are user reviews, product "likes"—whether by friends or strangers—and Pinterest pins (see Figure 10-1).

E-commerce websites see major improvements in conversion rates when they offer user-supplied ratings and reviews. Studies have shown the vast majority of such reviews are positive—four or five stars. And the power of word of mouth can be multiplied now, thanks to integration with Facebook and other social platforms.

Social Media Cues that Inspire Consumers to Trust a Brand

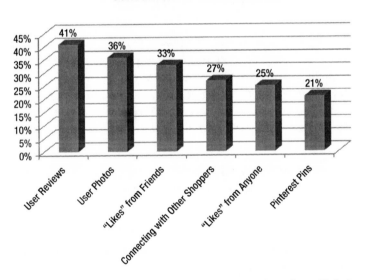

Figure 10-1. Traditional advertising is out, and *social proof* is in. Today's purchase decisions are inspired by user-submitted product reviews, shared videos, "likes," Pinterest pins, and other social media cues.[1]

---

[1] "To Build Consumer Trust, Reviews Are the Key," eMarketer, July 31, 2012, www.emarketer.com/Newsletter_htm/20120731.html?ecid=a6506033675d47f881651943c21c5ed4.

Bazaarvoice, a software system for product ratings and reviews, has integrated with Facebook for more than 400 clients, including AT&T, Best Buy, Macy's, Nationwide Insurance, and Zales. With Bazaarvoice SocialConnect, consumers can opt to share their purchases, ratings, and reviews on their friend networks. SocialConnect allows companies to merge a consumer's social graph with the Bazaarvoice suite to provide a "social shopping" experience across merchant websites and social networks. Shoppers can filter product categories or search results based on the behavior and ratings of their friends or other shoppers. Extensions of the Bazaarvoice platform can weave customer conversations into mobile apps, online and offline advertising campaigns, in-store merchandising, and more.

In my experience using reviews from PowerReviews (recently acquired by Bazaarvoice) and Facebook OnSite, over 16% of our reviewers opt to share their product reviews with their Facebook friend networks. (That's significantly higher than the 7% average, perhaps because coffee is more inherently social than some other product categories.) With this feedback multiplied by the hundreds of friends of each Facebook member, we've achieved tremendous reach and brand equity for very little investment.

Benefit Cosmetics deployed Bazaarvoice ratings and reviews on its website and its Facebook page, allowing fans to share their product reviews with friends and other Benefit Cosmetics fans. On Facebook, the reviews were accompanied by *Buy Now* buttons linking directly to product pages on BenefitCosmetics.com. The company saw a tenfold increase in click-through rate for *Buy Now* buttons on Facebook, compared with their average online ad.

While it's a best practice to solicit reviews from customers a couple of weeks after purchase, don't overlook the role that product reviews and ratings can play in a longer-term relationship—a relationship cultivated by social media.

Filson, the outdoor clothing and work-clothes brand, was founded in 1897 in Seattle to serve Klondike gold-rush prospectors with sturdy mackinaw clothing, blankets, boots, and sleeping bags designed for the frigid north. Still producing sturdy American-made clothing over a century later, Filson enjoys a devoted following—lifelong fans who love to testify to the quality of Filson's products in online reviews. "Folks like to review these products even ten years after they bought them," says Harry Egler, vice president of direct sales at C.C. Filson. "It can take a while to wear our products in, and really get a sense of their value. And your satisfaction with them just grows over time." [2]

---

[2] Harry Egler, remarks at National Etailing and Mailing Organization of America (NEMOA) directXchange conference, Groton, Connecticut, September 19, 2012.

Third-Party Social Plug-ins

While Facebook, Twitter, LinkedIn, and other networks offer perfectly good widgets, there are now a number of third-party tools that make the process easier, generate more powerful or flexible widgets, or add value through analytics or other features.

I discuss a few notable options below.

AddThis

I'm a fan of the AddThis widget, which is flexible, supereasy, and free. Its row of small, colorful icons can sit innocuously under whatever content you think is share-worthy (blog posts, articles, images, products). Users are familiar with it, and some of them key into the number of Facebook "likes" and Google +1's displayed, as an element of social proof that, hey, this thing looks pretty popular...

The AddThis stats package—detailing how much sharing you get, and on which networks—is eye-opening. As you'd expect, Facebook is the dominant sharing venue, followed by Twitter. Sites like Google+, Reddit, del.icio.us, Digg, Posterous, and LinkedIn all get traction here and there. Under the *More* button lurk hundreds of lower-tier networks, including many you have never, ever heard of. (Fark? Spreadly? Really?)

One thing I love about AddThis is the e-mail and print icons. You'd be stunned by how many people, in this Web 2.0 world, are still e-mailing links and printing web pages. But, hey—whatever makes it easy for your visitors to appreciate your content and spread it around.

Gigya

Another way to add social sharing and other Facebook Connect and Twitter integration to your website is to use a third-party platform like Gigya. Gigya and similar platforms make it easier to add common social features to your website without having to work directly with the Facebook APIs.

The heart of a Gigya installation on your website will be social sign-in, allowing your visitors to log into your site using their credentials from Facebook, Twitter, LinkedIn, Google, Yahoo, Foursquare, and about 30 other networks.

Social sign-in powers a wealth of Gigya functionalities, including user management, social management, and social gamification.

Gigya boasts an impressive client roster: *Forbes*, Nike, Martha Stewart, Pepsi, New Balance, White Castle, Bud Light, *USA Today*, and on and on.

■ **Tip** To download the Gigya software developer kit (SDK) and view the documentation, visit http://developers.gigya.com.

Extole

A social marketing tool I discussed in Chapter 9, Extole is also developing some exciting new features with Facebook Open Graph integration, making it easy to embed social buttons and sharing calls to action in the product pages or conversion pages of your website.

Facebook has extended the Open Graph to embrace what it calls "arbitrary actions and objects"—custom actions that go beyond the "like." Extole's Social Expressions tool allows you to code your pages so your customers can share their likes, loves, craves, opinions, wish lists, purchases, donations, subscriptions, and other "social expressions" across Facebook.

Almost any word or phrase can become a custom, shareable action on Facebook. For the wine site www.TastingRoom.com, Extole created a "Wines I Recommend" social expression.

Extole can also power social coupon promotions on your site; when claimed, coupons generate organic impressions in the Facebook newsfeed.

All these "stories" can also become the engine of a Sponsored Stories paid ad campaign on Facebook.

Connecting with Facebook via Open Graph

The *Like* button lets a user share your content with friends on Facebook. The simplest incarnation of the button is served up as a widget that allows anyone to share your page's URL as a story in their Facebook newsfeed—along with a link and a thumbnail image of the page that Facebook creates by screen-scraping your site every day.

When your web page represents not a random URL but a "real-world entity"—things like movies, bands, brands, companies, sports teams, celebrities, and restaurants—you can use the Open Graph protocol to pass information about your page back to Facebook. With Open Graph tags on your web page, it becomes equivalent to a Facebook page. When a user clicks a *Like* button on the page, it will be as if the user "liked" the entity on Facebook itself:

- Your page will appear in the "Likes and Interests" section of the user's profile

- You can publish updates to the user

- Your page will show up in Facebook search results and elsewhere on the Facebook site

- You can target Facebook ads to people who "liked" your content

---

■ **Tip** When you embed a *Like* button with Open Graph tags on your web page, the "like" count displayed on the button includes all likes and shares of the entity on Facebook. The "like" connection reported on the Open Graph API counts only the number of "likes" for your specific URL object.

Social Sign-in

Among users of social sign-in, most users opt to sign in with their Facebook account (48%), followed by Google (30%) and Twitter (9%).

Fab.com, a design website, emphasizes the "log in with Facebook" option on its sign-in page with big, bold graphics and prominent placement. Fab also offers a social shopping Facebook app. Here's how it was introduced on Fab's site:

1. Follow what your friends are purchasing and faving on the Fab live feed.

2. Show off your latest design finds on your Facebook timeline.

Fab never shares "adult" or gift purchases without permission (an early flaw of Facebook's discontinued Beacon program). Along with an image and a blurb like "Jane Doe bought Fab's Bijouterie Stationery Box," the shared story features icons so that others can tweet it, pin it on Pinterest, "like" it on Facebook, or (of course!) buy it on Fab.

Fab is a paragon of social shopping. The site does a superb job integrating the complete social experience with its website—going full circle, from login to promotion to sharing out on the platforms to ultimate sales conversion back on Fab. When you build social integration into your site, ask yourself *why* someone would want to log in using his social network credentials? What functionality are you trying to make easier? What consumer need or impulse are you satisfying by enabling social sharing of users' actions on your site with their friends and family social networks?

If nothing else, social shopping makes it *easier* for new customers to buy from you, without having to jump the hurdle of establishing a new account and password. Social check-in has shown to increase registration rates a whopping 20–40%.

And, at best, social sign-in allows you to benefit from the influence and emotional energy that friends share with one another.

With Fab, it's obvious: Fab shoppers are passionate about design, style, and the shopping experience—they want to share their finds and wish lists with like-minded friends. By the same token, they gain inspiration from what their own friends are buying.

The same holds true for movie recommendations on Redbox or Netflix, travel photos on TripAdvisor (or earning globe-trotting bragging rights using TripAdvisor's "Cities I've Visited" Facebook app), wine ratings, anything people are passionate about. That's the core value proposition of making your website more social.

Facebook Open Graph and API

You'll need to move beyond plain-vanilla widgets to truly unlock the power of social network integration: the ability to filter your site's content—recommended products, highlighted content—based on what a site visitor or her friends, or others like them, have bought, reviewed, liked, or commented on. That's where social proof and the "aha!" factor of users recognizing someone they know really tips the scales of the customer experience.

There's another key advantage of building rich, custom Facebook applications within the fabric of your website: when a Facebook user agrees to grant your app access to her Facebook account, you'll be able to access data on the user's likes, interests, gender, age, birthday, friends, and more. Be respectful of privacy, of course. Use this information judiciously. But I'm sure you'll find that it helps you be a better, more effective marketer.

The Open Graph and Facebook's API are powerful and enormously ambitious programming platforms. If you're a developer, you will be excited to dig into Facebook Developers central: http://developers.facebook.com/docs/opengraph/.

However, if you don't have coding resources at your disposal, or if you wish to work with a developer with prior Facebook development experience, you should consider working with a Preferred Marketing Developer. PMDs are web development firms—now numbering in the hundreds—that have been officially certified as developers for the Facebook API framework. The four areas for qualification are Pages, Ads, Apps, and Insights.

For the complete global directory of Facebook PMDs, visit https://apps. facebook.com/pmddirectory/. It can be a cumbersome marketplace to navigate when you're looking for a developer for a specific purpose, but it's a good starting point for seeing who all the players are, then visiting their websites to better assess their offerings.

In short, whether you do the work in-house or hire outside contractors, you can lean on a large and dynamic Facebook development community to help you:

- Add robust social features to your website

- Build social games, sweepstakes, contests, or other campaign-focused digital properties

- Share activity from your web pages back with the Facebook platform

Web Platforms with Built-In Social Integration

Software platform developers have not stood by idly while businesspeople ponder how to make their websites more social. Major e-commerce platforms are building comprehensive tools right into their software that will let website owners capture the Facebook-stored data of site visitors and put it to mind-blowing use in their businesses.

This requires visitor permission, of course—courtesy of Facebook's "Do you want to allow...?" dialog box. But as consumers become more and more familiar with such integrations, and the dialogs are presented in a fairly user-friendly fashion, Facebook data-sharing is becoming increasingly frictionless and commonplace.

Take the example of Art Technology Group (ATG), one of the leading e-commerce packages. Website owners using ATG can configure their websites so that users can log in with either their merchant-specific logins or their Facebook credentials. Once logged in, Facebook data can be written permanently into the customer record of your site's database.

- Age

- Gender

- Interests

- Employer and career information

- Music and literature preferences

- Education and alma mater

- Friends

- Facebook UserID

This data is stored alongside information that you as a merchant already know about the customer, which could include:

- Name

- Address

- Purchase history

- Browsing or onsite searching history

- Customer source (including whether a particular search query brought the customer to you from Google or another search engine)

- Wish list

These data points become a potent aggregate of evidence about the customer's intentions, interests, and demographics.

Imagine that Julia visits one of her favorite online stores. She logs in with her Facebook account and is greeted by name and with the news that three of her friends, pictured on the site, have "liked" items on the store's website. Her friend Laura, in fact, has shared that she bought a new messenger bag. This piece of news appears on the merchant website and on Facebook for all Laura's friends to see. If any of those friends "like" or comment on the purchase, those positive word-of-mouth brand impressions are published deeper into the Facebook activity feed.

Friend networks on Facebook are interconnected exponentially, so a single shared comment multiplies three-hundredfold as it is echoed or retweeted throughout these networks.

Building a Proprietary Network

"Build or buy?" is an increasingly rare question when it comes to social net-working, because of the power of the network effect—the sheer numbers of people already devoted to major networks like Facebook and unwilling to switch to anything you might build.

Still, specialist sites like Bodybuilding.com have invested in their own networks and been successful at it. The Ning software platform is available at little cost for brands to design their own communities. The advantages of building your "walled garden" are significant—you'll own the relationship with the customer, as well as the contact data; you'll get the benefit of organic search traffic to your domain (not someone else's); you can customize the platform with features to suit your audience; and you're insulated from the impact should one of the major networks change its terms, start charging onerous fees, or even go out of business.

Nike has built an outstanding online community at http://nikeplus.nike.com/plus/ that lets members log goals, milestones, running routes, and more. Graphics constantly refresh to display total miles run, calories burned, and goals hit by the community as a whole.

Bodybuilding.com, Fab.com, Gilt Groupe, The Clymb, The Motley Fool, and AARP are other examples of special-interest businesses that have built their own full-fledged social networks.

That said, I find it hard to urge anyone to go the "walled garden" route. I am mindful of all the equity, search traffic, customer permission, and other assets we're shoveling into the Facebook treasury. But I believe there's no substitute for the audience size, feature set, and pace of enhancements offered on the public networks. Furthermore, I honestly believe that with Open Graph and app development, you get two major benefits: (1) you can develop any custom functionality your particular customers need, and (2) integration will be tight enough and two-way enough that you can bring the customer relationship, customer data, and marketing permission into your system.

One best-practice example to consider is Starbucks. Instead of trying to reinvent the wheel, the company participates in the major social networks. It operates thriving communities on Facebook, Google+, and Twitter (where it maintains five special-focus accounts, including @starbucksjobs). Its YouTube channel has garnered nine million views, and its Pinterest board has 15,000 followers.

However, Starbucks isn't afraid to build custom community tools to suit specific purposes. It maintains a crowd-sourcing forum at www.MyStarbucksIdea.com, as well as other unique digital and social offerings, such as:

- AT&T Wi-Fi: a network of free hotspots at Starbucks locations across the United States

- An entertainment portal: the tunes and compilations heard in Starbucks coffeehouses, streamed free

- Starbucks Digital Network in Partnership with Yahoo!: free access to subscription news sites, video, and streaming iTunes music.

To bring all these social properties together, Starbucks hosts a Community portal at www.starbucks.com/coffeehouse/community.

Social Commerce

How to monetize the stunningly large audience for social media has been a conundrum for several years. Facebook users are loath to leave the site and don't tend to reward external URL ads with purchases.

A throng of software platforms has come on the scene to solve the problem. Moontoast, 8thBridge, Usablenet, ShopSocially, and ShopIgniter are just a few of the platforms serving up "F"-commerce. Some of them are simple iframe approaches that require very little intervention from your information technology people. Others are more comprehensive.

But they all bring e-commerce transactions directly to the Facebook wall or tab, or as a "light box" (a modal web dialog sometimes misdescribed as a "popup") allowing users to check out and buy without ever leaving the Facebook experience.

My sense is that the time for Facebook commerce is coming soon. We aren't there yet, but before long, Facebook will truly come of age as a platform for online commerce.

Summary

To be successful in social media, a brand must be *on* social media—participating in the major social networks, establishing connections with fans. But your presence on Facebook, Twitter, and the rest is only part of the equation. We've come full circle.

To be truly successful and maintain a 360-degree view of your customers, you must incorporate social features into your own website: social sign-in, coupon sharing, gamification, social proof—and richly personalized marketing based on your knowledge of each customer's likes and interests.

Bringing It All Together

Web 3.0—Are We There Yet?

Developing a social media presence today will position your company for success in coming years, when virtually everything—phones, electronics, cars, and homes—becomes interconnected. All those connections will have a social dimension. Our digital experience will be entirely personalized to our unique tastes and interests.

The emergence of the World Wide Web—call it Web 1.0—was characterized by static web pages. Web 2.0 has witnessed an explosion of dynamic web content, quick and easy to publish, including people-powered blogs and social media.

But even while most of us were still getting our heads around Web 2.0, thought leaders were envisioning—and creating the technical frameworks for—a Web 3.0. Tim Berners-Lee, creator of the World Wide Web, describes the next frontier as the *Semantic Web*, an interconnection not of "pages" related by links, but of ideas and data interlinked by logical, hierarchical, and personal relationships.

That Future Is Here: The Open Graph

The social fabric of the web already has its organizing framework: the Open Graph.

Travis Katz, CEO of the travel site Gogobot, sees a future of the Internet "where every page is going to be personalized. If you plan a trip to Paris, you shouldn't see 900 hotels. You should see six hotels based on where you stayed before; the places you checked in at on Facebook and Foursquare, and the places where your friends have stayed . . . It's something that makes sense for almost every part of the Internet."[1]

In the next wave, social connections won't be merely a feature of the Internet—they'll be a core organizing principle of the online experience.

"The Social Web is not just about relationships, but about the applications and innovations that can be built on top of these relationships," wrote the W3C Incubator Group, part of the World Wide Web Consortium, an international body dedicated to the development and promotion of Internet standards.[2]

That was in 2010. Today, the Google "Rich Snippets" markup allows web pages to encode attributes—including information about people—that are used to customize the display of search results.

Google, Bing, and Yahoo search results can display a person's name, profile photo, location, job title, and company for pages (like profile pages on LinkedIn) that delimit such data in their markup.

New frameworks and attributes are emerging from the WWW Consortium and www.Schema.org, with the aim of building a smarter web, one capable of parsing data into fields and relating entities to one another.

A smarter, more social, and more personalized web will be a more powerful web. Walls are coming down all over the Internet. Most of the major "walled garden" networks have made their logins available through social sign-in using the OAuth protocol for open authentication. Utilities like Gigya and Janrain now enable social sign-in for 25 social networks large and small, including Facebook, Twitter, LinkedIn, Google, Yahoo!, and Windows Live.

Eventually, most of our online lives will be tied to a single account with a universal username and password. The idea of unique usernames and passwords for each website we frequent will be as quaint as a horse and buggy.

---

[1] "Web 3.0: The 'Social Wave' and How It Disrupts the Internet," July 6, 2011, http://knowledge.wharton.upenn.edu/article.cfm?articleid=2808.

[2] "A Standards-based, Open and Privacy-aware Social Web," W3C Incubator Group Report, December 6, 2010, www.w3.org/2005/Incubator/socialweb/XGR-socialweb-20101206/.

Embedding Social Media Throughout the Enterprise

Just as social is becoming inextricable from the web experience, it's becoming permanently embedded in our work lives. Eventually there will be no corporate "social media team"—because social media tools and techniques will be so broadly distributed across your entire company.

Chris Boudreaux, a customer relations management and social media expert at Accenture, sees a pressing need for large businesses to ramp up their social media programs to enterprise scale, and to do so with operational excellence. "A lot of people talk about measurement being the biggest challenge with social media," notes Boudreaux. "But in the years ahead I'd say the bigger challenge is doing the hard work of industrializing it, scaling it, and embedding it across the enterprise."[3]

We are at an exciting turning point. The major social networks have achieved massive scale, reaching close to 100% of online adults. Based on its membership of over one billion people, if Facebook were a country it would be the world's third largest, after China and India.

Yet the size of social media, its pervasiveness, and its interconnection with our online lives are far from mature. In the years to come, social media will be informing everything we do in marketing, public relations, and CRM.

Summary

Social media are the biggest story of the Internet in the last ten years. They are now one of the biggest, most timely topics in marketing.

Certainly, the landscape is still changing and evolving. There is no sure blueprint for business success in this space.

But if your company approaches social media in a customer-centered way— listening more than talking, patiently cultivating relationships with customers rather than closing in for the quick sale—you will win in this game. If you develop campaigns that entertain, or stir cause-related passions, you will capture new leads and delight your existing customers. In the end, you'll find social media will be among the lowest-cost, fastest-impact, and highest-return channels in your business.

---

[3] Personal interview, August 21, 2012.

Business Plan Example

A Template for Documenting Your Social Media Plan

Think of your social media effort as a business within a business. As you would with a start-up business or a major internal initiative, write up a project charter and business plan for your social media program. This is especially important because 1) Social is still a new medium whose goals and measurements won't be understood and shared across the enterprise unless you document them in writing, and 2) The fast pace of change, and frequent emergence of new platforms and tactics means you must define your priorities—and stay disciplined in pursuit of those priorities.

Here's an example of the social media business plan of a fictitious adventure-travel business, Ends of the Earth Tours. (Some of the statistics are also fictitious.)

Executive Summary

[This section summarizes your main points about the marketplace, the opportunity, your strategy, and expected outcomes. Often it's best to write this section last.]

Ends of the Earth Tours is one of the oldest adventure travel companies in America, and we enjoy a 95% approval rating from our travelers. However, we have been slow to venture into social media, and today we find that many of our competitors have higher profiles than we do on major social networks. They appear to be attracting prospective travelers, as well as engaging with existing travelers and generating repeat business.

Adventure travel is an $89 billion industry worldwide, according to *Travel Industry Journal*. The industry is fragmented, with many companies competing to serve a limited supply of travelers. Social media represents an attractive new frontier for acquiring new customers at a fraction of the cost of traditional media. Social media also shows promise for building brand loyalty and winning repeat vacations from our existing travelers.

We aim to invest modest financial and personnel resources to establish a social media presence as vibrant and brand-positive as our offline reputation. In the next three years, we will catch up to and surpass our competitors.

We will chart our progress in four areas: 1) Total social media audience, 2) Leads and new business generated from social media, 3) Higher loyalty and lifetime revenue from customers who engage with us in social media, and 4) Brand awareness and positive brand image, as measured by consumer survey sentiment and mentions of our brand name in social media.

Positioning Statement

[As with a business's "unique selling proposition," your social media positioning statement succinctly describes your audience, what you do, and how you provide a special, unique benefit to the consumer.]

For active travelers ages 28 to 48, the Ends of the Earth online community is a source of expert information and inspiration, which helps people plan their next vacation, encourages them to share travel experiences with others, and rewards them for their loyalty.

Mission

[Your mission statement serves as an "elevator pitch" describing your program goals. It also provides a valuable orientation for all the staffers and agency people working on the project.]

Ends of the Earth aims to extend its reputation for world-class customer service, and unsurpassed adventure travel expertise, by building the largest and most passionate online adventure travel community.

The purpose of our social media program is to:

- Deepen engagement and stimulate more loyalty among our existing travelers,

- Stimulate positive connections among travelers before, during and after their vacations, and

- Gain increased visibility, word-of-mouth and "earned media" attention among prospective travelers who may be researching their next vacation.

Market Analysis

[Describe the size and nature of your market, especially as it manifests itself on social media. Talk about growth rates and opportunities, as well as the nature or segments of the online audience. This can be one of the most effective sections of your plan, because no one wants to be left in the dust by rivals. Watch your competitors over time so you can remark on particular social media campaigns, and their apparent impact on fans, followers, and subscribers.]

Adventure travel and tourism is an $89 billion dollar business. Over 36 million Americans booked vacation travel in 2012, and an estimated 6.3 million purchased a group tour or other organized vacation package.

Studies find the internet plays an increasing role in researching and booking vacation travel. In 2011, 76% of travelers reported researching their vacations online. 37% booked tours or accommodations online.

The increased use of the web as a vacation-planning tool dovetails perfectly with consumers' growing reliance on word-of-mouth recommendations and "social proof" to guide their buying decisions. Some 68% of consumers trust, and are influenced by, online ratings and reviews from other consumers.

We identify three main audience segments we aim to engage with on social media:

- *Customers:* Loyal Ends of the Earth travelers, who receive our catalogs and emails several times a year and travel with us on average once every three years.

- *Qualified prospects:* Experienced adventure travelers who frequently travel with other tour companies, and are good candidates to travel with us, assuming we can "meet" them and explain our value proposition.

- *Self-guiding travelers:* These adventure travelers are experienced, and interested in the destinations and activities we offer. But they have not booked group tours in the past.

Competitive Analysis

[Return on investment can be hard to calculate, but this section can paint a compelling picture of the other ROI—Risk of Ignoring. By describing what all your major offline rivals are doing in social media, you make the case for participating. The point here is to note their efforts and achievements and use them as benchmarks for your own.]

Adventure travel and tourism is a competitive space, and the social media landscape already reflects that competition. Our major rivals are already active, in varying degrees, on Facebook, Twitter, Flickr, YouTube, Pinterest, as well as specialty channels like TripAdvisor and GORP.

It is urgent we ramp up our own efforts so as to not cede visibility to rival companies. At the same time, we see that some of the biggest names in our industry have rather small and anemic online programs—which represents a major opportunity for us to leapfrog the competition.

To compare our social-media positioning to that of some of our key rivals:

Ends of the Earth Tours: We currently have 12,000 Facebook fans, 235 Twitter followers, and no activity on YouTube. We have 58 ratings on TripAdvisor with an average rating of 3.75 stars, but we do not post to the site ourselves, nor do we have an active advertising presence on the site.

Acme Adventure Travel: Acme has 85,000 Facebook fans and 600 Twitter followers. Every season, they post about six videos to their YouTube channel featuring travelers and guides on their tours. These videos have received 655,000 views, and some rank highly in searches like "Nepal trekking tour" or "Amazon raft tour." In May, Acme promoted an "Ultimate Adventure Sweepstakes" with a grand prize of a free trip to Bhutan. During the four-week promotion, their Facebook fans increased about 20% to almost 100,000 fans. Acme apparently has no activity on Google+, Pinterest, Flickr Yelp, or other networks.

Backcountry Tours [Example…]

Sojourn [Example…]

Country Walkers [Example…]

Goals and Objectives

[Focus on SMART goals—Specific, Measurable, Attainable, Relevant, and Timely. You must have a means to be able to declare victory. For a business plan, you'd forecast a few years out, but for your social media program, just one year is probably sufficient.]

Year 1:

- 150,000 Facebook fans (more than 10x our current level)
- 1,200 Twitter followers
- 40,000 sweepstakes sign-ups
- 36,000 email newsletter sign-ups
- 750 vacations booked directly from social media pages or indirectly via email from social media leads

Social Media Strategy

[How will you employ social media to meet the goals outlined above?]

Engage with existing travelers to encourage them to spread the word about us through referrals and positive reviews, to bolster their fond memories of their travel with us, and to increase their likelihood of booking with us in the future.

For *travelers currently booked* on an upcoming trip, establish and promote small Facebook communities dedicated to specific destinations and bookings. Use these to establish group cohesion, chemistry, high morale, and burgeoning friendships, even before a tour group hits day one. We expect this tactic will make for successful group dynamics that will lead to more positive customer satisfaction surveys and greater likelihood that customers will be repeat travelers in the future.

Acquire new customers. Our strategy is to attract vacation researchers through social media with travel sweepstakes, email newsletters, travel deals, fare-watcher tools, Q&A, customer ratings and review sites, and other attractive content that will inspire interaction, email subscriptions, and catalog sign-ups. We will augment all this free content with paid promotion on Facebook and Twitter.

Platforms

[Name the main social networks and media sites on which you'll be active, and what role each will play.]

Facebook: Facebook will be the focus of most of our efforts for daily community interaction, content posting, and support of sweepstakes campaigns. Facebook will serve goals of acquiring new customers, and engaging with existing customers. In addition to our main Facebook community, we will maintain several small ones dedicated to specific tours in order to build cohesion and community within our tour groups.

Twitter: We will limit our Twitter posts to travel tips, trivia, and vacation deals. The purpose will principally be to attract new travelers to our email list, or to inspire existing travelers to book a discounted trip.

Pinterest: We will maintain pinboards for each of our destinations, posting our catalog images and candid photos of travelers and guides. Our goal will be to cultivate relationships with top travel-and-tourism members, generate re-pins for the sake of new customer inquiries, and encourage customers to pin their own images of our trips.

TripAdvisor: We have claimed our page on TripAdvisor and will optimize it by uploading images, responding to reviews, and installing the review widget on our main site. The purpose is to generate more reviews, thank customers for positive reviews, and attract new travelers.

YouTube: Upload videos of our travelers hiking, riding, paddling, etc., in all our destinations. The purpose is to improve search-engine ranks, build a cookie pool for paid remarketing advertising, and attract new travelers.

Flickr: Post our catalog photos as well as candid shots of each trip.

Ends of the Earth Blog: Develop more fully the editorial content that is posted to Facebook. Have a publishing platform for more in-depth profiles of travelers, guides, and destinations. This can also be the destination URL for many of our Twitter posts.

Out of scope: Google+, Foursquare, Yelp, LinkedIn, and other social networks not mentioned here, are not in scope for the current year.

Staffing Plan

Currently, our social media efforts are run through one full-time social media staffer and partial-time allocation of three other staffers, and as-needed third-party services. Here's how it lays out:

Marketing Director: The project charter/owner of our social media program, she is responsibility for business planning, strategic leadership, budget allocation, and attainment of goal metrics. She dedicates approximately 5% of her time to social media, and anticipates this rising to 10% by next year.

Social Media Specialist: 100% of the SMS's time is dedicated to the social media program. He is responsible for execution of the business plan, participation on the strategy team, and daily community engagement.

The SMS's key roles are participation on the strategy team, drafting and executing the content calendar, daily posting, community interaction, and liaison with our Customer Service team and other internal stakeholders.

Graphic Designer: We will use 10% of the time of our in-house graphic designer for wall posts, tab design, campaign landing pages, and sweepstakes website design.

App Developer: For sweepstakes, games, contests, newsletter sign-up forms, and other development-intensive projects, we will rely on an outside vendor, Anytime Interactive, whose fees are accounted for in the Budget section below. By 2014, we anticipate building this capability in-house within our developer team.

Operations Plan

[Briefly describe the main functional elements of your social media program—how you will perform your daily tasks, what software tools you'll need, how you'll deal with a crisis, etc.]

We will organize our program around a monthly posting calendar. We anticipate a few regular features including "Destination of the Week," "Last-Minute Travel Deal," and "Fan Friday." We also anticipate recognizing local holidays and festivals, sharing recipes and travel tips, and asking questions and polls of our community members.

All staffers and consultants will be trained and certified under our new Social Media Certification program.

We will work with our counterparts in Customer Service, Legal, and Public Relations to ensure

- That customer service questions and complaints are resolved speedily, with friendliness and personality, and

- Any issues that must be escalated elsewhere in the enterprise are identified promptly and handed off effectively.

Working with the IT department, we will source a social media software platform that will help us:

- Efficiently publish to all social networks from one dashboard

- Monitor the web for mentions of our brand and our rivals

- Manage communications with our community members

- Track the impact of social media on our business

Marketing Plan

[Within your broad strategies, spell out particular tactics you will pursue, and their specific timing. If you'll execute four seasonal sweepstakes, test a mobile text-messaging promotion, or field a guerilla marketing street-team, say so!]

We will leverage free or low-cost promotion by mentioning our online communities—and specific sweepstakes or other campaigns—on the footer and homepage of our website, in booking confirmation emails, in our print ads, print catalog, and press releases.

We will attract attention through four large sweepstakes a year, where we give away a grand prize of a free trip for two to one of our more popular, trendy, or otherwise timely destinations. We will encourage positive word-of-mouth by making it easy to share the promotion with friends, and giving advocates additional prize entries for each "share."

These campaigns will also be supported by paid advertising. We will test paid advertising on Facebook and also use Google AdWords banner advertising triggered by cookies from watching our YouTube videos. We also expect we will pay for Promoted Account exposure to get our small Twitter community off the ground.

In addition to formal campaign promotion, we will also devote a small "Surprise and Delight" budget to giving free gifts, receptions, webinars, and discount offers to our biggest advocates in social media, VIP bloggers, travel media, and other influential people.

Budget

[Showing positive ROI is the holy grail, but it may take time to track and demonstrate the revenue impact of your social media, and to reach critical mass. For now, you'll likely show social media as a cost center. Budget accurately, by month and for the year as a whole.]

Personnel and outside agency costs	$105,800
Advertising	$58,000
Creative design and programming services	$23,525
Prizes and free goods	$12,000
Software licenses	$5,500
TOTAL	$204,825

Task Checklist

A To-Do List to Launch or Relaunch a Successful Program

Successful social media programs stand at the junction of marketing, promotions, public relations, customer service, and CRM—with a healthy dose of technology, finance, and legal compliance thrown in. Here's a checklist to help ensure you're covering all the bases.

Planning

- Obtain brand or domain: Facebook.com/yourname
- Obtain brand or domain: Twitter.com/yourname
- Obtain brand or domain on secondary platforms
- Social media mission statement
- Social media business plan
- Policy document for social media representatives
- Budget

Operations

- Interview and hire key social media staffers and/or agency
- Training and certification for social media staff
- Formal liaison and escalation path with customer service staff
- Formal liaison and escalation path with legal team

- Consider technology and staffing for a social media "command center"

Community Management

- Daily community management staffing/CRM plan
- Write monthly publishing calendar
- Monthly publishing calendar, legal review
- Research, survey, and customer insights projects
- Monthly CRM performance review

Advertising

- Top-line advertising cost and sales budget
- Ad campaign strategy brief
- Creative design briefs and production
- Technology requirements writing, vendor selection or in-house development, user-experience testing, UAT testing/debugging

Campaigns

- Campaign strategic plan and timeline
- Prizes or giveaways budgeted and finalized
- Research, survey, and customer insights projects
- Promotions and campaign strategy briefs
- Creative design briefs and production
- Campaign app requirements writing
- Vendor selection
- Campaign app development, user-experience testing, UAT testing/debugging
- Develop "like gated" Facebook tab
- Sweepstakes or other application or microsite
- Mobile application

Measurement and Reporting

- Technology requirements writing
- Vendor selection
- Website analytics setup and campaign tagging protocol
- Establish KPIs
- Brand monitoring
- Competitive analysis
- Develop and distribute social media dashboard reports
- Perform after-action reviews (AAR) of each major campaign

Index

CPSIA information can be obtained at www.ICGtesting.com
Printed in the USA
LVOW081154090613

337667LV00002B/296/P